From Colonies
to Commonwealth

New Studies in American Intellectual and Cultural History

Thomas Bender, Consulting Editor

From Colonies
to Commonwealth

Familial Ideology and the Beginnings
of the American Republic

Melvin Yazawa

The Johns Hopkins University Press
Baltimore and London

© 1985 The Johns Hopkins University Press
Printed in the United States of America

The Johns Hopkins University Press
701 West 40th Street
Baltimore, Maryland 21211
The Johns Hopkins Press Ltd, London

The paper in this book is acid-free and meets the guidelines
for permanence and durability of the Committee on Production
Guidelines for Book Longevity of the Council on Library Resources.

Library of Congress Cataloging in Publication Data

Yazawa, Melvin.
　From colonies to Commonwealth.

　(New studies in American intellectual and cultural
history)
　Bibliography: p.
　Includes index.
　1. United States—Politics and government—Colonial
period, ca. 1600–1775. 2. United States—History—
Revolution, 1775–1783—Causes. I. Title. II. Title:
Familial ideology and the beginnings of the American
Republic. III. Series.
E188.Y39　　1985　　　　973.3'1　　　　84-21846
ISBN 0-8018-2626-8 (alk. paper)

To Jennifer

Contents

Acknowledgments

I am pleased to be able formally to thank those persons who have contributed to the completion of this book. The staffs of the libraries and archives I visited were all helpful and congenial. I am especially grateful to the staffs of the Historical Society of Pennsylvania and the microfilm room, Milton S. Eisenhower Library, the Johns Hopkins University. In the early stages of my writing I was fortunate enough to have Rhys Isaac read and criticize several chapter drafts. J.G.A. Pocock was both gracious and generous with his time; his incisive comments, offered in the course of several lengthy discussion sessions, never failed to broaden my understanding of the social context of republican ideology. William W. Freehling provided additional commentary, and I have benefited from his encouragement. I am also grateful for the support I received from my friends and former colleagues at Southwest Texas State University: Kenneth Margerison, Ronald C. Brown, and department head Betty Kissler. William D. Liddle and Craig Donegan, busy with their own work, seemed always to find the time to listen to my ideas. Henry Tom and Jane Warth of the Johns Hopkins University Press expertly managed to ease the transition of the manuscript into print. Finally, I owe special thanks to the two persons who have contributed most, directly and indirectly, to the development of this study. I am indebted to Jack P. Greene not only for his illuminating suggestions and scholarly guidance but also for the counsel and encouragement he has uniformly provided throughout the years of our association. My wife, Jennifer, knows how much she has done and why this book is dedicated to her.

Introduction

A mid-seventeeth-century Massachusetts law stipulated that if "child[ren] above sixteen years old . . . shall curse or smite their natural father or mother they shall be put to death." This provision by itself has sometimes been enough to convince the casual observer that children in colonial New England lived in fear. At the very least, prescribing the death penalty for a relatively "minor" infraction seemed to indicate an appalling absence of affection within the early American family. Both of these conclusions, however, are well off the mark. In the first place, there is no evidence of the law ever being enforced to its full extent. On the contrary, even in cases of extreme provocation, magistrates were more than willing to resort to lesser punishments. Also, contrary to first impressions, the law was a statement about the paramount importance of familial affections. Precisely because such affections were taken to be sacred, so much a part of the order of things, lawmakers could justify their harsh prescription. Logically, a society founded on the primacy of domestic affections cannot afford to treat the cursing of one's parents lightly. The ultimate penalty was thus prescribed for an ultimate crime.

But, again, no child was ever executed under this law. What this suggests is that the law was intended not so much to frighten children into obedience, or even to deter them from violent expressions of disobedience, as it was to warn parents. As the law made clear, misbehaving minors would be exempt from the capital punishment provision if "it can be sufficiently testified that the parents have been very unchristianly negligent in the education of such children." The onus of disobedience, in other words, weighed as heavily upon parents as upon their children. Indeed, in view of the law's history, the implication here is that parents stood indicted for negligence if, after sixteen years of domestic instruction, their "child" remained ignorant of the basics of filial affection.

The Massachusetts law serves as an effective introduction to this study of early American social perceptions. Above all, it should be quite obvious that we must begin with a broad definition of education, one geared not to the mechanics of reading, writing, and arithmetic, but rather to the dynamics of socialization. Education in this sense is nothing less than the process by which the uninitiated are transformed into full participating members of a given society. The principal feature in the education of colonial Americans, it will be argued, was the inculcation of familial "affection." Not only domestic peace, but also harmony in the larger public world was dependent upon the dissemination of this fundamental social virtue. Parents, as educators of the first order, along with magistrates and ministers, were responsible for nurturing the proper affections in their charges, thereby preparing them for a useful adulthood.

The term *affection* in this social context signified more than *intimacy* or *love;* it was a generic term comprising a whole spectrum of dispositions—desire, hope, gratitude, joy, grief, hatred, anger, and so forth. And just as the ligaments of the natural body held it together, the "bonds of affection," by holding the collective body of men together, were thought to be the proper ligaments of society. Without such bonds, civil society would amount to nothing more than a multitude of discrete parts. For colonial writers the ideal polity incorporating all of the essential affective components was summarized in the familial paradigm of patriarchal authority. Church and state, they were fond of saying, were but a "great family," and the "family well ordered may be called a little commonwealth."

In Part One, then, I have described the theoretical foundations of the notion of affectionate authority. As with any paradigm, it should be emphasized, the familial construct prescribed as well as described certain ideal forms of behavior. These forms, mutually binding upon superiors and subordinates—"fathers" and "children," civil as well as natural—were drawn from an elaborate version of the social imperatives implicit in the Fifth Commandment. Children learned that the "father" and "mother" mentioned in the commandment included "all our superiors." By extension, the same lesson taught all superiors to consider themselves bound by parental obligations. The scope of the familial commandment was inclusive. All relationships were in truth familial; all persons bound together and in place by affection.

Building on this theoretical base, Part Two details the operation of the familial paradigm in everyday life. In their lessons on the social implications of the Fifth Commandment superiors and subordinates alike learned *what* was required of them in their dealings with one another. In complementary lessons, they learned *how* to fulfill those obligations. As a general rule, inward esteem had to be manifested in outward expressions. Demeanor was of paramount importance, for a properly "obediential Frame and Carriage" was thought to be the best measure of affection. Civil and ecclesiastical authorities were thus alive to the meanings of various nonverbal expressions, and often tempered their government accordingly.

I believe that the scholastic community provides us with an ideal setting for an extended examination of the themes introduced thus far in the text. As a familial institution, *in loco parentis,* the school accommodated instances of paternal supervision and filial submission that corresponded to the affectionate patterns replicated throughout the rest of society. But the school was also an artificial social environment with clearly demarcated limits both in time and space. Its behavioral imperatives had to be more formally and explicitly stated than in the case of the natural family, where shared identifications were intense enough to allow such rules governing interaction to be left unspoken. Thus the process of socialization in this special environment, the methods used by the "fathers" of the schools to indoctrinate novices into the standing order, lends itself quite readily to close scrutiny.

The convergence of events, demographic and political, in the middle decades of the eighteenth century provided at least an oblique endorsement of the domestic counselors' warning that the fate of the commonwealth was inextricably intertwined with the fate of the family. Part Three begins with an examination of the ways in which the familial paradigm contributed to the movement toward independence. The bonds of affection were supposed to govern the actions of superiors and subordinates, and therefore to establish the limits of authority as well as subjection. Because of this special arrangement, parents were neither "tyrants" nor "masters," and children neither "slaves" nor even "servants." In the course of the imperial crisis, the colonists came increasingly to believe that the king and his ministers were not bound by the dictates of affection. The rhetorical charges customarily associated with the radical Whigs were thus strengthened by an appeal to the older tradition of patriarchalism.

Perhaps ironically, the familial paradigm lost much of its explanatory power as a result of the Revolution. The erosion of patriarchal authority in the eighteenth-century family dovetailed nicely with the dissolution of the imperial family. Social evolution and political revolution combined finally to necessitate an alternative mode of perceiving civil relationships. The new paradigm was revealed during the Revolution as Americans committed themselves to republican principles. This commitment, the equivalent of a religious conversion for many, rendered inappropriate the earlier behavioral guidelines established while America was dependent upon Mother England and Americans functioned as members of a familial empire. The revolutionary "catharsis" entailed the forming of a new identity. Independent republicans were no longer held together or in place by affective prescriptions. Instead, republicanism seemed to require a depersonalization of the diverse public patterns of authority and subordination, patterns founded ultimately not in affection but in "mechanics." We can trace the formal emergence of this new understanding most clearly in the evolution of the doctrine of constitutionalism between 1776 and 1787.

The dimensions of the change in mentality that accompanied political independence and the nature of the social imperatives summarized under the rubric of republicanism are discussed in Part Four. Constitutional improvements notwithstanding, the Revolutionaries maintained that a virtuous citizenry was essential to the survival of the American republic. But while the celebration of virtue continued unchecked, the social context of the concept itself was transformed. The Revolutionary idea of virtue was at once less communal and more conspicuously political. In the familial social order, the advancement of virtue was a collective enterprise, a product of mutual interdependence. In the new republic, however, virtuous citizens were by definition autonomous in their personal bearing and independent in the exercise of their wills. Dependence of any kind supposedly rendered one susceptible to all sorts of temptations and impositions. Thus dependence was despised by republican ideologues, and dependent persons became objects of suspicion because they were seen as easy targets of corruption. Benjamin Rush's voluminous reflections on the "Mode of Education Proper in a Republic" constitute the most coherent and sustained presentation of these ideas. His references to "republican machines," in particular, amounted to a shorthand description of the ultimate goals of social education in the new nation.

Autonomous citizen participation in the "great machine" of the state, a "becoming independency," had to be complemented by a binding and habitual attachment to the republic itself. Monarchies endured over long periods, and unfortunately even despotic governments were prone to be long-lived, because kings and princes were exceedingly fond of the states over which they ruled. For a republic to be equally durable the people, as sovereign, must be similarly disposed. Impressed by conventional wisdom concerning the sacrifices needed to support republican systems, the Revolutionaries were keenly aware of the political potential of education. That they had committed their lives and fortunes to a historically ephemeral form of government, and one that placed the old ligaments of the familial commonwealth in low repute, only made the need for a self-consciously patriotic education more acute. In the end, the bonds of what Tocqueville labeled a wearisome "garrulous patriotism" came to replace the older severed bonds of familial affection.

I

AFFECTION

A Narrative of the Case of John Porter, Jun.

*John Porter, Junior, the sonne of John Porter, Salem, in the county
of Essex, in New England, yeoman, being about thirty yeares of age,
& of sufficient capacity to understand his duty unto his superiours,
according to the fifth commandment, but he, being instigated by the
divill, & his currupt heart destitute of the feare of God, did not only
prodigally wast & riotuously expend about fower hundred pounds of
money & goods committed to him by his Father, for his improvement
in two voyages to the Berbadoes, & so for England, where by his evill
courses he ran himself further into debt, (& was there imprisoned,
from whence being relieved by the charritable assistance of some
Friends of his Father,) all which debts his father did voluntarily
discharge. After this, returning to New England, his parents enter-
tained him with love & tenderness as their eldest sonne, & provided
for him [what] was expedient & necessary. All these things have been
clearely demonstrated to the Court: but notwithstanding the said John
Porter, Junior, did carry himself very perversly, stubbornely, &
rebelliously towards his naturall parents, who are persons of good
repute for piety, honesty, & estate.*

*He called his father theife, lyar, & simple ape, shittabed. Frequently
he threatned to burne his fathers house, to cutt downe his house &
barne, to kill his catle & horses, & did with an axe cutt downe his
fence severall times, & did set fire of a pyle of wood neere the
dwelling house, greatly endangering it, being neere thirty roads
[rods].*

*He called his mother Rambeggur, Gammar Shithouse, Gammar
Pissehouse, Gammar Two Shoes, & told hir her tongue went like a
peare monger, & sayd she was the rankest sow in the towne; & these
abusive names he used frequently.*

*He reviled Master Hawthorne, one of the magistrates, calling him
base, corrupt fellow, & said he cared not a turd for him.*

*He reviled, & abused, & beate his fathers servants, to the
endangering of the life of one [of] them.*

*He was prooved to be a vile, prophane, & common swearer &
drunkard; he attempted to stab one of his naturall brethren. All which
things are prooved by the oathes of sufficient wittnesses upon record.*

*In this vile & unsufferable course he continued severall yeares, but
more especially the two last yeares, sixty two & sixty three [1662 and*

*1663]. At length, his father. in the sence of his sonnes wickedness &
incorrigiblenes, & the dayly danger of himself, his estate, & family,
by his meanes, sought releife from authority, first more privately,
which was ineffectuall, & afterwards more publickly, before the
County Court held at Salem, & by that Court was committed to the
house of correction at Ipswich, where he was kept some time; & afterward, being set at liberty, did persist in his former wicked course, &
being againe complained of by his father to the said Salem Court the
fower and twentieth of the ninth moneth, 1663, where his offences
being found to be of a high nature, he was committed to prison at
Boston, there to remaine for a triall at the Court of Assistants, where
he was called to answer upon the fowerth of March, 1663 [1664].*

*The complaints against him, the said Porter, were produced, the
wittnesses brought face to face, & his charge prooved; also, his owne
naturall father openly complained of the stubbornes & rebellion of
this his sonne, & craved justice & releife against him, being over
pressed thereunto by his unheard of & unparrelled outrages before
named. Unto which complaints the said John Porter, Junior, had
liberty to answer for himselfe. He impudently denied some things,
others he excused by vaine pretences, & some he owned, but gave no
signe of true repentance; whereupon the said Court proceeded to give
sentence against him, the summe whereof is, to stand upon the ladder
at the gallowes, with a roape about his neck, for one hower, &
afterwards to be severely whipt, & so committed to the house of correction, to be kept closely to worke, with the diet of that house, & not
thence to be releast without speciall order from the Court of Assistants
or the General Court, & to pay to the country as a fine two hundred
pounds.*

*If the mother of the said Porter had not been overmooved by hir
tender & motherly affections to forebeare, but had joyned with his
father in complaining & craving justice, the Court must necessarily
have proceeded with him as a capitall offendor, according to our
law. . . .*

By the Court
EDW: RAWSON, Secret[ary]

1

The Bonds
of Affection

Aboard the *Arbella* en route to New England in 1630, John Winthrop described the bases of a Christian utopia. In this ideal society, stability depended upon a divinely ordained pattern of inequality. "God Almightie hath soe disposed of the condicion of mankinde," Winthrop said, "as in all times some must be rich some poore, some highe and eminent in power and dignitie; others meane and in subjeccion." To support his assertion, Winthrop posited three interrelated propositions. The first two stemmed rather directly from the traditional understanding of the Great Chain of Being. All things in this world were created and arranged in an infinite series of gradations that ranged from the lowest inanimate object to the loftiest animate being. Thus, "to hold conformity with the rest of his workes," God must have made inequality an inherent characteristic of the human condition. If the "variety and difference of the Creatures" reflected the "glory of his wisdome," the ordering of "all these differences for the preservacion and good of the whole" revealed the "glory of his power." Winthrop's third proposition constituted the bulk of his presentation. Social gradations effectively demonstrated that God intended men to remain dependent upon one another, to "be all knitt more nearly together in the Bond of brotherly affection." [1]

Winthrop's rhetoric was noteworthy, but there was nothing extraordinary about the message itself. Because of this, however, because Winthrop drew upon a commonplace set of ideas, his address becomes even more significant. The argument contained in Winthrop's "Model of Christian Charity" was a derivative of the popular perception of society as an organism whose structure and operations ought properly to be understood in comparison with the constitution and functions of the natural body. William Perkins, the English divine, had summarized this traditional notion earlier in the century. "All societies of men are bodies," Perkins explained; "a family is a bodie, and so is every particular Church a bodie, and the Common-wealth also." As such, distinctions "betweene man and man in every societie" originated in the order of creation. More than a century after Winthrop's statement on "charitie," Nathaniel Chauncey declared without reservation that the idea that a *"Collective*

Body" of men ought to resemble the *"Natural Body* of Man" was both current and convincing because it accurately described the "various *Parts or Members* that belong to the Body." [2]

A society without distinctions, then, was long held to be contrary to the patterns of nature and to the intentions of nature's God. Levelism under any circumstance was unacceptable. In addition, for these seventeenth- and eighteenth-century commentators the organic imagery was prescriptive as well as descriptive. Society was not only composed of various members, but each member had to do his part to secure the well-being of the whole. Although the inhabitants of any society would naturally occupy different "Places of Distinction," William Balch observed, they must nevertheless *"all* consider themselves as making but *one Body."* Even those members whose appointed stations appeared to be "Feeble" were necessary to the health, "Safety and Happiness of the whole Body Politic." Abraham Williams added that a "society without different Orders and Offices, like a Body without Eyes, Hands and other Members, would be uncapable of acting, either to secure its internal Order and Well-being, or defend itself from external Injuries." Moreover, Williams said, these several members must perform their "natural Functions" and attend to their "respective Duties." The eye, for example, cannot assume the operations of the ear, or the ear the responsibilities of the eye. Such actions would result in "Discord and Confusion," with the "usurped office" rendered vacant and useless. The lesson was clear. Schisms and distempers afflicted the body, natural and collective, whenever individual members forsook their "proper Sphere" or acted "out of Character." [3]

The prescriptions incorporated into the organic vision were compelling, ultimately, because they were providential. God valued efficiency as well as order. There could be nothing superfluous about his creations. Every part of the natural and civil body was accounted for in the divine estimation of perfection. "Attend . . . to the formation of man, his very body," Joseph Huntington advised, and we cannot fail to recognize the imprint of divine wisdom. "How useful? How beautiful? How complete in every part?" Huntington continued: "We desire not a member more than we have, and we are very averse to the loss of any one, though it be the least. What symmetry and proportion do we observe? What mutual harmony and sympathy? What convenience in the location and office of every limb and every member? We could not be willing to have one organ, limb or member placed any where in the body but where it is." The beauty of the human structure was such that even the thought of the slightest "alteration in the number and situation of any of our members" causes us to "shudder." The head, legs and arms, fingers, toes, and internal organs, all were perfect members perfectly situated. It was the perfection of this integration that held the whole together. Every part felt the need of every other part. Deviations from the norm were intensely displeasing to us because they resonated throughout the entire body by unnaturally depleting the "nutriment" that sustained the whole.[4]

The principle of providential efficiency and its corresponding social implication of mutual dependence, coupled with the idea of natural distinctions between man and man, were expressed in the Puritan doctrine of "personal callings." As William Perkins observed, "if all men had the same gifts, and all were in the same degree and order," then they would also all have "one and the same calling." But, of course, such an initial assumption betrayed a gross lack of reverence for and appreciation of God's glory. Men were inherently distinct from one another, just as the "hand is the hand, not the foot, and the foote, the foote, not the hand." Therefore, a "diversitie of personall callings" must accommodate the diversity "betwixt the members" of society. "Every person of every degree, state, sexe, or condition without exception, must have some personall and particular calling to walke in," Perkins declared. Only by pursuing his proper calling could the individual contribute to the advancement of the common good.[5]

This understanding of the dictates of the calling and of the organic nature of the social order supported a vigorous condemnation of the solitary withdrawal of "Monkes and Friars." Perkins sternly rebuked those who sought to approach a state of perfection by separating themselves from their fellow creatures. These misguided souls lived a "damnable" life, damnable because they violated the strictures of providence. "God in his word hath ordained the society of man with man," and yet, the reclusive monk insisted on living "apart from the societies of men." To make things even worse, such monkish isolation was hardly an innocuous gesture; it was never solely a private affair because the general good was dependent upon the combined efforts of all the diverse ranks and orders of men. Communal well-being was a compound product of the several separate but mutually reinforcing personal callings. "No man is born for himself alone," Peter Clark explained. Having given us at least a capacity, if not an inclination, for "social Converse and mutual Assistance," God had "thereby laid an Obligation upon us to seek each one another's Welfare." Personal isolation could be realized only at the expense of the happiness and perfection of the whole. Truly, those who refused to live up to the responsibilities of their sphere and thus failed to contribute to the good of the whole were like "rotten legges and armes that drop from the body."[6]

The basis of good order, social stability in "collective Bodies or

Societies," then, could be found in the simple imperative that all men must be, as Abraham Williams put it, "connected together, related & subservient to each other." This much ought to be obvious. However, since Adam's fall, mankind had either failed to recognize this simple truth or refused to live by its stipulations. Adam's "Apostacy hath much blurred" the rules of good order, Samuel Willard said. Thus, when "Adam Rent . . . himself from his Creator," Winthrop agreed, he "rent all his posterity allsoe one from another." Adam, in short, according to Thomas Foxcroft, had destroyed the "habit of Original righteousness" and thereby introduced confusion, corruption, and "deformity" into society. Furthermore, Samuel Sewall added, once men had departed from God's way, "there was such an aversion in them to return, that every kind of Authority was necessary to reclaim them." [7]

Original sin, therefore, made all of the various forms of government necessary. In view of mankind's fallen state, "if there were none in Authority, Justice and Righteousness would soon forsake the Earth; Rapine & Violence, Falsehood & Oppression could every where prevail & triumph," Jonathan Todd exclaimed. Indeed, Noah Hobart was convinced that "Public Happiness" could not "possibly be effected without erecting & supporting Civil Government." Corrupted and corruptible, given to gratifying their own irregular appetites, men were naturally inclined to anarchy. Unrestrained, every individual would seek to advance his own interest at the expense of others, unaware of the intimate connection between the parts and the whole of society. Ignorant of the consequences, every "domineering Wretch" would, Todd warned, attempt to "set up his own Will for a Law." [8]

Given this sad state of affairs, with sinful man unwilling or unable to recognize the necessity of self-restraint, it was left to God to promote public peace and the general good. He did this, in part, by sanctifying civil government. Although God had not ordained a particular form of government, it was commonly acknowledged that, as William Welsteed noted, government "abstractly considered" bore the "plainest Signature or Impress of divine Authority." According to Charles Chauncy, civil government "means the same thing" as "order and rule" in a world that had been threatened with chaos ever since the apostasy of Adam. Government thus could not be merely a human "contrivance"; it had to be "essentially founded on the will of God." "Public Communities," Daniel Lewis emphasized, could not possibly subsist without some form of government; therefore, "Civil Government is not an *accidental* Thing which Men have hit upon by Chance, but is of Divine Institution." [9]

The notion that governments were divinely inspired had at least two important implications. Divine ordination meant, in the first place, that the distinction between rulers and ruled was blessed rather than arbitrary. The office of the magistrate must not be seen as the creation of "crafty and ambitious Men," explained Samuel Phillips. Magistrates instead were God's agents. William Perkins went so far as to refer to them as "gods upon earth." And before Perkins, Henry Bullinger had argued that God, aware of the necessity of government, "doth attribute to the magistrate the use of his own name, and calleth the princes and senators of the people gods." The authority of the magistrate was thus a "sacred Thing" and, Jonathan Todd advised, must be "reverenc'd accordingly." The ruled were obliged to respect and venerate their rulers, and, above all, to remain obedient to them in the interest of good order. The people themselves might have a hand in electing their rulers, but they had to remember that magistrates were ultimately obligated to God and to God alone. "It is yourselves who have called us to this office," Winthrop told the freemen of Massachusetts Bay, but once called, "we have our authority from God." [10]

Divine ordination also meant, however, that rulers, even more than the ruled, were saddled with certain responsibilities. As Bullinger observed, to call magistrates "gods" might teach their subjects to hold them in "reverence," but at the same time, "they by the very name should be put in mind of their duty." While it was the "Duty of *all* to seek the Welfare & Prosperity of the Community whereto they belong," William Balch elaborated, that "Duty is heighten'd and increases upon Men in Proportion to the Advantages and Opportunities, which any enjoy for it." Clearly, "Rulers have Power and Authority, and many Advantages . . . which other Men have not." Therefore, they were obliged, "beyond others," to "serve the Public and promote its Welfare." Samuel Whittelsey argued that a magistrate needed only to reflect honestly on his situation to realize the truth of this assertion. When "he considers that neither God nor Men have so exalted him for his own sake," he will be forced to conclude that he is so placed "that he might be under advantage to do more good, and others receive the more benefit by him." It would be "blasphemous" to suppose otherwise, Noah Hobart said, an insult to God to think that in ordaining governments his "intention was to give some men a Right to gratify their Pride and Ambition." Good rulers must be, as Elnathan Whitman put it, "publick Benefactors." [11]

Rulers were thus called to a most "difficult & labourious Task," William Welsteed noted. If governments had been instituted to cope with the confusion that arose in the wake of Adam's fall, it was primarily the ruler's responsibility to initiate programs aimed at combating that confusion. The purpose of the magistrate's office, the "true *design* of that power some are entrusted with over others," was to restore the "Original righteousness" of man's estate. Rulers, Charles Chauncy said, were elevated to office for this purpose: that they might promote the *"general good* of mankind" by keeping "confusion and disorder out of the world." [12]

Success in this laborious undertaking depended in large part upon the ruler's ability to evince a "Publick Spirit." Only public-spirited men, it was widely argued, would be concerned enough about the welfare of the community-at-large to place it above their own interests. The organic nature of society meant, of course, that all members of the community must possess this spirit to some degree. It was, Samuel Whittelsey explained, a "vertue of universal extent . . . incumbent on those who wear the Ensigns of Dignity and Authority, and also upon those who are Hewers of wood & Drawers of water." But despite the universality of its application, this was a virtue that figured especially prominently in descriptions of the good ruler. In this, as in all other duties and requirements, a man was burdened "according to the measure of his ability." Thus while a "public Spirit . . . ought to animate all the Members," Abraham Williams pointed out, it must be "more conspicuously the Character of those intrusted with public Affairs." Because God had granted rulers advantages and opportunities *"above* and *beyond* what others enjoy," Jeremiah Wise concurred, they were obligated above and beyond all others to prove themselves "useful and serviceable in the World." It followed also that if rulers should fail in their appointed roles, William Burnham added, their faults and failings would be "more Heinous in the sight of God, than the same for kind & degree would be, if committed by men of lower Rank." [13]

In proving themselves serviceable through displays of public spirit, rulers went a long way toward restoring order in the world, for "man was made for *Imitation.*" Whittelsey suggested that the "superior example" of the ruler would probably evoke a complementary response on the part of the ruled. William Balch similarly recommended a "Public Spirit" to all men, but added that the *"Example* of Rulers is a great Thing; and . . . will go a great Way towards reforming those, who are placed under them." It was a known truth, Samuel Phillips declared, that *"Precepts teach,* but *Examples move Men."* More importantly, "there is a peculiar *Force* in the Examples of Superiours, and especially of Rulers." Thus, because the world had been rendered confused and contentious by sin, rulers ought to be, remarked Nathaniel Appleton, examples of "regular & peaceable living." In a world short on virtue, Phillips agreed, rulers should be "bright Examples" of "Vertue"; in a world wanting original righteousness, rulers must be *"Patterns of Righteousness."* [14]

[14]

II

Public spirit in the civil realm was a manifestation of that most precious of social virtues, "affeccion." By referring to the organic model, John Winthrop illustrated the significance of affection in society. "Noe body," he said, "can be perfect which wants its propper ligamentes," and men's affections, by holding the collective body together "as one man," were the ligaments of society. To be sure, these ligaments bound men in place so that "some [are] highe and eminent in power and dignitie; others meane and in subjeccion." But while they bound men to their appointed stations in life, they also bound them together. Without such bonds of affection, civil society would amount to nothing more than a multitude of discrete parts. It is affection, Winthrop observed, that "knitts these partes together . . . because it makes eache parte soe contiguous to other[s] as thereby they doe mutually participate with eache other." Well-affected members were infused with a "sensibleness and Sympathy of each others Condicions" and thus worked to "strengthen, defend, preserve and comfort" one another. This "speciall relacion" founded in affection made the body perfect, for it alone made the whole greater than the mere sum of the individual parts.[15]

"Affections," then, as Abraham Williams pointed out, "powerfully incite to, and plainly indicate, that Man was formed for Society." But what were the affections of men? Jonathan Edwards, who dealt with this subject at length, supplies us with some answers. The affections, Edwards said, were the "more vigorous and sensible exercises of the inclination and will of the soul." Here Edwards managed to summarize two fundamental ideas. First, because affections manifested themselves through the operations of the inclination and will, they were not to be confused with that other faculty of the soul—the "understanding." Whereas the latter enabled the soul to perceive and speculate, to view and judge things, the former "is the faculty by which the soul does not behold things as an indifferent unaffected spectator, but either as liking or disliking, pleased or displeased, approving or rejecting." In raising the soul above the state of indifference, these exercises of the inclination and will thus fell into two categories: "those by which the soul is carried out to what is in view, cleaving to it, or seeking it; or those by which it is averse from it, and opposes it." On the one hand, "love, desire, hope, joy, gratitude, [and] complacence" were exercises of approbation, of "pleasedness," Edwards explained; on the other hand, "hatred, fear, anger, grief, and such like" were attitudes of aversion, of "displeasedness." There were, in addition, some complex affections, combining elements of both categories. "Pity," for example, entailed compassion for the "person suffering" and aversion "towards what he suffers." [16]

It should be apparent that the term *affection* referred to a whole class of attitudes, all of which in turn reflected certain "kinds of actings of the will." Winthrop and Perkins, among others, sometimes employed the synecdochic technique of substituting "love" for "affection." And this was understandable, for as Edwards observed, "love is not only one of the affections, but it is the first and chief of the affections, and the fountain of all the affections." Nevertheless, we must not lose sight of the full range of dispositions encompassed by the class term itself. Otherwise, we will fail to grasp the scope of the imperatives stemming from the affectionate bond.[17]

The second idea Edwards incorporated into his definition of affection was the notion that the actings of the will and inclination had to be "vigorous" and "lively." Human nature was such that man, unaffected, tended to be "very inactive" at best. Affections were the "springs that set men agoing, in all the affairs of life, and engage them in all their pursuits." Thus, if we took away "all love and hatred, all hope and fear, all anger, zeal and affectionate desire . . . the world would be, in a great measure, motionless and dead." However, all of the operations of the will and inclination did not automatically qualify as "affections." There were differences in degree and manner. There were "some exercises of pleasedness or displeasedness, inclination or disinclination, wherein the soul is carried but little beyond a state of perfect indifference." Such exercises, Edwards said, rather than being "affections" were merely "wouldings." The will and inclination were engaged, but barely; consequently, the soul was abandoned in a conditional state of "would do" rather than doing. The distinction was as basic as the difference between idle wishing and active performance.[18]

Despite these reservations and qualifications, especially in regard to the "understanding," Edwards never separated the affections from the intellect; that is, from the mind and the powers of reason. He insisted that "it is not the body, but the mind only, that is the proper seat of the affections." Because the body of man was incapable of "thinking and understanding," it was incapable also of generating true affections. The "motions of the animal spirits, and fluids of the body" always accompanied the exercises of the affections, but they were "concomitants of [and] . . . entirely distinct from the affections themselves, and no way essential to them." An "unembodied spirit may be as capable of love and hatred, joy or sorrow, hope or fear, or other affections, as one that is united to a body."

However lively the "actings" of the will were, then, no matter how far above the state of the conditional "wouldings" they progressed, the affections remained properly under the power of the mind. This was the crux of the distinction between the "*affections* and *passions.*" The term passion signified those actings of the will that were "more sudden, and whose effects on the animal spirits are more violent." Consequently, displays of passion, unlike the exercises of affection, occurred only when the mind was "overpowered and less in its own command." [19]

Edwards thus positioned the affections so that they were carefully, if somewhat precariously, balanced between inert understanding on the one hand and irrational passion on the other. This carefully constructed balance was crucial because it seemed to distinguish man from the lower orders of creation. As John Taylor noted, in the absence of such a balance men were "only Brutes in a different Shape." Sentiments such as "love, sorrow, fear, and the rest are common to us with brute beasts," Plymouth's minister John Robinson elaborated; hence our "understanding must order [them] that they be not brutish." In some men, Robinson continued, the faculty of the "understanding" was so weakened by corruption that it no longer exercised any control over "brutish affections." Such men sought only to satisfy their own "appetite" because they could not impartially determine what constituted the general good, nor could they fathom the bonds between self and society.[20]

Observers such as Edwards and Robinson were offering a conventional interpretation of original sin, one that was conveyed in the lessons of the *New England Primer:* since the fall of Adam, passions have prevailed over affections. Once the habit of "Original righteousness" was broken, men were at a loss "to restrain their unruly Lusts," John Barnard said. If they were "left to live, and act, as they please, 'tis undoubted, the different Views and Interests, Humours and Passions of Mankind . . . would unavoidably produce a continual Jarr and Strife." In this dark state of nature, everyone would attempt constantly to "promote his own, and gratify Self, and so a perpetual Preying of the Stronger upon the Weaker" would ensue. Sin, therefore, was tantamount to disorder because it corrupted the understanding and, according to Nathaniel Chauncey, left man without the "rectitude of his will." Thus abandoned, mankind submitted to the "power and influence of Passion, Lust and corrupt Affection," and the world descended into "Disorder, Confusion and Misery." [21]

The first step in correcting this situation was suggested by the malady itself: passions had to be restrained. With this in mind, God, as we have seen, was said to have ordained the establishment of governments. One needed only to consider "how much stronger Influence Men's Passions have over them than their Reason" to realize the necessity of such restraints, William Welsteed declared. "The Lusts and Passions of Men are such," Jonathan Todd said, "that if entirely let loose . . . the World it self would scarce be a habitable Place, but rather a confused Scene of Intemperance, Lewdness, Oppression, Robbery, Murder, and all Manner of Exorbitances." Since the introduction of sin into the world, John Barnard asserted, the "Passions of Men" have run "rampant." Hence, unless governments were instituted to keep these passions "within due Bounds," human society would be thrown "into the last Disorder and Confusion." Because fallen man often would not or could not depend upon the faculty of "understanding," civil laws, duly enacted and enforced by the proper authorities, must serve "to tame this fierce Creature, to bound his Appetites, & [to] bridle his Passions." Jared Eliot warned that without the aid of these external restraints life would be beastly; "the weak would become a Prey to the strong. . . . Men would become *as the Fishes of the Sea,* the less . . . devoured by the greater." [22]

Important as this first step was, it was still not enough merely to enforce restraint. Governments, "every kind of Authority," were divinely appointed for the ultimate purpose of restoring the habit of original righteousness. Passions had to be bridled, to be sure, but more than that, the bonds of "affeccion," which alone elevated human societies above the conglomerations of brutish beasts, had to be restored. It was precisely in the undertaking of this dual responsibility that magistrates, "gods upon earth," came closest to resembling the God in heaven. As John Winthrop explained, God worked first "upon the wicked in moderateing and restraineing them soe that the riche and mighty should not eate upp the poore, nor the poore, and dispised rise upp against theire superiours." But his work in promoting good order was inseparable from his success in rejuvenating affection among the regenerate; thus the mighty would be known for "theire love, mercy, gentleness, temperance etc." and the "poore and inferiour sorte [for] theire faithe, patience, obedience etc." The bonds of affection were thus as much a part of the divine original as social gradations, and for commonwealths to be rightly structured they would have to manifest both characteristics. Only then, as Noah Hobart concluded, would mankind enjoy the "Benefits and Advantages that are peculiar to the *Social* Life." [23]

2

Honor Thy Father

"Government comes from God," Abraham Williams proclaimed in 1762. The establishment of civil government in particular had become necessary in the wake of Adam's fall. It would "never have been needed," as Stephen White said, "if Man had continued in a state of Innocency." Because mankind was no longer innocent, without "good and wholsome Laws, all manner of Confusion and Disorder rushes in among a People like a Flood." Civil magistrates empowered to enforce such laws were, according to Jonathan Ingersoll, clothed by God with "that Authority wherein they are to act in some Measure like himself." However, these agents of the divine had to remember that in practice the stern face of the law had to be softened by a "tender Concern" for the welfare of the people.[1]

When colonial writers sought a model for their conception of a polity that combined restraint with affection they turned to the traditional familial paradigm of patriarchal authority. The family, they were fond of saying, was the "First-born" and most natural of human associations. Moreover, if governments were divinely ordained, surely one could do no better than to conform to the "Pattern of the *Divine* Rule and Government." "God is the Father of the whole Creation," William Balch said, and "he has appointed Rulers to be Fathers in their respective Charges and Provinces." The "whole World is his [God's] Family," Peter Clark affirmed, "which as the universal Parent, he presides over, sustains, and provides for, with a paternal Bounty, Wisdom, and Care." And, Clark continued, "such being the Ends of the divine Government, earthly Magistrates may be said to rule with him, when they harmonize with the supream Ruler." Given this providential connection, paternal and political rule seemed so closely linked that their imperatives were interchangeable. The family, as the basic unit of society, was acknowledged to be, as George Lawson put it, the "seminary both of the Church and civil State." Beyond that, Lawson added, "as a State, or Church, may be said to be a great family; so a family well ordered may be called a little commonwealth." The use of the familial referent was, we know, widespread in the political discourse of Stuart England. Because the colonists looked to the mother country for cultural guidelines, it is not surprising to find that this imagery was also common currency in America. Civil and ecclesiastical authority, along with natural paternity, constituted the "Three Chiefe Fatherhoods."[2]

As with any paradigm, the familial construct prescribed as well as described certain ideals and modes of behavior. Whether in the great family or little commonwealth, filial obligations had to be respected. "A Household is a kind of little Common-wealth," John Ussher said, "and a Common-wealth a great Household"; therefore, "what in the one a Husband, a Father, and a Master may expect from those who have such relations to him: the like, by due proportion, is to have place in the other." John Cotton presented the same forthright message in his popular catechism for children. When asked to elaborate upon the Fifth Commandment, specifically, to identify those included in the prescription to "Honor thy father and thy mother," "Boston Babes" were taught to respond: "All our superiors, whether in family, school, church, and commonwealth." The roles of subordinates in domestic, civil, and ecclesiastical situations were essentially identical. If rulers or magistrates were "Civil Fathers," Daniel Lewis advised, then it was the people's "Duty to *honor* them *as such.*" Instead of "*Murmuring* and Railing . . . we ought to pity and pray for them, to *reverence* and *honour* them."[3]

The pervasiveness of the familial paradigm was reflected in the steady stream of admonitions covering the filial responsibilities of the ruled. Richard Bushman has correctly suggested that colonial New Englanders responded as subordinates to a "series of stern fathers who stood over them in the homes of their childhood, in the church, in society, and in the state." The point that needs to be made here, however, is that the close identification of natural and political "fathers" led to two related developments: first, an emphasis on the affections required of all "children," civil as well as natural; second, a corresponding emphasis on the affections required of all "fathers."[4]

Principally, subordinates in civil and natural families were supposed to exhibit what William Gouge labeled a "compound disposition," a seemingly contradictory blend of "love" and "feare." There must be in all children a "*loving-feare*" or a "*fearing-love,*" Gouge declared. In part this insistence on a combination of disparate affections represented a call for moderation. "*Love* like Sugar, sweetens Fear, and *Fear* like Salt, seasons Love," Isaac Ambrose said in 1762, reiterating the phrases Gouge had used more than a century earlier. But more than moderation was involved, for love and fear often appeared in references to God. John Robinson, for example, advised his Plymouth followers to "trust to God with fear, love him with fear, obey him with fear." Because man's trust, love, and obedience to God should be anything but moderate, the austere Robinson's counsel could hardly have been one of moderation. Rather, as

Robinson noted, "fear," in this context, was a "threefold apprehension." First, there was a general fear of God "as our glorious Creator," a fear akin to awe, which was "natural" in the presence of his majesty. The second and third elements of man's "threefold fear of God" were more specifically linked to the affection of love. One could be moved by a "servile" fear of the consequences of sin; that is, punishment at the hands of a "just and angry Lord." Or, one could react to the stimuli provided by "filial" fear, a fear of sin itself that stemmed from a desire not to displease the "gracious Father." In the case of the latter, we "love God more than ourselves," whereas, in servile fear, we "love ourselves more than God; considering, that by sin God is offended, and we by punishment." [5]

This complex association of affections formed the basis of the familial order. In his description of the *Well-Ordered Family,* Benjamin Wadsworth noted, first, that "Children should love their Parents," and second, that "Children should fear their Parents." Following the arguments of Robinson, William Gouge, and Samuel Willard, Wadsworth went on to describe a kind of filial fear founded on parental love. Children should "fear to offend, grieve, disobey, or displease" their father and mother because such disregard bespoke a base ingratitude that was altogether unnatural. The child's fear could thus be distinguished from the servant's. Children were fearful of violating the natural order of things, but servants were inclined to "stand in awe of their Masters and Mistresses" and to fear their power to inflict punishment.[6]

Isaac Ambrose offered the same distinction between filial and servile fear. The *"love-like Fear* . . . so proper to Children" was a fear "mixt with *Love."* Children were therefore affected by the prospect of being the cause of an "offence which a Parent may take." The servile fear of servants and slaves, by contrast, was a *"Fear* . . . ordinarily mixed with Hatred." Foremost in the slave's mind was an apprehension not of the offense as such, but of the "Punishment which his Master may inflict upon him." [7]

The familial paradigm, itself modeled after the pattern of divine rule, thus required more than mere obedience to superiors; it required affectionate obedience. "It should be the very Joy of your Life, to yield *Obedience* unto the commands of your *Parents,"* Cotton Mather declared. Ideally, the "inferiour sorte" would learn to manifest in speech and carriage a filial fear of their superiors. Demeanor, therefore, was of great importance in colonial relationships, and that subject shall be examined in succeeding chapters. For the present, we must move on to a consideration of the dual nature, the mutual obligations, of the affectionate imperatives encompassed in the familial paradigm.[8]

Affections were at least as important in rulers as they were in the ruled.

Social harmony was the product of a jointly sustained effort; it could be realized only if both groups performed their appointed tasks with "mutual Kindness and Usefulness." Children learned very early in life that the "father" and "mother" mentioned in the Fifth Commandment signified "All our superiors." By extension, the same lesson taught all superiors to consider themselves bound by parental obligations. John Cotton's catechism suggested as much, but the "Shorter Catechism" of the *New England Primer* was quite explicit:

Q. What is required in the fifth Commandment?

A. The fifth Commandment requireth preserving the Honour & performing the Duties belonging to every one in their several Places and Relations, as Superiours, Inferiours, or Equals.

Q. What is forbidden in the fifth Commandment?

A. The fifth Commandment forbiddeth the neglecting or doing any thing against the Honour and Duty which belongeth to every one in their several Places & Relations.

Clearly, the scope of the commandment to honor one's "father" and "mother" was inclusive. In his lengthy critical examination of the "Shorter Catechism," Samuel Willard dwelled upon this aspect of the requirements and restrictions of the familial commandment. Its stipulations must be understood, Willard said, "Properly" to include natural parents, "Metaphorically" to include "all Superiors," and "Synecdochically" to include "all the Duties which are mutual between Persons." Not only parents and children, husbands and wives, but also magistrates and subjects, ministers and church members, masters and servants, rich and poor, aged and young, well-descended and lowly, talented and not-so-talented, all must recognize that "there are reciprocal Duties incumbent on them." All relationships were in truth familial; all men bound together and in place by affection.[9]

Under the terms of the Fifth Commandment, civil subordinates were forbidden to murmur and rail against their superiors; at the same time, superiors were reminded of their parental duties. As Ebenezer Gay asserted, a "Mutual good Affection between Prince and People, engaging them to their respective Duties, and shewing itself in the Expressions of a tender Concern for the Safety and Comfort of each other" was a precondition of good order. There must be a certain "*propriety* and *fitness* of action, which is immutably and eternally required, in such a *constitution of things,* as *rulers* and *ruled,*" Charles Chauncy pointed out. If the ruled, therefore, were bound to obey the instructions of their rulers with filial fear, rulers were obliged to manage the affairs of their charges with fatherly concern. Propriety and the fitness of things required that superiors conduct themselves in this manner, for God had not only appointed rulers to be fathers in their respectives realms, William Balch explained, but "it is with a fatherly Affection and Tenderness that he expects they should treat their People." It was not a matter of personal choice or individual magnanimity for "Rulers to exert themselves in the service of the public," Jonathan Mayhew declared. It was, instead, a natural obligation incurred by civil fathers, an "indispensable duty of justice which they owe" to the public "by virtue of their station." [10]

Good rulers, as "Fathers of the Commonwealth," were expected by God and the people, according to the tenets of this doctrine, to discharge their responsibilities in congruence with the priorities of paternity. *"Natural Fathers,"* we know, said Daniel Lewis, are "willing to run all Hazards to preserve" the lives of their offspring and "to promote their Welfare." Political fathers ought likewise to be absorbed in the care and protection of the people. However, they would be similarly preoccupied only if they were similarly affected. Unless civil rulers were "affectionately concern'd for the People's Safety and Welfare," insisted Ebenezer Gay, they would not be inclined to make the kinds of sacrifices necessary in order "to do all that is incumbent on them, with Self-Denial, Patience and Resolution." Elnathan Whitman concurred that good rulers "must be animated and influenced by a paternal Love and Affection for the People committed to their Care," for this attitudinal posture, more than anything else, would "excite" them into pursuing the "great End of Government . . . the publick Good & Welfare," and "put them on laying out themselves to the utmost to promote it." So disposed, rulers would be paragons of public spirit, able to withstand the "Difficulties, Discouragements & Temptations [encountered] in the faithful discharge of the duties of their Place and Station." [11]

Whitman's emphasis on the "faithful" discharge of duties was a basic theme in the literature on affectionate authority. Faithfulness in rulers was as essential as filial fear in subjects. And like filial fear, it was a complex affection. Rulers, if they hoped to succeed in gaining the "Hearts" of the people, Lewis said, must exercise their authority with "prudent Lenity." Afflicted with a "churlish and imperious Manner," a ruler would find it impossible to inspire the "love" that was by definition an integral part of a filial, as opposed to servile, relationship. "Temper therefore your Family Government with a suitable Degree of Mildness," advised John Barnard. For civil and domestic rulers, the same principle of faithfulness applied: "Let your mildness procure their Love to you, at the same Time that your steady Authority excites them to fear you." [12]

In the *Faithful Ruler Described and Excited*, Nathaniel Chauncey elaborated on this theme. "Faithfulness," he said, "is not a simple, but a compound Vertue." It comprised such disparate yet complementary traits as "Humility & Modesty, Sincerity & Self-denial, Diligence & Watchfulness, Justice & Benevolence, Prudence & Constancy." These excellent qualities carried with them more than a hint of "Original righteousness," and indeed, Chauncey observed, "Faithfulness lies either in speaking or acting according to the truth." The faithful man "may be believ'd in what he says" and, because he understood the imperatives of the original order of creation, "may be depended upon for the doing of what he is any ways obliged to do." Faithfulness in a "larger & more extensive sense," then, meant that a man's actions must be "answerable not only to his Promise, or his Post, but to every Relation that he sustains." In this larger sense, faithfulness was a universal social virtue. But, again, given the power of superior examples to move men and the propensity of inferiors to follow such attractive leads, faithfulness was especially "to be regarded in the advancing of persons to places of Trust." Moreover, because faithfulness in rulers tended to generate faithfulness in the commonalty, Nathaniel Appleton noted, good rulers indirectly but effectively suppressed "Disorders . . . Jealousies, and Discontents" among the people and made them more inclined to yield a "cheerful and ready Subjection to their Authority." [13]

Of course, one could not dimiss "fear" in the makeup of good rulers. The fear of God was an important complement to faithfulness. In the first place, like all men, rulers were supposed to maintain a filial fear of the Father of Creation. As Chauncey stated, they must experience "such a sense of God on the heart, as serves Effectually to restrain from whatever is displeasing unto God," and thus "to put on the doing of their duty." But rulers, unlike the majority of ordinary men, were exposed to additional temptations quite simply because of their elevated stations in life. Pride, an inordinate sense of self-importance, was often an unfortunate byproduct of preferment. Fear in rulers, therefore, seemed to encompass the full range of meanings associated with that affection. The lowly servant was all too ready to slip into abject servile fearfulness; consequently, he needed little encouragement in that direction. This was not the case with rulers, however. Their preferred status, coupled with the accoutrements of authority and distinction, had to be balanced personally with a healthy dose of humility. This might be accomplished, William Balch suggested, if the "greatest of Men, or of Princes" were made aware of the "essential Properties of their Nature," particularly their own mortality. Magistrates may stand as gods on earth in their relations with ordinary subjects, yet, regardless of the variety in their worldly conditions, they should know that "They Rule over Beings like themselves." Ebenezer Devotion's discussion of the ruler's mortality played upon an aspect of servile fear. Although the "Civil Ruler" was a "Dignify'd Servant of the Lord," he was still a "Dying Man." Moses died, and "so must civil Rulers of every Order." The "Lofty Pine as well as the lowly Shrub must bow its Head. Purple and Ermine give way to the Shroud." The meaning of Devotion's message was unmistakable: the "wise and contemplative Ruler" believed in his own mortality and acted "under the Influence of such Belief." If in his exalted station he was tempted ever to overestimate his importance there was "enough in the Thought that the Ruler is the dying Man to prevent false Greatness, and allay the Pride of Grandeur & high Title." By contemplating his ultimate and inevitable confrontation with God, the faithful ruler would remain in awe of the Creator. This thought would not "keep him from acting in his proper Sphere of Elevation," but it might "keep him from over acting of it." [14]

Properly affected by a fear of God, the faithful ruler was inspired to live up to the expectations implicit in the Fifth Commandment, to perform the duties belonging to him as a superior, and to refrain from encroaching upon the rights belonging to others in their several "Places & Relations." There was, as Jonathan Mayhew observed, "but little probability, that those who fear not God, will much regard man; or that they who have not an habitual sense of His authority over themselves, will exercise that which he has given them over others as they ought to do." Fear of the Lord, however, did more than provide an appropriate perspective for understanding the foundations of civil authority. It also encouraged faithfulness by holding men's passions in check. There were "no restraints . . . like those which the true fear of God lays upon men's lusts," Charles Chauncy said. True fear, a combination of natural, servile, and filial fear, "habitually prevailing in the hearts of rulers, will happily prevent the outbreaking of their pride, and envy, and avarice, and self-love, and other lusts." Faithful rulers, therefore, as "true fearers of God in this life," might well personify the Original Order. Adam's fall had subverted man's understanding and subordinated his affections to his passions, but faithfulness and fear of God tended to reverse this unhappy circumstance and to restore righteousness. [15]

Good rulers, faithful and fearful of God, were thus, as Nathaniel Appleton exclaimed, a "Great Blessing" to the people. Having arrived at the character of being political fathers, they could effect a far-reaching moral reformation. Just as "Children . . . have a strong Propensity to approve and practice what is done by their Parents," Daniel Lewis noted, subordinates were inclined to adopt the manners of their "*Civil* Fathers." Where rulers managed to govern their affections and subdue their passions, the people themselves soon learned to act accordingly. They, too, Jonathan Marsh pointed out, would come to "govern their Affections" and to subdue "their corrupt Humours and Passions." Society would comprise a group of people who were "Sober, Temperate, Peaceable, Chaste, Diligent . . . Truth[ful] . . . Kind and Charitable . . . Humble and Meek." And God, taking especial "Delight in such a People," might then proceed to "crown the Years that Pass over them with his Goodness." The blessings secured by good rulers were health and happiness, peace and prosperity.[16]

But if political fathers were a blessing, rulers not paternally inspired were surely a curse. They left their charges bereft of appropriate role models, but more than that, they became the chief instigators of social unrest. If rulers "are not vertuous *themselves,*" Samuel Phillips warned, "then the People will incline to think, that their Rulers aim at nothing more than to keep them in Awe, and to oblige 'em to support them in their Vice." Suspicions such as these were inevitable, for authority unaffected by a paternal desire to promote peace and prosperity among the people soon evolved into an object of "Contempt." The logic of the situation seemed irrefutable. As Daniel Lewis asserted, if paternal affections ensured that "*Rulers* will not grasp after *more* Power than properly belongs to them, nor the *People* be under a Temptation to wish it *less* than it is," then the apparent absence of such affectionate restraints must give rise to constant, acrimonious confrontations.[17]

The bonds of affection were thus as fragile as they were essential. They could be maintained only through the cooperative efforts of superiors and subordinates. Whenever "those under Authority perceive their Rulers [to] have no paternal Concern for them, they will be apt to have but little Affection for their *Civil Fathers;* which must needs be productive of great Confusion and Disorder in the Body Politic," Lewis warned. It appeared as though once the affections were alienated, the passions of man again reigned supreme and social harmony became impossible. "When *Power* is visibly abused *Submission* will be found an hard Task," Lewis observed, for without the ligaments of affection each party "will be jealous of the *other.*" So essential indeed was the affectionate bond that without it the familial commonwealth degenerated into a tyrannical domain. Disaffected rulers, Lewis said, may be properly "look'd upon rather as *Tyrants* than *Fathers.*" Superiors could be cast as fathers or tyrants, subordinates as children or slaves, and the role of affection was as ever decisive.[18]

All of this implied that civil subordinates might at times be tempted to interpret filial fear, combining "Honour and Reverence" with "Obedience and Submission," as a conditional obligation. It was due ultimately,

Elnathan Whitman observed, only to superiors who "faithfully discharge the duties of their Places, and approve themselves Blessings to their People." Human nature was such that, Nathaniel Appleton argued, a "willing and obedient People" presupposed the existence of "wise and good Rulers." The bonds of affection being mutual, the "People have their Rights as well as Rulers," Stephen White added. Therefore, the divine precept calling for submission to the commands of an affectionate civil father was plainly not the same thing as the "absurd" doctrine demanding subjection to the dictates of an abusive tyrant. The people were "bound to submit" only to "civil Rulers acting in Character. I say, acting in Character with special Emphasis." Magistrates were well-advised to heed the warning incorporated into this formulation of the commonwealths of affection.[19]

II

DEMEANOR

Excommunication of John Farnum

*His offence for which he was dealt with, was many moral evils (and
so a complicate[d] offence) breaking forth at once: viz. 1. Renouncing
Communion with the Church; 2. Holding familiarity with Excommunicate Persons; 3. Slanders against several holy and worthy men;
4. That having been often reproved for these things he still persisted.
When the Elders reproved him for these slanders he replied, that* they
might be offended at a thousand things, he cared not: *and that* there
was never an Elder in *New England* was willing any should read the
Scripture, but themselves: *After this, he was called before the Church,
tenderly dealt with, and those Scripture Rules which he had
transgressed were applied to his Conscience: but in vain. At the third
Church Meeting on his account (Octob. 16, 1665) the Pastor (Mr.
Mayo) told him it was expected that after so much patience he should
manifest repentance. His reply was, that* he desired none of their
patience, he was humbled for his sins. *The Teacher (Mr. Mather)
saying to him, we must see it by the fruits, he retorted, you see it! you
shall never see it: some Brethren told him his speeches and carriage
were very sinful, they had never seen the like, he replied,* I did not
come hither to be snub'd and snarl'd at by every one, *and so he
turned his back to depart: the Pastor wished him to stay and hear
what further they had to say, and seeing him still proceed, charged
him in the Name of the Church and of Christ to stay: he rejoyned,* do
not use the Name of Christ to me, I am not one that can bow and
stoop to every one; & exit. *The same day he told some of the Brethren
that he wished the Church would Excommunicate him, and then he
should be of a better society. On all these accounts was he laid under
Admonition. Two months after which, being called before the Church,
he, in words, confest the evil of some of the particulars, but was
observed at the same time to turn about and laugh: where then was
his Repentance? The Church (this notwithstanding) waited divers
months longer, till he went on to that height of impiety and
prophaneness, that one of the Teaching Officers setting before the
Church the Rule concerning Excommunication* Farnum *makes a* leg *[?]
to him (in the Assembly) in way of derision. . . . Upon these things the*

Church concluded upon his censure, only allowing him another months patience: after which (no repentance appearing) they proceeded.

SAMUEL WILLARD, *Ne Sutor Ultra Crepidam* (Boston, 1681)

3

Inward Esteem,
Outward Expressions

On a December day in 1705, a fracas took place on a country road outside of Roxbury, Massachusetts. At first glance, the incident involving Governor Joseph Dudley, his son William, and two farmers, Thomas Trowbridge and John Winchester, appears to be of scant significance. After all, the fracas itself and the civil trial that followed produced no long-lasting changes in the public life of the Bay Colony. However, because some of the most deeply held assumptions concerning mutual obligations in an affectionate commonwealth were involved, the episode is especially revealing. We can follow the action through Samuel Sewall's *Diary,* for Sewall presided over the case when it came before the colony's Superior Court.

Despite some variations of detail in the opposing depositions, the outlines of the event are clear. On 7 December, Governor Dudley's coach, attended by his son, approached Meetinghouse Hill, a slight elevation about a mile from the governor's estate. There he encountered "two Carts in the Road loaden with wood" and driven by Trowbridge and Winchester. The governor sent his son to meet the oncoming carters and to order them to "give him the way." When the men refused, the fracas ensued. Harsh words were exchanged, the governor drew his sword, and Winchester "layd hold on the Govr. and broke the sword in his hand"; finally, local authorities intervened and "sent the Carters to prison."

According to Governor Dudley's account the two carters were guilty, if not of assault, then at least of gross insubordination. It is important to note that the governor not only recorded the circumstances of the men's refusal, but also carefully elaborated upon the manner in which the refusal was issued. Thus, when William Dudley first asked the men to give way, Winchester allegedly "says aloud, he would not goe out of the way for the Governour." Even after the governor himself calmly explained that they must give way because his coach was "so heavy loaden" that it was "not fit to break the way," the carters remained obstinate: "Winchester answered boldly, without any other words, 'I am as good flesh and blood as you; I will not give way; you may goe out of the way.'" Furthermore, the carters did not stop there, but came menacingly "towards the Governour." In the interest of defense, only to "secure himself," Dudley drew his sword. He had no intention of "hurt[ing] the carters, or once pointing or passing at them," the governor testified, for he still "justly" supposed that "they would obey and give him the way." And because he was thus indisposed to inflict any harm upon the carters, Winchester was allowed to take hold of the sword and break it. As a final insult, Winchester and Trowbridge attempted to drive their carts "upon and over the Governour."

The demeanor of the carters, clearly, was of first importance. The carters are said not only to have refused to comply with the governor's repeated requests, but also to have done so in an ostentatious manner, loudly and boldly. In support of his indictment, Dudley thought it necessary further to inform the Superior Court justices that during his "talk" with the carters, both men impudently refused even to identify themselves. Trowbridge reportedly went so far as to mock the governor's inquiry, "saying he was well known." The depth of their incorrigibility might be measured, Dudley thought, by the fact that the carters did not "once in the Govrs. hearing or sight pull off their hatts or say . . . any word to excuse the matter." Surely, if Dudley's testimony was accurate, Winchester and Trowbridge had violated some of the most fundamental tenets of propriety in the affectionate familial commonwealth.

It seems, however, that Dudley's record of the incident was far from complete. The governor, for example, failed to describe the physical setting of the confrontation, which in this case was obviously relevant. The Roxbury road split into "two plaine cart paths" at the foot of Meetinghouse Hill. The carters, descending along the "path on the west side," saw the governor's oncoming coach approaching the fork in the road. Thereupon, Trowbridge, the lead carter, explained, "I drove leisurly, that so the coach might take the path on the east side," which was the better path anyway, once it began its ascent. When the carts "came near where the paths meet in one" at the base of the hill, Trowbridge said he "made a stop, thinking they would pass by me in the other path." This was not to be, however, for the Dudleys seemed to prefer the west side path up Meetinghouse Hill, the same path the carters were already using in their descent. It was then that the governor's son William "came rideing up and bid me clear the way," Trowbridge said. When Trowbridge suggested that it might be "easier for the coach to take the other path than for me to turn out of that," young William drew his sword, threatened to stab Trowbridge and his horses, and indeed made "severall passes."

Winchester substantiated Trowbridge's account and added that he stepped in only after "hereing Mr. William Dudley give out threatening words." Seeing William persist in his "rash" behavior, Winchester decided to approach the governor, "hoping to moderate the matter." To the carter's dismay, the governor proved to be as hostile and passionate as his son. When Winchester observed that it would be "very easie" for the governor's party to take the better path on the east side "and not come upon us," Dudley allegedly flew into a rage and called him a "rouge [sic] or rascall." Unwilling to press the matter, Winchester claimed he asked for "a minute or two . . . [to] clear the way" for the coach. But as he was returning to the carts, the governor cried "run the dogs through," and with "his naked sword stabed me in the back." Winchester turned to face his assailant but instantly received a "bloody wound" on the head. Fully "expecting to be killed," and wanting only to "prevent his Exelency from such a bloody act in the heat of his passion," the carter caught hold of the sword "and it broke." Still the governor's "furious rage" was not spent. He continued to deliver "divers blows with the hilt and peice [sic] of the sword remaining in his hand."

Meanwhile, Trowbridge, attempting to come to the aid of his friend, had been detained by William Dudley and stabbed in the hip. The governor subsequently shifted the focus of his assault and began to strike Trowbridge with the "hilt of his sword" and with the carter's own "driveing stick . . . as he had done to Winchester afore."

The story told by the carters differed significantly from the report filed by Governor Dudley. There was, however, this important similarity: both accounts placed a high premium on demeanor. Rather than being guilty of disobedience or disaffection, Winchester and Trowbridge appear in their recollections to be models of filial restraint. Verbally, they conveyed their respect for the governor through the use of "Exelency" in references pertaining to Dudley. All requests and suggestions were appropriately couched in a rhetoric of humility, prefaced always by "may it pleas your Exelency." Nonverbally, too, the carters noted, they had been properly deferential. As Winchester emphasized, when he "passed to the Governour" he proceeded carefully "with my hat under my arm." Both men also explicitly professed their affection for the governor. Winchester recorded that during the entire assault he pleaded with Dudley: "I told him twas very hard that we who were true subjects and had bene allways ready to serve him in any thing, should be so run upon." Trowbridge likewise insisted that such declarations were made, that Winchester in at least one instance during the attack had told the governor that he was a "true subject to him, and served him and had honoured him, and now he would taked [sic] his life away for nothing." If Winchester and Trowbridge were to be believed, Dudley was anything but a faithful ruler.

[35]

Dutiful subordinates had been put upon and abused by a superior who, unable to subdue his passions, was incapable of exercising affectionate authority.

The Superior Court justices apparently found the carters' account of the fracas more convincing than Dudley's. Winchester and Trowbridge were respectable farmers. Dudley, however, already had something of a reputation for his outbursts of "great passion." In addition, there were other telling bits of evidence. Judge Sewall, conducting his own investigation of the incident, visited the "ground where the three carts stood." It was indeed a "difficult place to turn," especially if one were transporting a load of cordwood, as the farmers were doing that day. Besides, Sewall thought, the "Govr had a fair way to have gone by them if he had pleas'd." Several months later, with the case still pending, Sewall by chance found himself behind the governor's coach as it approached Meetinghouse Hill. He "follow'd the Coach . . . and observed that the Coachman of his own accord" took the east side path up the hill, the very same path "which was refus'd December 7." Trowbridge's assertion that the east path was the better path thus gained added credibility, for, Sewall noted, there was nothing now to influence the coachman's choice "but the goodness of the way." The ever-curious Sewall made a point of observing the governor's coach during the return trip. Again the east path seemed preferable as the coachman "took it also returning." The bulk of the evidence indicated that the confrontation had been needlessly provoked by the governor. In November 1706, nearly a year after the incident itself, the Superior Court discharged Winchester and Trowbridge "by solemn Proclamation." [1]

The Dudley-Winchester-Trowbridge incident highlighted some essential premises of the affective commonwealth. Social inequality was inherent in the order of creation, and magistrates were divinely appointed, but the duties belonging to the several orders were not to be ignored. Maintaining the bonds of affection was a joint responsibility. It required the combined efforts of rulers and ruled, and such efforts "cannot be mutually discharged as they ought," Samuel Willard declared, "without a due respect born each to other, according to the Order wherein they stand so related." This was, as we have seen, the lesson contained in the commandment to "honor thy father and thy mother." [2] The Dudley case also illustrated the importance of personal bearing during interpersonal exchanges. That both parties in the dispute dwelled on outward appearances was a reflection of their belief that the best measure of affection, of filial fear on the one hand and paternal regard on the other, was demeanor.

In their lessons on the Fifth Commandment, children learned what was required of them in their dealings with superiors. In complementary lessons, they learned how to fulfill those obligations. As a general rule, Benjamin Wadsworth said, children were expected to "show respect and reverence" for their parents, civil as well as natural, "both in *Words* and *Gestures.*" Samuel Willard agreed, that children were obliged to obey and serve their superiors with an "Obediential Frame and Carriage." The precepts pertaining to this obediential carriage were many. John Dod and Robert Cleaver, in their popular treatise on "houshold governement," described a few of the basic rules of interaction. When approached by "elders and betters," for example, children were admonished to "rise up," "bend the knee, in token of humilitie and subjection," and "uncover their head[s]." William Gouge's guidelines on demeanor were nearly identical to Dod and Cleaver's, and Gouge explicitly recognized the communicative significance of nonverbal token exchanges. By their "countenance and gesture of the body," Gouge said, children and other subordinates in civil hierarchies expressed their respect and readiness to obey.[3]

Eleazar Moody produced perhaps the most popular behavioral guide in eighteenth-century America. Moody's *School of Good Manners,* first reprinted in the colonies in 1715, continued the tradition established by earlier writers such as Dod and Cleaver. Moody's book, for the most part a compilation of rules, covered a wide spectrum of settings. As one might expect, however, there was a good deal of overlapping advice offered in parallel situations. Whether at home, school, or meetinghouse, subordinates were supposed to remove their hats immediately upon being confronted by a superior. They were cautioned neither to sit while in the presence of superiors, nor to speak "till thou art spoken to, and bid to speak." At such bidding, they were to "Speak neither very loud, nor too low," to "Speak clear[ly], not stammering, stumbling nor drawling," and finally, to "Speak not without, Sir, or some other title of respect." Above all, Moody warned, an indolent posture while in the presence of a superior was totally unacceptable: "Loll not when thou art speaking to a superior or spoken to by him."[4]

Because facial expressions could be especially meaningful, subordinates were advised to keep them under strict control. In most exchanges, "Let thy countenance be moderately cheerful, neither laughing nor frowning." If one's superior should utter something "wherein thou knowest he is mistaken, correct not . . . nor grin at the hearing of it; but pass over the error without notice or interruption." Similarly, "if any immodest or obscene thing be spoken in thy hearing, smile not," but rather "settle thy countenance as though thou did'st not hear it." Stray glances, Moody knew, could be inadvertently offensive; therefore, he mentioned them specifically in several instances. At the meetinghouse, "Fix thine eye on the minister, let it not wildly wander or gaze on any person or thing." At the table, "Fix not thine eyes upon the plate of another, or upon the meat on the table." While drinking, "Lift not thine eyes, nor roll them about." Also, "Look not earnestly on any one that is eating." When in the company of others, "leer not at any person whatsoever." And, perhaps most important in view of the commitment to duty and place, "Look not boldly or wishfully in the face of thy superior." [5]

The overriding impression one might get from a cursory examination of these rules governing "words and gestures" is that they were repetitious, mechanical, and petty; hence, that they may profitably be ignored. However, this is simply not the case, for the very nature of these behavioral guidelines reveals to us the fundamentals of an affectionate social order. We can begin with Moody's "Admonition to Children": "by a timely and early accustoming yourselves to a sweet and spontaneous obedience in your lower station and relations, your minds being habituated to that which is so indispensable in your duty; the task of obedience in further relations will be performed with greater ease and pleasure." Moody summarized two salient points in this declaration. First, "spontaneous" obedience was a product of custom and habit. This was not as contradictory as it might sound. For if men were, as most writers believed, creatures of habit, then habitual responses were indeed "spontaneous" in the sense that they were unthinking reactions to certain kinds of stimuli. Second, the force of habit was capable of transforming what was initially disagreeable into something agreeable. Thus the "task" of obeying one's superiors became a matter of ease and pleasure once the mind was properly habituated.[6]

The implications of these commonplace axioms were obvious. Habits could be good or bad. If habits of virtue were not instilled in the child, then, as James Burgh warned, "habits of Vice and Profaneness . . . must of course take possession of an uncultivated mind, as naturally as weeds do of an uncultivated ground." Although it was true that, as Charles Chauncy put it, good habits prevented the "out-breaking of . . . pride, and envy, and avarice, and self-love, and other lusts," until eventually they weakened and destroyed the "inward propensities themselves to the various acts of vice," it was also true that vicious habits could be equally potent. "As Years advance, Habits gain Strength," regardless of whether they were virtuous or vicious, John Taylor said. Therefore, it was incumbent upon parents in educating their child to "choose the best" and to "habituate him to it" so that eventually it became "easy and pleasant." Otherwise, Benjamin Wadsworth cautioned, children become "us'd or accustomed to a course of . . . scandalous wickedness" that, once established, was "very hard" indeed to change.[7]

It followed that "cultivation" had to be undertaken early in life, before the "weeds" of profanity became perennial. Fortunately, these were the years when the child was most susceptible to, and most likely to benefit from, what Samuel Phillips called a *"due Regimen."* Childhood was known to be, as Cotton Mather observed, "the *Waxy,* the *Ductile* Age, the Age that is most easily *Moulded* into any Form." "Babes are flexible and easily bowed," John Cotton agreed; therefore, "it is far more easy to train them up to good things now, than in their youth and riper years." During their "tender Years," Josiah Smith confirmed, children were "less habituated to corrupt Practice," and the "Root of Vice" may thus be quite "easily plucked up." Then, too, while their "Hearts" were tender, children were "more apt to receive the Impressions of Vertue." But, Smith cautioned, the "Time of Instruction is *short.*"[8]

It followed also that parents or parental surrogates were forced to assume an enormous educational responsibility, for they enjoyed opportunities that were not, and perhaps never again would be, available to anyone else. The "utter incapacity of Youth," James Burgh said, "lays them almost wholly at the mercy of their Parents or Instructors for a set of habits to regulate their whole conduct through life." Thus situated, "every Parent or Guardian" must be to the "last degree solicitous what *Habits* first take root in the minds of those he has charge of." The very essence of parenthood was bound up in this responsibility. "Either instruct your Children or lay down the Name of Parents, a Title and Character you have no Right to," declared Josiah Smith. An undisciplined youngster, then, could rightfully be viewed as a shameful reflection of his parents' failure. But even more important, the tragedy was not a personal one confined within the limits of the home. The ungoverned child became an ungovernable adult. Not having learned the value of submitting to the will of his natural parents, he was not likely to submit to the authority of his civil fathers. Chaotic families inevitably reduced the commonwealth itself to chaos.[9]

Faithful parents were thus obliged to begin the process of restoring the habit of original righteousness. In order to do this, their children could not be left to themselves. Uncontrolled by a wise household government, uninformed by a set of suitable precepts, their passions would naturally hold sway. This was the sad legacy of Adam's fall. Adam's disobedience, it will be recalled, was thought to have subverted man's understanding, allowed his passions to prevail over his affections, and reduced man to the level of brutes and beasts. Until the affections were restored to their proper place, ordered under the faculty for "understanding," men would remain beastlike, driven into action, as John Taylor remarked in the *Value of a Child, or, Motives to the Good Education of Children,* by the dictates of their weakened constitutions, "inslaved and devoured by ravenous Appetites." "It belongs to us" as natural or civil fathers, therefore, "to light the Understandings of our Children" and thereby "to moderate and direct their Passions." [10]

This process of lighting the child's understanding had to start with lessons on submission. Immediately following the alphabet in the *New England Primer* the "Dutiful Child" had to learn "by Heart" the promise to "fear GOD, and honour the KING . . . honour my Father & Mother . . . Obey my Superiors . . . Submit to my Elders." John Taylor advised his parental audience to "teach your Child Submission to yourself, or you will be able to teach him nothing besides." All children, as sons and daughters of Adam, were under the influence of their passions, which they discovered, John Barnard noted, "very soon . . . even before they can speak." Consequently, they would not, were unwilling to, accommodate any of the moral advice offered them until this natural inclination of their wills was subdued. John Robinson's observations on this theme are well known. There was, Robinson said, "in all children . . . a stubbornness, and stoutness of mind arising from natural pride, which must, in the first place be broken and beaten down. . . . For the beating, and keeping down of this stubbornness parents must provide carefully for two things." They must restrain the "wills and wilfulness" of their children, and they must inure them "to such a meanness in all things, as may rather pluck them down, than lift them up." [11]

We should add, however, for it is often overlooked, that Robinson's intention was not to destroy the will of the child. He did speculate, it is true, that it might be best if children did "not know . . . that they have a will in their own." But even then he expressed some doubt that such knowledge "could be kept from them." More to the point, what Robinson advocated was the destruction of the influence that passion exerted on the will. This was the "fruit of natural corruption," of Adam's sin, which had to be destroyed lest we "plant a nursery of contempt of all good persons and things" and revert to mere "brutishness." Once the grip of passion was broken, the will was free to respond to the understanding and the affections. "Inflexibility and obstinacy" would be supplanted by "humility and tractableness"; thus the foundation of education would be laid and the habits of virtue could begin to be inculcated. [12]

In these particulars there was nothing extraordinary about Robinson's observations. Indeed, his prescriptions and the premises that supported them received their fullest explication in the advice offered by that gentler Englishman John Locke. In *Some Thoughts Concerning Education,* Locke argued that "few of Adam's children are so happy as not to be born with some bias in their natural temper." Specifically, human nature tended to be both selfish and short-sighted. Mankind by and large was unwilling to allow the dictates of "reason" to overrule the desires of the "appetite," unwilling "to resist the importunity of present pleasure or pain, for the sake of what reason tells him is fit to be done." It was the principal "business of education," then, "either to take off, or counterbalance" this unfortunate bias.[13]

Locke recommended, as the crux of a properly conceived educational system, a mode of childrearing aimed at curbing the passionate wilfulness of children. This could be accomplished with the least amount of pain if a program of submission was commenced very early in the life of the child, Locke observed, for "Children (as soon almost as they are born, I am sure long before they can speak) cry, grow peevish, sullen, and out of humour, for nothing but to have their wills." Therefore, it was best for children to "go without their longings, even from their very cradles," so that they might grow accustomed to submitting their "desires" and accepting what their parents thought was "fit for them." During this crucial period, the child's "ignorant Nonage," parental will must prevail and "stubbornness . . . must be mastered." When the issue at hand was a "contest for mastery betwixt you, as it is, if you command, and he refuses; you must be sure to carry it," Locke warned, "whatever blows it costs." A "perverseness in the will" of the child must be beaten down; "there is no other remedy." The immediate cause of the confrontation might be an "indifferent matter," but the punishment remained the same regardless. If there was evidence of "wilfulness mixed with his fault" so that the result was a "designed, resolved disobedience, the punishment is not to be measured by the greatness or smallness of the matter wherein it appeared, but by the opposition it carries, and stands in, to that respect and submission that is due to the father's orders." Obstinacy—and for Locke this alone justified resorting to the use of the rod—had to be rigorously opposed; the "blows by pauses laid on, till they reach the mind, and you perceive the signs of a true sorrow, shame, and purpose of obedience."[14]

Locke, as the last statement indicates and as we shall see in the section to follow, was not suggesting a "slavish" system of discipline geared primarily toward breaking the child. Rather, he insisted that the "true secret of education" was to find a way "to keep up a child's spirit . . . and yet, at the same time, to restrain him from many things he has a mind to, and to draw him to things that are uneasy to him." The strongest case for the early commencement of disciplined obedience was founded on the belief that a firm hand applied in the beginning would "keep their [children's] wills right" and thus make harsh punishments unnecessary. The need to use the rod against "untractable" children was, Locke said, "usually the consequence only of former indulgences or neglects."[15]

The solution to Locke's "secret," therefore, lay in the Robinson formula of substituting "tractableness" for the obstinacy that was rooted in passion. Given the inherited temper of the "sons of Adam," Locke asserted, good order in this world must not be left to "unguided nature." The human mind had to be made "pliant" through the intervention of an external source, in this case the visible hand of caring parents. The effort to make children "perfectly comply with the will of their parents" was not an end in itself, however. Restraints and punishments were well applied only to the extent that they prevailed "over the wills" of children and taught them to "submit their passions, and make their minds supple and pliant to . . . their parents' reason . . . and so prepare them to obey what their own reason shall advise hereafter." [16]

The progression of the educative process was crucial. First came the lessons on submission and obedience, because the grip of passion, Adam's legacy, had to be broken; then, after the mind was rendered supple and open to instruction, other lessons, moral as well as eclectic, could begin. The very organization of his *Thoughts Concerning Education* conveyed this central message, for Locke spent the first half of his book describing the bases of childrearing and the nature of childish wilfulness before proceeding to a discussion of the particulars of "virtue, wisdom, breeding, and learning." Furthermore, this progression seemed supported by the stages of human growth. Submission was not only the first step in education, but it was also most easily learned in the beginning. "A compliance, and suppleness of their wills, being by a steady hand introduced by parents, before their children have memories to retain the beginnings of it, will seem natural to them, and work afterwards in them, as if it were so," Locke explained. In the same vein, the natural bias of children's tempers might incline them toward perversity, but if faults were dealt with "one by one, as they appeared, they might all be weeded out, without any signs or memory that ever they had been there." By entering upon a course of prudent firmness early enough parents established the education of their children on a solid foundation. Thenceforth, increasingly, the voice of "reason comes to speak" in their children "and not passion." [17]

In his *Thoughts on Education*, James Burgh repeated Locke's advice. "Previous to every other step, that is to be taken in the education of a young person, is the forming and breaking [of] his temper," counseled Burgh. The latter was accomplished by "crushing and nipping in the bud the luxuriant or pernicious" exercises of passion, such as "Anger, Pride, Resentment, Obstinacy, Sloth, Falshood, and so forth." In contrast, the forming of a young person's temper could best be done by "cherishing and encouraging the good qualities of it," such affections as "Humility, Tractableness, Meekness, Fearfulness of offending, and the rest." Also, Burgh, in common with Locke and others, warned that this educational process must be started early. "If this work be neglected by parents till the age of Six be past," Burgh said, "it need hardly be attempted at all." The reason for this was simple: with the passage of time the "mind soon acquires a sturdiness and obstinacy that is not to be conquered." "Bad *Habits* become quickly, as it were, a part of the very soul." [18]

Human nature, then, had been corrupted by Adam's fall, but education might restore a semblance of the original order if it could advance good habits until they became, as Benjamin Wadsworth put it, *"second Nature."* Good habits derived from an external source, the "something put into him" that Locke said must be interwoven into a person's "nature," would act to counterbalance the inherited "bias" of Adam's descendants. Moreover, this second nature was vital to the effort to maintain the bonds of affection. As Winthrop noted in his discussion of "workes of mercy": the "force of Argument from the goodness or necessity of the worke" was often not enough because it was not uniformly reliable. Only a "habit in a Soule as shall make it prompt upon all occasions to produce the same effect" was an acceptable guarantee. [19]

This conceptualization of the force of habit and second nature harks back to Eleazar Moody's claim that habitual responses were "spontaneous." If the affections were properly framed, virtuous deeds would be promptly performed in response to the appropriate stimuli; they would be "nativEly" brought forth "as any cause doth produce the effect." Rational arguments would not have to be repeated over and over again, for these responses would be incorporated as an intimate part of man's second nature. As Locke pointed out, "habits . . . being once established, operate themselves easily and naturally, without the assistance of the memory." Habitual actions, then, were spontaneous because individuals performed them "without reflection." This is not to say, however, that such actions would be irrational. On the contrary, the affections, by definition, must be under the influence of the understanding. Thus, affectionate responses founded upon habits of virtue were unthinking, but only displays of passion rooted in the reprobative nature of Adam's sons were truly mindless. [20]

In addition to these assumptions pertaining to the force of habit, the particulars of the several rules governing behavior were founded upon a second premise more directly related to the measurement of affection.

Bent knees, uncovered heads, and all of the other gestures of the body were attitudinal markers. Children, Locke declared, were under a "perpetual Obligation of *honouring their Parents*," and this entailed an "inward esteem and reverence to be shewn by all outward Expressions." The Fifth Commandment itself seemed to necessitate an intimate connection between inner feelings or affections and outward bearing. The fine line between filial and servile fear was dependent upon just such a connection. It was not enough, Ebenezer Gay said, merely to give one's parents or superiors "high Titles and loud Applauses." This kind of "cringing" obedience was servile. Such "external Significations of Reverence" were proper only when accompanied by "more substantial Demonstrations of Respect and affectionate Concern." In a *Well-Ordered Family,* Isaac Ambrose likewise argued that the "duties of Children to Parents" were twofold: "inward, as *Love and Fear*" and "outward, as *Reverence, Obedience,* and *Recompence.*" Moreover, Ambrose explained, the "outward *Duties*" must be manifestations of the inner state of "Love and Fear." Children imbued with filial fear, or a fear "mixt with Love," would invariably honor their parents through such means as the use of "reverent and honourable Titles" and "meek and humble Speeches," together with a recognizably obediential "Carriage." [21]

Thus, although the rules on demeanor depicted a ritualized form of interaction, we cannot afford to dismiss them as insignificant. The rituals themselves were meaningful. They provided clues to the state of an individual's affections. Children's words ought to be properly reverential, Cotton Mather observed, but their carriage "must yet more Emphatically *Speak* the *Reverence*" they had for their superiors. Eleazar Moody never lost sight of the ultimate purpose of his numerous selections on deportment. In his final "admonition to children," Moody reminded his charges to "Let your body be on every occasion pliable, and ready to manifest in due and becoming ceremonies, the inward reverence you bear towards those above you." [22]

The principals in the Dudley-Winchester-Trowbridge fracas were right to emphasize demeanor. In an affectionate familial commonwealth, where bonds of affection formed the basis of stability, personal bearing was a proper item of concern in any indictment. The degree and kind of punishment meted out often hinged on questions of demeanor. The Superior Court's decision to discharge the carters was in essence a comment on the governor's conduct. If Winchester and Trowbridge had breached the bounds of propriety, they were, it appeared, more than ordinarily provoked by Dudley's disaffected behavior. The governor was blameworthy for having initiated the confrontation in the first place, and then for causing it to escalate into a serious conflict. The governor's provocative actions bolstered the suspicion that he was not in control of his passions. His "rash" response to the requests of the carters seemed to indicate that he was filled with an inordinate sense of pride and self-importance. Only a proud and imperious ruler, John Robinson had said, would become "fierce and violent" whenever he was a "little crossed." The "humble-minded" civil father bore such injuries "moderately, as thinking moderately of himself." Dudley's "meekness" and "humility" had been tested and found wanting. He failed to act as a faithful ruler, and because he first violated the tenets of paternal decorum, filial obedience was not forthcoming.[23]

The court's decision amounted to a judgment against the deportment of the governor. It should be noted also that the fundamental social values of the familial commonwealth were reinforced by the handling of the case. Disciplinary proceedings were in this way an important part of socialization.

II

Ever since Adam's fall and the decline of the habit of original righteousness, discipline had become, as John Norton said, "an essential part of the nurture of the Lord." Verbal instructions, even moral advice accompanied by virtuous examples, often proved inadequate in the post-Adamic world. A comprehensive system of social instruction, therefore, had to include an affectionate method of disciplining those who violated the written or unwritten codes of propriety. Fortunately, the divine plan of nurture provided man with an eminently appropriate model. According to Jonathan Marsh, God dealt with his misbehaving charges as a *"tender and compassionate Father."* He patiently moderated their "peevish Tempers and forward Dispositions" under conditions that would have been unbearable had he been less affectionately concerned. In his program of discipline, he turned to the rod as a last resort, only after he was convinced that "Milder means won't do; Reproofs, Admonitions, Warnings, Threatenings won't do." And even then he acted "as a Father . . . and not as an incensed Judge." His primary affection in this instance was pity, and pity, we know, was a compound affection consisting of empathy for the miscreant and antipathy for the misdeed. Moved finally into using the rod, the Lord nevertheless "limits and sets bounds to his Anger, as to the time and the measure of it." Moreover, he carefully ensured that his correction was timely. "He will not do it too soon; so as to be sudden and hasty in it; nor will he defer it too long." Instead, his actions were always "seasonable and proper to carry light and conviction with it," for it was a matter of supreme importance that those being punished "read or see their Sin in the punishment of it." [24]

That Marsh identified this carefully orchestrated program of discipline and enlightenment as "Fatherly" was an indication that domestic government ought to be just as purposeful. Ultimately, the very welfare of the whole was dependent upon the "conscionable performance" by parents of their "domesticall and household duties," William Gouge declared. Chief among those duties was the establishment and maintenance of good order in the family. Social harmony and security, the ends of the institution of government, could be achieved only if children learn "their places, and practice Subjection and Obedience at home," Samuel Whittelsey asserted. It can be truthfully said, Nathaniel Chauncey proclaimed, that "*Families* (are as it were) *Nurseries,* where the *young Trees* are raised & nourished." And "much according to the Ordering they have here, they prove *Useful* or *Hurtful*" to the church and state. As Benjamin Wadsworth cautioned, "Young Persons wont much mind what's said by Ministers . . . nor will they much regard good Laws made by Civil Authority, if they are not well counsel'd and govern'd at home." [25]

Because the stakes were so high, with the "good ordering of Church and Common-wealth" resting in the balance, parental neglect in this matter could not be tolerated. Good order in the home, sustained by a program of discipline that was educative as well as corrective, was never solely a household affair. Colonial laws empowered local officials to oversee the actions of parents and guardians, intervening with fines, admonition, and ultimately removal of children, whenever domestic government was judged faulty. It must quickly be added, however, that the yoke of family government was never supposed to be onerous or oppressive. By definition, submission to an affectionate governor must be "chearful" rather than "forc'd." By law, excessively cruel parents or masters were even more culpable than those who were immoderately indulgent. Indulgence was foolish but understandable; cruelty was unnatural and incomprehensible. [26]

Perhaps the clearest summary of a program of domestic discipline founded on affection was, for eighteenth-century Americans, provided by John Locke. In his *Second Treatise on Government* and especially in *Some Thoughts Concerning Education,* Locke described the limits of parental authority and bemoaned the use of the rod in maintaining the familial order. At best, corporal punishment might bring about a temporary peace and a grudging compliance on the part of the child. What was far more likely, however, Locke said, was that such a "lazy and short way" of correction would encourage the worst propensities in our charges. Obedience rendered for "fear of whipping" was based on no other principle than the desire to secure "greater corporal pleasure" and to avoid "greater corporal pain," a selfish principle that was at the "root . . . [of] all vicious actions and the irregularities of life." The distinctly servile quality of obedience thus obtained was unsurprising; "slavish discipline makes a slavish temper." [27]

In a truly efficacious and paternal system the fear of offending must outweigh the fear of the rod. Such filial fear might be established, Locke advised, by cultivating a sense of shame in children. The "shame of suffering for having done amiss" should be paramount in the mind of the offender. Even in cases of outright obstinacy or rebellion, where the child "should be beaten," the "shame of the whipping, and not the pain, should be the greatest part of the punishment." For it was the "shame of the fault," the fear of appearing offensive in the eyes of one's parents and justly "deserving chastisement," that was the greatest restraint on childhood infractions and the most durable guide to laudable behavior.[28]

When it came to specifics, Locke made it clear that he thought parental demeanor was at the core of any system dependent upon filial fear. If a frequent resort to the rod was counterproductive, "constant rebukes and brow-beatings" were similarly objectionable, tending only to blunt the apprehension of shame. In their place, Locke suggested that parents "show wonder and amazement at any such action as hath a vicious tendency, when it is first taken notice of in a child." This "first" and "best remedy" would convey to the offending youngster the impression that "it could not be imagined he would have done" such a thing "and so shame him out of it." If the fault should appear a second time, it must be "discountenanced with the severe brow of the father . . . and all about him" and accompanied by a "cold and neglectful" carriage suited to discrediting the misdeed, "and this continued till he be made sensible and ashamed of his fault." If words were used, and Locke conceded that verbal reprimands were "sometimes" necessary, "they ought to be grave, kind, and sober" rather than the sort of "Passionate chiding" that tended to confuse the child, leaving him unable to determine "whether your dislike be not more directed to him than his fault." Ultimately, both verbal and nonverbal chastisement, to be effective, must highlight the "unbecomingness of the faults" and, consequently, magnify the "shame of doing amiss." [29]

Colonial commentators seemed to subscribe wholeheartedly to these Lockean prescriptions. Jonathan Edwards believed that ideally the discipline that prevailed in the home should be conducive to making obedience an easy task. Visitors' accounts confirmed that the yoke of government in the Edwards household was perhaps the closest thing to ideal in this world. Edwards was "careful and thorough in the government of his children," Samuel Hopkins said. He took "special care" in establishing his authority early. "When they first discovered any considerable degree of will and stubbornness," Edwards would "attend to them till he had thoroughly subdued them." He thus encouraged in his children a spirit of humility that was naturally "yieldable, subject, [and] obediential." In spite of such thoroughness, or more likely because of it, Edwards never seemed to resort to severity. On the contrary, as a result of his "prudent" mode of domestic rule, his children "reverenced, esteemed, and loved him." Edwards, it appeared, had successfully "established his parental authority" on affection and "produced a cheerful obedience ever after." [30]

That the Edwards home was an "abode of order and neatness, of peace and comfort, of harmony and love" was also in no small part due to the efforts of Mrs. Edwards. Sereno Dwight noted that Sarah Edwards was in every way a model wife, "in every sense a *help meet*" for Jonathan. Most praiseworthy, Dwight thought, was her handling of the children. She was fully aware of the importance of her duty, for she knew that "in many respects, the chief care of forming children by government and instruction, naturally lies on mothers, as they are most with their children, at an age when they commonly receive impressions that are permanent, and have great influence in forming the character for life." Sarah Edwards, like her husband, "knew how to make them regard and obey her cheerfully, without loud angry words, much less heavy blows." [31]

The key to this "excellent way" of governing children, it soon became apparent, lay in the nurturing of affection. Parents had to be firm, but if punishment was ever meted out, it was accomplished in good Lockean fashion; it was administered calmly with affection rather than suddenly with passion. Otherwise, it would be impossible to right the inverted order that obtained in the world since the fall of Adam. According to Dwight, Sarah understood this imperative well; thus she never punished her children "in a passion." She refused even to use "angry, wrathful words" in admonishing them because, given the passionate nature of Adam's progeny and the imitative nature of youngsters, such words managed only to "provoke children to wrath, and stir up their irascible passions, rather than abate them." Whenever she had occasion to "reprove and rebuke, she would do it in few words, without warmth and noise, and with all calmness and gentleness of mind." Also, because the affections were so closely associated with the understanding, and because the divine model of parental nurture called for "light and conviction" to accompany all corrections, Mrs. Edwards would, in a "gentle and pleasant" manner, "address herself to the reason of her children, that they might not only know her inclination and will, but at the same time be convinced of the reasonableness of it." Consequently, while parental authority and discipline was "strictly and punctiliously maintained," this "kind and gentle treatment . . . seemed naturally to beget and promote a filial respect and affection." [32]

The yoke of family government in the Edwards household, rather than being burdensome, had succeeded in instilling filial fear in the children. They did not merely or grudgingly obey, they obeyed "cheerfully" without a hint of "murmuring or answering again." It is possible, of course, that the visitors saw only what they wanted to see. In that case, however, the predisposition itself would be important, for it would be a reflection of their domestic ideal. Most observers, indeed, would have found only confirmation of the general assumption that, as Dwight noticed, affection seemed naturally to beget affection. "Let them see your Affection and Regard in your Admonitions," Josiah Smith told parents, and even in the process of correcting your children you will manage to "win their Hearts." If we are able to temper our authority with affection, with "Kindness, and Meekness, and Loving Tenderness," Cotton Mather had said, then we may expect "our children" to *Fear* us with *Delight.*" John Taylor, in his remarks concerning the "Motives" behind a good education for children, elaborated further. "A parental Dominion, well supported by Reason and good Sense, is the best Hold we can have of our Children," Taylor said. If parents hoped to nourish a sense of filial attachment, they must effect a balance between love and authority. Such a balance, as we have noted, was the essence of affectionate rule. "If we so love . . . [our children] as still to maintain our Authority"—that is, if we refuse to indulge them foolishly—and if we "so maintain our Authority as sufficiently to discover our Love"—that is, if we are mindful of our humble status and reject a haughty and imperious carriage—then, Taylor declared, "they are probably our own for Life." When parental "Love and Authority conspire together, the one steadily forbidding, and, in good earnest, correcting what is wrong, and the other chearfully encouraging and smiling upon every Thing right and commendable," children soon learn to subdue their passions and to develop habits of "Wisdom and Virtue." Thus educated, a child "can never be ungrateful to its best Benefactors." [33]

Parents who adhered to this divine program of "Fatherly Care" were justly honored. Then, more than at any other time, they approximated William Ames's description: "Parents in regard to their Children, soe beare a singular image of God, as hee is the Creatour, Sustainer, and Governour." Under these circumstances, children feared not the punishment but the grief the offense would give their parents. This filial fear, properly cultivated, made severity of discipline unnecessary as well as undesirable in accordance with the supposed bliss of the Edwards household. Only the incorrigible feared the ferule more than the fault. Hence in Cotton Mather's well-known program of gentle coercion, which itself echoed Locke's advice on parental demeanor, the *"first Chastisement"* for an "ordinary Fault" consisted of mock dismay. "I . . . lett the Child see and hear me in an Astonishment," Mather confided. In a world alive to the meanings of nonverbal signals, Mather's show of parental displeasure conveyed the sense that he was "hardly able to beleeve that the Child could do so *base* a Thing, but beleeving that they [*sic*] will never do it again." Where filial fear rendered the child apprehensive about losing parental favor, Mather said, the "sorest Punishment" that could possibly be inflicted upon the misbehaving youngster was the shame of being "chased for a while out of *my Presence.*" The exercise of this *"Sweet Authority"* normally was enough to restrain the passions of children. Only in cases involving *"Obstinacy* or some gross Enormity" did Mather confess to giving "a child a Blow." He minced no words in expressing his distaste for the "abominable" systems of discipline that encouraged "raving and kicking and scourging." In agreement with Locke, Mather labeled such methods a *"slavish* way of Education," for at best they instilled only servile fear.[34]

A prudent course of discipline was thus a vital part of the process of social education. Without it, domestic government was impossible and civil order would disintegrate. "Fatherly" discipline checked the vicious propensities of fallen man and at the same time held out the promise of reformation. Such a program of punishments and positive reinforcements, however, depended upon the existence of two closely related conditions. First, a just system of discipline had to allow for the exercise of discretion on the part of the punishing agent. Indeed, discretion was the soul of a "Fatherly" administration. "Sapience, or wisdom," John Robinson remarked, was "gathered from principles" and stood merely in "bare contemplation of things excellent." Wisdom, in other words, was a function of the faculty for perceiving, speculating, and judging, or what Jonathan Edwards had called the "understanding." "Discretion," however, was revealed in "practice" and ought, Robinson said, to be "restrained to things fit or unfit." It was more properly a function of the affections.[35]

In the realm of punishment, discretion tended to ensure a "fitness" between the crime and the penalty, a fitness that could not be secured by referring to principles only. One needed instead to make reference to the offender. William Perkins provided a concise statement of this idea in his discussion "Publicke Equity." Laws, with "punishment and penalty" affixed to them, were needed to "uphold the common wealth, and all societies" of fallen man, Perkins noted. In the execution of these laws, however, "publicke equity" demanded that penalties vary "according to the quality of the fault, greater or lesse." Magistrates and all others in a position to inflict punishment could insist on the "extremity of the law" or on the "mitigation of the law." Both of these powers, Perkins said, were conferred upon them "by God himselfe." Thus it was essential for them to realize that what the law allowed in a particular case was not always the same thing as what was just. Whether to execute the law "straightly & precisely, according to the literall sense & strict forme of the words, and the exactest meaning that can be made out of the words," or to proceed with moderation "when there is good and convenient cause of mitigation, in regard of the person offending," must ultimately be left up to the "discretion" of the punishing agents.[36]

Perkins urged flexibility. "He offends as well, that neglects to *mitigate the extremity,* when just occasion is, as hee that neglects to *execute the extremity,* when there is need." Certainly, a person with no knowledge of the law was unfit to be entrusted with the power to punish, because he had insufficient understanding to discern his duty. But a person who knew only the law was equally unqualified, because he "can doe nothing but urge the law, & the plain words of the law, and is not able to mitigate the rigour of the law, when need so requireth." It was, therefore, the "glory of Judges and Magistrates," civil or otherwise, both to "execute the Lawes, and to temper them with . . . discretion." Justice, public equity, would prevail only when the cold law was affectionately administered.[37]

The case for discretion presupposed the existence of some criteria that the magistrate might draw upon for guidance in his rulings. Perkins insisted that "justice alwayes shakes hands with her sister mercy," but he also cautioned against a "certain foolish kinde of pity" that would have the "extremity of the law executed on no man." Such foolishness, inordinate indulgence in civil and natural fathers, tended to undermine the effectiveness of all laws and "to pull downe authority, and so in the end to open a doore to all confusion, disorder, and to all licentiousnesse of life." John Robinson similarly warned that discretion might easily become indiscretion if care was not properly exercised. There was, he said, such a thing as "merciful cruelty," whereby a just punishment, justly administered, saved the "persons themselves that are punished, and others" who might witness the action. Conversely, there was such a thing as "cruel mercy, when men by sparing, spoil both the persons offending and others who by their impunity take boldness to offend." "Foolish pity," said Robinson, was often the cause of ruin in the "city" as well as in the "family."[38]

The need to distinguish between merciful cruelty and cruel mercy, the one as admirable as the other was detestable, leads us to a consideration of a second condition inherent in a prudent program of discipline. "Fatherly" discretion rested on the ability of parents and magistrates to discern the presence, or to gauge the sincerity, of certain attitudes in their "children." Here, once again, the presumed connection between outward posturing and inward esteem came into play, for demeanor seemed to affect the nature and duration of the punishment inflicted. Except in cases of "gross enormities," the personal bearing of the offender was as important as the offense itself in establishing the boundaries of acceptable deviance. The ignorant but well-affected deviator might be reformed; therefore, a mitigation of the penalties prescribed by law was quite appropriate. In contrast, the unaffected and practiced deviant was incorrigible; hence the extremities of the law must be applied lest authority in general be brought into contempt. Discretion, then, was informed by an evaluation of the criminal's character, which in turn entailed a close scrutiny of his deportment.

That "*First-born* of all humane Societies," the family, was again the paradigm for the larger world of the commonwealth. As the situation in the Edwards household indicated, children responded to correction without murmur or protest when confronted by a firm but prudently gentle governor. However, even under less ideal circumstances, the emphasis on an obediential carriage seemed to apply. Samuel Willard believed, almost without exception, that children "should take reproofs kindly," resolve "not to displease or grieve" their parents ever again, and "be Thankful to God for the faithfulness of their Parents." William Gouge allowed that an innocent child might plead his case in order to avoid unjust chastisement, but he must do so "mildly, reverendly, and seasonably: not too peremptorily crossing or thwarting his parent." Eleazar Moody advised children to bear with patience "thy parents reproofs or corrections" even if "it should so happen that they be causeless or undeserved." All were agreed, moreover, that outward expressions, the attitude in which corrections were borne, ought to influence the course of discipline. Wayward children, if "corrigible," showed signs of contrition. They received correction readily with "meekness and patience." Others, less capable of reformation, betrayed their intractability by "murmuring or sullenness." Moderation would work in the case of the former, but only the extremity of the law would do any good in the case of the latter.[39]

This sensitivity to outward expressions, rooted in the discretionary dictates of public equity, kept authorities alert to the prospect of dissimulation. In stressing the significance of countenance and carriage, Locke had warned of "affectation," which, he said, was not the product of inadvertence or of "untaught nature," but rather of deliberate deception. Through close observation, however, this "counterfeit carriage" could be exposed, because affectation, being less than genuine, would lack the "natural coherence" that should obtain "between the thing done, and such a temper of mind, as cannot but be approved of as suitable to the occasion." In other words, the dissimulator would reveal himself to the sensitive observer because his behavior would appear "awkward and forced" as a result of the "disagreement between the outward action, and the mind within." [40]

No more striking examples of paternal discipline, discretionary justice, and the importance of demeanor can be found than in the pronouncements of excommunication by church fathers. Excommunication was an appeal to the extremity of the law; hence, before this sentence could be prescribed church fathers had to be convinced that anything less would constitute foolish indulgence, that all of the lesser penalties—public confession, admonition, and suspension—would be worse than ineffective, they would prove harmful to the welfare of the whole.

The case of Isaac Theer illustrates some of these axioms. In Braintree, Massachusetts, in 1683, Theer "was called forth in public" by the Reverend Moses Fiske. Theer, who had been convicted of stealing pewter, cheese, and a horse in a series of "notorious scandalous thefts," had already been counseled in private, "especially by the officers of the church." However, these efforts to "bring [him] to a thorough sight and free and ingenuous confession of his sin" failed to reclaim Theer. Thus he was now required publicly to "acknowledge his sin and [to] publish his repentence." Accordingly, when Theer appeared before the congregation "he owned his sin of stealing," said he was "heartily sorry for it," and "begged pardon of God and men, and hoped he should do so no more."

It appears as though Theer met all of the requirements of the ceremonial act of public contrition. Yet, "sentence was declared against him." Why? It is clear that Theer's effort fell short of expectations. But it was not so much because of what he said or did not say; after all, he confessed his sins, expressed repentance, and held out the promise of reform. Rather, it was Theer's demeanor, his nonverbal performance, that hastened his conviction. When called forth, Theer "moved pathetically" and so conveyed immediately his reluctance to conform to the rules of the ceremony. Before the congregation, he "stood impudently"; that is, he leaned "against the lower end of the foreseat." Finally, although his words were words of contrition, he spoke "with a remiss voice, so that but few could hear him." The Braintree church fathers felt there was good reason to doubt the sincerity of Theer's apology. His outward actions seemed to belie the existence of true inward repentance. And their worst suspicions were confirmed when they asked Theer for a more detailed confession, for Theer refused to comply with their request, "saying his sin was already known, and that there was no need to mention it in particular."

The church "at length" determined that Theer was a "notorious, scandalous sinner," and based on his performance in public, beyond reformation because he remained "obstinately impenitent." Here was an example of Locke's awkward dissimulator. William Gouge had also warned his audience about such men who joined "Faire words . . . with contrary deeds." Whenever there was a "contrariety betwixt words and deeds," Gouge advised, "the one will be a witnesse against the other, and that man's condemnation the greater." All that was left was for the Reverend Fiske to pronounce sentence upon the incorrigible Theer by spreading "before him his sin and wickedness." As soon as Fiske began, however, Theer, "guessing what was like[ly] to follow," refused to be detained any longer. He "turned about to goe out" and despite Fiske's command that he "tarry and hear what the church had to say to him," Theer "flung out of doors, with an insolent manner, though silent." [41]

It is worth noting that, aside from the complex of verbal and nonverbal images conjured up by the Theer case, the public ceremony of contrition operated on two levels. First, it offered the corrigible offender an opportunity to demonstrate that he was truly repentant and, therefore, deserved to be reclaimed. Second, it ensured that the incorrigible deviant would stand exposed before the congregation prior to being repudiated by the church. On both levels, communal values were reaffirmed, either by the offender through his confession or by the church fathers through their condemnation. This ceremonial imperative was so well understood that disciplinary proceedings continued even in the absence of the criminal. Theer, for example, refused to play his role in the final charade of sentencing. Instead of standing silently while his sins were "spread before him," he stormed out of the meetinghouse. By this time in the proceedings, however, communal reaffirmation was the principal goal of the church fathers. Thus after Theer had left, the Reverend Fiske simply "applied himself to the congregation" and "spread before them his [Theer's] sin." The pastor's intentions were twofold: "partly to vindicate the church's proceeding . . . and partly to warn others." Theer's presence, in short, was no longer crucial because the remainder of the ceremony dealt only tangentially with him. [42]

A similar emphasis on demeanor during disciplinary hearings was evident in the case of James Penniman. In 1713 the church fathers of what was to become the town of Quincy heard various charges lodged against Penniman and found him guilty of "unchristian carriage towards his wife, and frequent excessive drinking." They ordered Penniman to appear before the congregation so that he might acknowledge his sins and begin to make amends. When he made his appearance, however, Penniman was hardly contrite. "He behaved himself very insolently before the church . . . and was far from discovering any signs of true repentance." As a result, the congregation was unanimous in its condemnation and Penniman was "laid under solemn admonition by the Church."

Apparently this lighter sentence managed to hold Penniman in check for a while, but in 1723 the church was moved by his "contumacy in sin" finally to consider excommunication. This time Penniman willingly acknowledged his faults, "presented a confession" to the congregation, and "prayed that they would wait upon him awhile longer." In sharp contrast to his earlier appearance, he "behaved himself tolerably well." Penniman "seemed considerably affected" by the gravity of the proceedings and "gave some slender hopes of Reformation." Consequently, the church accepted his confession, decided against excommunication, and resolved only that Penniman be "again publicly admonished, and warned against persisting in the neglect of Public Worship, against Idleness, Drunkenness and Lying."

But the delay was in vain. About two months after the second sentence of public admonition, the congregation "met together to consider what is further necessary to be done by the Church towards the reformation of James Penniman." Penniman presented himself before the assembly and once again read a confession desiring "their patience towards him." However, his performance was now judged inadequate. Penniman's confession, the church concluded, was a "trifling confession," for its contents were contradicted by the absence of a posture of contrition. Penniman's outward bearing "manifested no sign of true repentence." The congregation moved unanimously that Penniman "should be cast out of the Church for his incorrigibleness in his evil waies" and authorized the Reverend John Marsh to proceed as he saw "good to do it." Marsh decided to "wait upon him some time," but by early the following year, convinced of Penniman's incorrigibility, he had the "fearfull sentence of excommunication pronounced upon him." [43]

Aspects of deportment and demeanor so evident in the Theer and Penniman cases were vital to the process of determining whether the extremity of the law or a mitigation of it was in order. Such judicial discretion, founded on the familial paradigm of paternal authority, was not, of course, confined strictly to ecclesiastical matters. Civil fathers were supposed to effect the same balance of justice and mercy in their rulings;

therefore, they too had to be attentive to attitudinal indicators. When Jonathan Gilburt of Hadley, Massachusetts, appeared in county court in 1676 on charges of sedition, disturbing the peace, and "affronteing Authority," he managed to have his sentence moderated. Despite the weight of his conviction, the "Corte yet Considering his humble Confession and Acknowledgment, and manifestation of greate sence and Shame for his former actiones, Promiseing to Carry it Better for time to Come and Ernestly desireing that he may be put to the tryall upon that account" placed Gilburt on probation, "Bound in a Bond of ten Poundes . . . for his good Behaviour" for one year.[44]

The Gilburt case was not an isolated example. It was more the rule than the exception. As in the ecclesiastical trials, "humble" confessions, "earnest" pleadings, frank acknowledgments of wrongdoing, and heart-felt promises of reformation often resulted in mitigated penalties. Thomas Stebbing, Jr., disturbed the peace in Springfield in 1671 by publishing a "foolish . . . Rime casting reproch upon the Towne and the Maides in Towne" and was hailed before the county court. Magistrate John Pynchon nevertheless thought it best to deal "gently with him by a small fine" of twenty shillings, which would serve the purpose of "bearing Testymony against such disorders." Pynchon's reasoning was simple. Although Stebbings was at first a "little saucy yet afterward Confessing all and being admonished and told of the evill: he seemed very Penitent and promised to be more watch full against such like disorder."[45]

The interaction of penitence and punishment was revealed also in the case of Joane Miller. In 1656 Joane appeared before the Pynchon court to account for her "very evill behavior" while at home. Her husband, Obadiah, complained that Joane abused him with "reproachfull tearmes or names." She regularly called him a "foole toad and vermine" and, once, in a fit of anger, had fallen "uppon him indeavoringe to beat him at which tyme shee scratched his face and hands." John Lamb, a family acquaintance, confirmed that Joane frequently abused her husband by calling him names and by threatening to "knock him on the head." Thomas Miller, the plaintiff's brother, provided further corroboration. While Joane customarily referred to Obadiah as a "foole and vermine," Thomas testified, "he doth not remember he ever heard her call him husband." Indeed, in what may well have been the most damaging bit of evidence against Joane, Thomas Miller swore that she had openly proclaimed "shee did not love him [Obadiah] but hated him; yea she here said she did never love him and shee should never love him." Joane's truculence not only undermined the harmony of the Miller household, but, in the absence of affection for the "chiefe governor," eliminated what scant prospects there were of ever restoring good order.

The court found Joane guilty of "vile misbehaviour," vile because her actions subverted domestic government and thus jeopardized the basis of social stability. It ruled that she "be taken forth to the whippinge post, there to receive Soe many stripes on the naked body as the Commissioners should see cause to inflict on her." When the sentence was pronounced, however, Joane prostrated herself before the court. By her utter "humiliacion and earnest protestations for better carriage towards her said husband" she reaffirmed communal values. The court thereupon remitted the extremity of the law. Joane was placed on probation, "that for the least miscarriage to her husband after this tyme she should be brought forth agayne to receive a good whipping on the naked body well laid on." Joane's last-minute show of contrition had been decisive.[46]

Henry Sewall's plea to the Ipswich Court in 1651 went into greater detail than Joane Miller's and, therefore, provides us with further insights into the dynamics of public confession. Sewall, by all accounts, was a cantankerous old man often at odds with his fellow townsmen. In late 1650, at the age of seventy-four, Sewall was involved in a brouhaha at the meetinghouse in Rowley. The incident began when Sewall, acting on the belief that the Reverend Ezekiel Rogers was late, started to pace back and forth "in the foremost seat in the meeting-house near the pulpit." When Rogers was ready finally to step into the pulpit to begin prayers, he ordered Sewall to cease his "walking." Sewall responded immediately by saying "you should have come sooner, with more words to that purpose, but he not ceasing his walking." Rogers, perhaps taken aback by Sewall's abruptness, admonished him to "remember where you are; this is the house of God." But Sewall would not relent. In a "lowd voyce" he retorted, "I know how to behave in the house of God as well as you." Exasperated by the confrontation, determined not to allow the disturbance to continue, Rogers ordered: "putt him out." To which Sewall replied, "lett us see who dare." About this time a concerned "brother" attempted to intervene by speaking to Sewall in a "friendly way," but he would not be swayed. Instead, with a "stearne countenance and threatening manner," Sewall "saide he would take a course with some of us." What ensued in the wake of this challenge is not entirely clear. It is likely, however, that Sewall's removal was far from peaceful, for he was later charged with disturbing the meeting and with assaulting a member of the congregation and "drawing blood."

In early 1651 Sewall appeared before the Ipswich court and apologized publicly for his misconduct. "I doe now in the presence of god & this reverand assemblage freely acknowledg my evell according to the full extent of the Testimonies," he confessed. His actions, Sewall affirmed, constituted a "great sin against god," an offense against his "messinger," and an affront to the congregation. In particular, Sewall apologized for his "contemptuous speaches & gestures, to the reverend Mr. Ezeekiell Rogers & others in the publique meeting." Finally, the stout-hearted septuagenarian held out some hope of reformation. He "earnestly desire [d]" the prayers of his brethren to the effect that the "god of all wisdom & grace" might "guide me in his blessed wayes of Truth & peace for tyme to come." Properly humble and repentant, Sewall was welcomed back into the community.[47]

The import of these examples of judicial discretion in the family, church, and community is clear. In the first place, to insist upon the extremity of the law in a society where the institutional means of coercion were often inadequate, as was the case in colonial America, was at best impractical.[48] But even more important, severity was out of place in the intimate world of face-to-face interaction. Heavy-handedness, the indiscriminate meting out of all legally prescribed penalties, would be detrimental to the social order because it would alienate the very affections that were supposed to bind people together. Even if it were institutionally possible, therefore, a frequent resort to the extremity of the law was less than desirable. While it might secure compliance, that compliance would be forced rather than cheerful, founded on servile rather than filial fear.

In its proper context, the act of chastening an offender was an episode in social education. The entire procedure was geared for a society organized after the familial paradigm and constrained by the yoke of family government. That paradigm, with its potency already drained by the evolution of the family in America, would be replaced in the course of the Revolution by an alternative model, a republican vision.[49]

4

In Loco Parentis

The redoubtable Samuel Johnson felt perfectly comfortable in addressing the students of King's College, with "inexpressible tenderness," as "my sons." Student regulations at Yale College and the College of Rhode Island lumped the "President, Fellows and Tutors" together with "natural Parents." The College of Rhode Island also required the steward to "sit at meals with the students . . . and [to] exercise the same authority as is customary and needful for the head of a family at his table." Dartmouth College in 1771 "as yet has no Laws," observed Ezra Stiles, "but the Govt is declared *parental*" with its president Eleazar Wheelock "being *parent.*" When a student ignored Wheelock's advice concerning the course of his studies, his action was termed "disobed [ience] to parental Govt & so a Breach of a moral Rule; & thereupon Dr. Wheelock censured & dismissed him from the College." [1] This list of examples might easily be extended, and, considering the traditional *in loco parentis* role of the school along with the social imperatives contained in the Fifth Commandment, none of this would be surprising. It is this traditional conceptualization of the school, however, that makes it an ideal setting for an extended examination of the themes introduced thus far. As a familial institution, the school was organized according to the pattern of paternal supervision and filial submission manifested throughout the rest of society. But the school provides us with an especially illuminating example of the affectionate commonwealth. As an artificial social environment with clearly demarcated limits both in time and space, the scholastic family was forced to state its behavioral imperatives more formally and explicitly than was necessary in the natural family, where shared identifications were intense enough to allow such rules governing behavior to be left unspoken. Thus, the process of socialization, the methods used by the fathers of the schools to indoctrinate novices into the standing order, lends itself quite readily to close scrutiny.

The necessity of a concerted effort in socialization becomes quickly obvious when we consider the nature of the collegiate way. Student accounts give us a revealing glimpse into this special social setting. When thirteen-year-old Oliver Wolcott, having completed the required examinations for admission to Yale College, visited the New Haven campus in 1773, he was struck with "emotions of awe and reverence":

Men in black robes, white wigs and high cocked hats, young men dressed in camblet gowns, passed in small groups. The men in robes and wigs I was told were professors; the young men in gowns were students. There were young men in black silk gowns, some with bands and others without. These were either tutors in the college or resident graduates to whom the title of "Sir" was accorded. When we entered the college yard a new scene was presented. There was a class who wore no gowns and who walked but never ran or jumped in the yard. They appeared much in awe or looked surlily after they passed by the young men habited in gowns and staves. Some of the young gownsmen treated those who wore neither hats or gowns in the yard with harshness and what I thought indignity. . . . The domineering young men I was told were scholars or students of the sophomore class, and those without hats and gowns and who walked in the yard were freshmen, who out of the hours of study were waiters or servants to the authority, the president, professors, tutors and undergraduates.

Whether this brief exposure discouraged Wolcott we do not know, but he did postpone his entrance into Yale for one year.[2]

Wolcott's description highlights several important aspects of the eighteenth-century college community. The pomp and ceremony, the formalized orders, and the privileges of class are easily identified. Moreover, to the uninitiated observer the role of the freshman appeared to be marked by indignity. In 1784, a decade after Wolcott's experience, another entering freshman, Jeremiah Mason, recorded his first encounter with the norms of college life. On the afternoon of his first day Mason was approached by a "man booted and with a horsewhip," who asked him if he was a freshman. "I answered, 'yes, sir,'" Mason recalled. "Take off your hat, then, when in the presence of one of the government of the college," he was told. Mason was then ordered to ring the bell for prayers. "I was confused by this harshness and went immediately to what I supposed to be the chapel." Unable to find the bell rope, however, and "feeling a little indignant at the rude treatment I had received," Mason left the chapel and returned to his room. There he shared his story with a few of the other collegiate novices and voiced his "apprehension of trouble from my disobedience of orders." Mason's anxiety proved to be well-founded, for the man with the horse whip turned out to be a tutor, and Mason was soon to experience his wrath.[3]

Natural advantages, it seemed, did not mitigate the indignity of the freshman. A "slender sprig," Wolcott observed, could make demands of another "much his superior in Age and Strength." Wolcott therefore thought it necessary to caution his brother Frederick, in 1782, to remember the special context of his experiences. "I suppose this will find you a

Freshman with your Hat under your Arm under continual Apprehensions of some severe Discipline from those self-important Gentry who affect to stile themselves your Superiors," the older Wolcott commiserated. "You ought however to remember that this Superiority will be of short Duration." And though "you have an undoubted right to despise an ignorant Fellow, who values himself upon his priviledge of wearing a Gown," it would surely be "improper and imprudent to express any Contempt publickly." [4]

Collegiate laws outlined the parameters of the special social environment wherein, as the older Wolcott indicated, natural distinctions were often discounted. Aware of these special circumstances, and eager to ensure an acquaintance with them, college authorities required entering freshmen to transcribe the laws. A candidate for admission to Yale had to "transcribe and Keep by himself a Copy of these College Laws, which being Sign'd by the President and One or more of the Tutors Shall be the Evidence of his Admission into this College." The colleges of New Jersey and Rhode Island had identical requirements obliging students to transcribe and keep the laws close at hand as a guide to proper behavior. King's College not only had every candidate for admission transcribe the laws but also made him promise "all due obedience to them, which promise shall be expressed in writing under his hand." And although the University of Pennsylvania allowed its laws to be printed in 1788, it stipulated that "These rules shall be publicly read once in every three months, and a printed copy put in each of the schools." [5]

Detailed regulations governed freshman behavior in a manner reminiscent of Eleazar Moody's prescriptions for children in the *School of Good Manners.* At Yale, for example, freshmen were expected to "show all proper Respect to the Officers of College, the Residency Graduates and undergraduate Classes superior in standing to themselves." This meant that on stairways or in narrow hallways they must "stop and give way, leaving the most convenient side" for their superiors. They had to rise whenever a superior entered or left the room and were not allowed to sit while in the presence of a superior. Similarly, at the various gates and doorways of the college, freshmen had to be particularly circumspect: "When a Freshman is near a Gate or Door, belonging to College or College-Yard, he shall look around, and observe whether any of his Superiors are coming to the same; and if any are coming within three rods, he shall not enter without a signal to proceed." At the College of Rhode Island, the ritual was the same. A member of an "under class" was required to "stop and observe" whenever he approached any of the college's "gates or doors." He had to be especially observant at the chapel and dining hall, "looking round" for any member of a superior class and, if necessary, securing his permission to enter.[6]

Student attire was an even more readily recognizable indicator of status than these behavioral manifestations of deference. The thirteen-year-old Wolcott on his first visit in 1773 immediately noticed the young men with no gowns who appeared awed and apprehensive. Freshmen were forbidden to "wear a Gown, or walk with a Cane." The hat was also an essential token of the ceremonial idiom. A freshman was never to appear out of his room without his hat, which he was obliged to remove whenever he spoke to, or was addressed by, a superior. At Yale, the College of New Jersey, and the College of Rhode Island, freshmen could not wear their hats in the college yard "until May vacation," and all undergraduates were "forbidden to wear their Hats (unless in stormy weather) in the front dooryard of the President's or Professor's House, or within Ten Rods of the Person of the President, Eight Rods of the Professor and Five Rods of a Tutor." And even the parenthetical exception was best ignored, William Wheeler declared in 1781, for "(raining or not) we must never approach [the president] nearer than ten rods without pulling off our hats; and five rods for a tutor." Oliver Wolcott revealed his familiarity with the ceremonial role of the hat, then, when he wrote to his brother Frederick, "I suppose this will find you a Freshman with your Hat under your Arm." [7]

If freshmen had to be made aware of the special requirements of collegiate life, it was the duty of the upperclassmen to do most of the indoctrinating. Seniors, in particular, were entrusted with the "duty . . . to teach Freshmen the Laws, Usages and Customs of the College." Consequently, they could "order the whole Freshman Class, or any . . . Member of it, to appear, in order to be instructed or reproved, at such Time as they shall appoint; when and where every Freshman shall attend, answer all proper Questions, and behave decently." Seniors, of course, could also supervise the actions of juniors and sophomores. The senior class at the College of Rhode Island had the authority to "detain in the Hall after evening prayers, such of the under classes as they shall observe breaking any of the laws of College, and there admonish them of such offenses, as well as correct and instruct them in their general deportment." Not only were seniors to oversee the manners of the lower classes in "minute particulars," but these subordinate classes, for their part, were also to receive all admonitions and instructions "with modesty and submission, and punctually observe." This "overpowering authority & influence of the Senior Class," freshman David McClure confided in his diary, was used at times to coerce the lower classes into acting against their better judgment. Thus in 1766, a petition to the Yale Corporation calling for President

Thomas Clap's "dismission" was signed "by all classes," but "many of us of the Freshman Class," McClure noted, were "hastily persuaded." [8]

Although the senior class was thus singled out, whenever any lapses in deference occurred, juniors were empowered to reprehend "any of the classes below them." Further down the social ladder of the college community, superior only to the lowly freshmen, sophomores could also exercise some levers of control. The "domineering young men" that Wolcott had observed, it will be recalled, were sophomores. Formally, however, sophomores needed to "obtain leave from a Senior" before they went about disciplining a freshman. And even then, they were not supposed to detain him for longer than five minutes, "after which the Freshman may retire, even without being dismissed," provided only that he "retire in a respectful Manner." [9]

Yet sophomores, perhaps even more than juniors and seniors, seemed to relish their roles as "mentors" and "monitors" of the freshman class. Benjamin Silliman, a 1796 graduate of Yale, recorded that freshmen "were, early after their arrival, formed in line, in the long gallery of the old chapel; the senior class being arranged parallel to & fronting them, when one of their number—a man selected for his gravity & weight of character explained to the novices, the peculiar customs of the college, especially in regard to manners. . . . Thus far very well, but the interference of the inferior classes with the freshman class, and especially of the sophomore in lecturing—disciplining & sending on errands—usually vexatious & often insulting, was only mischievous." [10] The petty tyranny of the sophomores had been openly acknowledged by the officers of the college nearly four decades prior to Silliman's complaint. In 1756 the president and tutors "ordered that the Sophomores in teaching the Freshmen the Rules of good Manners & reproving them for any Misdemeanors shall not speak so loud as to be plainly heard in any adjoining Room, nor use any harsh insulting or opprobrious Language, nor Stamp at them, nor speak more than one at a Time, nor use any tyrannical Measures, but shall speak to them with Decency & Gravity, and ordinarily sitting down." Silliman's experience indicated that this order was being ignored. Lyman Beecher likewise commented on the "tyranny of the Sophomores." In 1793 freshman Beecher "was sent for to a room so full of tobacco-smoke you could not see across it. There I was asked all manner of questions . . . and received all manner of solemn advice. Then Forbes, a big fellow, took me as his fag, and sent me on errands." "Every day he contrived to send me on some business or other," Beecher recalled, "worrying me down to indignation." [11]

An even more complete indictment of the sophomores was provided by William Wheeler, a 1785 Yale graduate. Wheeler described the ritual of "trimming"—the details of which the president and tutors must have been familiar with, judging from their 1756 order prohibiting harassment by loud, insulting, or opprobrious language, stamping, or multiple speakers. According to Wheeler, every freshman was "sure to be ordered up and disciplin'd" by the sophomores. The collegiate novice was "generally too free with his Superiors—runs in at the Gate before them—sets without leave—or something," and thus presented the sophomores with numerous opportunities for trimming.

> After he has committed the Crime they assemble a dozen good Voices and summon him [the freshman] with a stamp and a step up to my Room—He entering trembles and is discomposed and 'tis ten to one commits a greater offence than the other,—perhaps he forgets to make a bow, then they all fetch a stamp, asking him what he meant to enter so without bowing,—if he bows to one, the rest are affronted and ask him if he likes that one better than all the rest—if he bows in an awkward manner they take great pains to shew him—keeping him bowing for half an hour almost to the floor. . . . If he is obstinate they put fists in his face, keep him constantly turning around to see those that are behind him—blow tobacco smoke in his face, make him hold a candle, toe a crack, bow to his shadow and when his back is turnd they are continually going in and out to trim him for not bowing,—two or three talking to him at once while he all passive obedience and non-resistance is obliged to stand mute and answer only to the questions they ask him.

Such abuse, reduced to a routine in abasement, convinced Wheeler that "a Soph is absolute and despotic as the great Mogul." [12]

By far the privilege most easily and frequently abused by the upperclassmen was, as Beecher's complaint indicated, the custom of "fagging"—that is, the practice of sending freshmen on errands. At the colleges of New Jersey and Rhode Island, freshmen were obliged to wait upon their superiors. "Every Freshman sent on an errand," the College of New Jersey specified, "shall go and do it faithfully and make quick return." Wolcott, on his first visit to Yale, had noted that freshmen "out of the hours of study were waiters or servants to the authority, the president, professors, tutors and undergraduates." Freshmen, in this way, were perhaps taught a degree of humility; they were certainly kept constantly occupied. We "have attained almost the happiness of negroes," one beleaguered freshman lamented. [13] But the custom of fagging played an important part in maintaining the ceremonial order of the college. First, because it made clear the privileges and distinctions of the several classes, it reinforced the internal structure of the college. Second, because the privilege could be bestowed or withheld, the period of subjugation terminated or prolonged, fagging was a formidable weapon in the defensive arsenal of the college authorities.

Yale required its freshmen to perform all "reasonable Errands for any superior." More specific and revealing, however, the regulation went on to declare that freshmen "are not obliged to go for the Undergraduates in study-time, without permission obtained from the Authority; nor are they obliged to go for a Graduate out of the Yard in study-time." The order of precedence was clearly marked: "A senior may take a Freshman from a sophomore, a Bachelor from a Junior, and a Master from a senior." [14] Such specifications were of primary importance in a deferential society wherein status arrangements generally determined the nature of interactions. The removing of the hat, for example, was not merely an act of etiquette, it was also a ritual dictated by the imperatives of status. A fundamental aspect of social organization and communication, sociologist Erving Goffman has said, is the allocation of "personal space." These "territories of the self," or the space surrounding an individual, when breached by another, causes the individual to feel encroached upon and leads to shows of displeasure or withdrawal. Under normal circumstances, therefore, it becomes the duty of the intruder to provide an account or apology for the intrusion, in short, to perform a "remedial ritual" to restore the routine of "normal appearances." [15] Personal space, it should be evident, varies not only according to the social context, but also according to the individual's status. Thus the remedial ritual of removing one's hat had to be performed at ten rods for the president, eight rods for a professor, and five rods for a tutor. This ritual, then, reaffirmed as well as recognized the status arrangements of the college.

It is noteworthy also that interaction between the various status levels was formally regulated, indicating that the affectionate commonwealth of the school was not a truly domestic institution. Ideally, individuals occupying one status level were allowed to penetrate the personal spaces of others on different levels only on a ritually licensed basis. Familiarity between the members of two distinct levels could not be sanctioned. Thus the Yale freshmen were cautioned: "A Freshman shall not play with any Members of an Upper Class, without being asked; nor is he permitted to use any Acts of familiarity with them, even in Study-Time." President Clap demanded further that "Scholars Shall Shew due Respect and Distance to those who are in Senior and Superiour Classes." A due "distance" had to be maintained because much of the logic and order of collegiate society depended upon it. The faculty of the College of Rhode Island in 1791 thought it necessary to "Admonish all the College for irregularities." These irregularities included unnecessary noise and neglecting of prayers and recitations in the college. The faculty was especially concerned with the students' practice of "associating together in each others rooms in study Hours," and the tendency to make "no distinctions, in their intercourse, between the higher & lower Classes." [16]

Status and distance were communicated in a number of ways. Gowns differently marked and canes separated the freshmen from the remainder of the undergraduates, and tutors from resident graduates. Also, the different orders were addressed differently. As Yale's laws pointed out, undergraduates were called by their surnames, Bachelors of Arts had the title "sir" affixed to their names, and Masters of Arts were addressed as "Mr." Nothing could better illustrate the importance of such distinctions than the confusion that arose over the ranking of tutors. Tutors occupied a special place in the hierarchy of the college. They were mediators between the "Authority"—president and professors—and the student body. As part of the process of maintaining proper role distance, the president and professors refrained from the everyday and somewhat menial task of supervising student behavior. This was left to the tutors, who were not so far removed from the students, either geographically or socially. Their position was indicated by the custom of fagging. Whereas a senior could take a freshman away from a sophomore, a Bachelor could take a freshman away from a junior, and a Master could take a freshman away from a senior, every freshman living with a tutor was "exempted from going [on] Errands for any but the Authority of [the] College." The confusion, Ezra Stiles recalled in 1781, involved the ranking of the tutors themselves. Because tutors were not always selected sequentially by classes, it became "a matter of doubt at Yale & is still so at Harvard, whether a Tutor of Senior Standing in the Catalog shall precede or take rank of one of Jun. Standing yet prior in his Election & Induction into the Tutorship." Until 1748, Stiles observed, class standing seemed to take precedence over the date of election into the tutorial ranks. Thus a 1741 graduate, "Mr. Welles," preceded a 1743 graduate, "Mr. Fisk," even though the latter had already been a tutor for a whole year by the time the former was elected. In 1748, however, a contest developed between "Williams," a 1745 graduate, and "Phelps," a 1744 graduate, for the position of Senior Tutor, which President Clap resolved in favor of Williams. "I well remember," said Stiles, "we tho't it wrong," for "Mr. Phelps had for three Quarters of a year taken Rank of Mr. Williams in sitting in the Hall, at Meetings, & in Processions." Stiles sensed that college routines were being violated. Yet, upon further reflection, it became clear that the affairs of the tutors superseded these routines, for "when the matter was canvassed among the Graduates, it was conceded, that the Dignity of the Tutorship exceeded that of Graduation in Arts; so that there never was a

doubt but that a Tutor tho' A.B. should take rank of a Master of Arts."
President Clap had determined "that in the co-equal order of Fellowship,
they [the tutors] rank according to order of Election not of the
Catalogue." And, Stiles later confessed, "I rather think this is a just Principle." Because the role of the tutor was so much a part of the everyday life
of the student, however, and because student routines were so basic to
everyday interaction, disruptions of those routines, no matter how justifi-
able, had to be kept to a minimum. As a concession, the college authorities began selecting their tutors by classes. "Now every Class of Graduates expects Tutors to be chosen from among them in their Order—& if
any Class is passed over it is disagreeable, & it would be considered
dishonorable if after electing a Tutor from a Class of Graduates of Jun.
Standing another should be elected from one of Senior Standing." [17]

The emphasis on role distinction and distance reflects the importance
of ceremonial gestures within the college. Student accounts testify to the
significance of the college rituals. Freshmen, for example, welcomed their
first class prerogative, the illumination of the college yard on commencement eve. But even more enthusiastically, they embraced the opportunity
ostentatiously to exercise their newly acquired privileges. Freshmen were
stigmatized, it will be remembered, by their dress. Therefore, on commencement eve they customarily participated in a sort of sartorial display.
Benjamin Silliman described the occasion: "On the evening preceding the
public commencement, they first assumed the toga, & the cane; and ostentatiously paraded the college yard in close phalanx—fencing their way
through crowds of people, assembled to view the illumination of the college windows, & the dazzling pyrotechnics of mounting rockets—and
burning wheels revolving with blazing corrunations & fiery serpents, fly-
ing through the air with comet trains along the line of the college yard."
As might be expected in this circus atmosphere, the freshman class often
carried these displays to extremes. The Yale Corporation complained that
on the eve of the 1760 commencement freshmen "walked together in
the College Yard with Clubs or Staves, and one of them walked Before
and brandished a naked Sword, and that they all or most of them made a
violent and scandalous Noise by jointly beating and striking on the College Fence." [18]

The corporation was well aware of the disturbances occasioned by
commencements and attempted to curb the excesses. In 1734, 1737, and
1739, it ruled on a central concern: "It having been observed, that on
Commencement Occasions there is a great expence in Spiritous distilled
Liquors in College, which is justly Offensive, For the prevention hereof It
is Agreed & Voted by the Trustees, that for the future no Candidate for a
Degree, nor any undergraduate Student, shall provide or allow any

Brandy Rum or other Spiritous distilled Liquors to be drunk in his Chamber during the Week of Commencement. And if any shall transgress against this Act, the person or persons so transgressing & being thereof Convicted shall be debarred from future Honours of the College." [19] In 1731 the corporation declared that "Considering the ill Practice of firing the Gunns at the anniversary of Commencement [and] to prevent the same for the future, we strictly forbid it." Any undergraduate convicted of having "a Hand in such firing of the Gunns . . . either directly or in-directly" would be degraded or otherwise punished, as the college authorities thought proper. In 1755 the corporation threatened the ceremony itself. Citing the "firing of the great Guns" and the "great Disorders" that accompanied the "Elumination of the College on the Evening before the Commencement," the corporation warned that if the disturbances continued "the Elumination shall be wholly suppressed." [20]

These efforts at curtailing commencement activities, however, were either circumvented by the students, or so vigorously opposed by them, that the college authorities were often forced to acquiesce and accommo-date the near riotous rituals of celebration. President Clap's attempt in 1760 to enforce an order limiting each senior to two gallons of wine led to a minor rebellion over "some contraband goods (a small cagg of rum)" and was productive, one observer noted, of "some humour and more con-fusion." In the end, despite "some demurrer," Clap secured a "humble confession" from the students responsible for smuggling the rum into the college, and he had the confession read at the graduation exercises in place of a salutatory oration. But it was a Pyrrhic victory. Clap's "unpolite manner" aroused an "almost universal resentment" among the students and, one participant observed, "both the matter and manner of this act of humiliation was such, that it was the chief subject of banter and ridicule that evening and to the end of Commencement—it occasioned some dispute (as there were a few that endeavored to justify the Pres [iden] t's measures), but more severe reflections and a great deal of fun." [21]

Similarly, freshmen were unwilling to surrender the traditional privi-lege of parading in their gowns and canes during the commencement eve "Elumination." Walter Bradley, an absentee Yale freshman, proudly pro-claimed after his class had triumphed in regaining this customary privi-lege: "I . . . am very happy to be informed that after so many and fre-quent petitions have been made to the President by the Class [we] have at last obtained liberty to walk the yard and to perform the other sports and amusements which we made application for." [22]

But it was not only the students who delighted in rituals. College authorities presided over a number of small-scale ceremonies that tended to reaffirm the internal order and social reality of student life. Ezra Stiles, ever sensitive to customs and traditions, recorded a few of these symbolic gestures. In 1788 Stiles "gave Permission to the Freshman Class to wear their hats in the College yard after the ensuing Vacation." Formerly, Stiles explained, freshmen were never allowed to wear their hats in the yard. From about 1775 they were "permitted to wear them after May Vacation. We now permit them after Jany. Vacation." The strictly appointed seating arrangements within the college hall afforded an even more ceremonious mode of marking the progression of the classes. In July 1782, Stiles noted that after the candidates for degrees had been dismissed, "I advanced & brot forwds the Classes, the Juniors to be the Senior Seats, &c. . . . & committed the Freshmen now Sophomores to the Discipline of the new Seniors." Again, in July 1784, Stiles recorded: "At Evening prayers I ordered the Classes to take their new seats, reserving sufficient Room for the Young Sirs who may tarry in Town." The young "Sirs," of course, were recently commenced Bachelors of Arts. Such titles, as we have seen, distinguished the undergraduates from the graduates. This circumstance afforded yet another opportunity for a small-scale ceremony. At the commencement dinner, Stiles explained in 1784, "I drank to Sir Goodrich one of the Candidates, in a Glass of Wine. This was the Punctum saliens for all the Classes to change their Appellations, & to commence the Juniors, Seniors, & so on." [23]

Rituals and routines, formal and informal, were, therefore, elements of the ceremonial idiom through which the individual student came to learn the authorized patterns of interaction and interdependence among the several social orders of the college. Within this community certain forms of "ill-behavior"—for example, the freshman display on commencement eve—actually reinforced the established order. The ostentatious show of gowns and canes tended, after all, to enhance the importance of these image markers. Bona fide misbehavior, however, was especially threatening to this intimate social world and therefore required a complex system of discipline.

II

The prescribed canons of behavior were supposed to maintain order and industry, harmony and regularity. Yet, despite the close regulation of student activities, and sometimes because of it, opportunities for mischief abounded. The problem for the college fathers in dealing with violators of the prescribed order was identical to that which had perplexed generations of civil and ecclesiastical fathers. A just system of discipline had to fit the penalty to the crime. This entailed more than a comprehensive code of laws; it required an affectionate administrator, one capable of exercising judicious discretion in meting out punishments. Whether the extremity of the law or the mitigation of it was called for remained a matter of personal judgment, which, in turn, was guided by the demeanor of the criminal. Collegiate discipline, in other words, was bound by the divine model established under the yoke of family government. An entry in the "Records of the Judgments and Acts of the President and Tutors of Yale College" serves as an appropriate introduction.

On the evening of 20 January 1752, "Goodrich, Wiggins & Spaulding with sundry other[s] engaged in a disorderly Noise." Ezra Stiles, then a tutor, ordered them to be still, but they would not quit their "disorderly Rout, & . . . stamping & jumping." With the help of a second tutor, Stiles again attempted to put an end to the disturbance, but the flushed students "contemptuously disregarded" the tutors' orders. When Stiles proceeded to record their names, Wiggins "behaved in a most indecent and disrespectful Manner" and would not cease. "At the same Time Goodrich & Spaulding behaved with great Levity & Disrespect, by smiling, laughing, Walking, odd Bowing &c." After taking down their names, Stiles ordered them to remain in the room until they were sent for, whereupon "Spaulding shoved up the Window, & halloo'd, 'Who has any thing to give the poor Prisoners.' " When they appeared before the tutors, again "they behaved with the utmost Insolence, Contempt & Disrespect— Wiggins, by appearing without any Gown or Hat, & by unseemly, disrespectful Gestures—Spaulding, by odd Bowing, Stepping too & fro &c." Threatened finally with expulsion, Spaulding was said to have replied, "I dont much matter that." Thus unable to control the "unsufferable Noise," the tutors "went & informed the President of them as incorrigible."

The response of the president could not have been unexpected. Noting first that "Students have been generally too much addicted to making a Noise," and that "such Riots heretofore . . . have not been suppressed by lesser Punishments," President Clap suspended Goodrich and Wiggins "for their repeated Violations of the express Orders, as well as disrespectful & contemptuous Treatment of the Tutors." They were henceforth "prohibited from coming within the Limits of the College Yard." Cited for his "disrespectful & contemptuous Treatment" of the tutors, for "his hallooing out at the Window, & for his making light of an Expulsion," Spaulding, the "principal Actor in the Riot," was expelled.[24]

As recounted in the "Records of the Judgments and Acts of the President," this 1752 incident brings into focus two fundamental aspects of collegiate society. First, the details on demeanor are especially important. Spaulding, Goodrich, and Wiggins were guilty of "repeated Violations";

they were convicted of ignoring express orders "4 or 5 several Times." To be sure, they were charged with a "Series of violent, riotous & rebellious" actions. But even more important was the manner of their rebellion. The clue words appear again and again throughout the record: "contemptuous," "insolence," "disrespect," "contempt," "unseemly," "indecent," "presumptuously." These words referred to specific actions of the students: "odd Bowing," "appearing without any Gown or Hat," "unseemly" gestures, "Stepping too & fro." Second, it is important to keep in mind the reasons that were given in justification of the expulsion and suspensions. College authorities seemed to be as reluctant to exercise these powers as church fathers were to employ the corresponding power of excommunication. Spaulding, Goodrich, and Wiggins were indicted for being "incorrigible," and thus creating "a Scandal to this College." Spaulding, in particular, was charged with crimes "which are scandalous to this College, & render You unfit to be a Member of It." This was a crucial allegation. Because he had already proven himself "unfit to be a Member," the president and tutors were able "utterly [to] expel, reject, & cast out you the said Spaulding from being a Member of this College." Not only was the relationship terminated and the remaining scholars forbidden to "entertain any free or familiar Conversation" with Spaulding, but even past traces of his presence were to be removed. The butler and monitor had to "erase & blot" Spaulding's name from their records.[25]

We will examine first the emphasis on demeanor. From what has been said concerning status distinctions and role distance in the everyday interaction of the members of the college, the stress on student demeanor is understandable. A familial commonwealth, dependent upon the restraints imposed by the bonds of affection, is especially vulnerable to "contumacious" behavior and must therefore protect itself against it. Thus the College of New Jersey demanded that "Every member of the College . . . treat the authority of the same, and all superiors, in a becoming manner, paying that respect that is due to every one considered in his proper place." When spoken to by a superior, the student should give a direct answer "with the word, SIR, at the end thereof." The College of Rhode Island required that every scholar "shew all due honor and reverence both in words and behavior to all his superiors." Among these were parents, magistrates, ministers, and "especially . . . Trustees, Fellows, President, and Tutor of this College." In "no case" would the student be justified in using "reproachful, revelling, disrespectful or contumacious language."[26]

King's College was most explicit in this respect. The 1755 college laws specified that if a student was convicted of such "scandalous immorality" as drunkenness, fornication, lying, theft, or swearing, he would be forced to make a public confession of his crime. If, however, the crime "is judged too heinous," the violator would be expelled, "especially if he be contumacious." Cards, cockfights, and dice were also outlawed; students engaging in these games of chance could be fined, admonished, suspended, or expelled, "especially if contumacious." Similarly, if a student was "disobedient" to his superiors, or treated them "with any insulting, disrespectful or contemptuous language or deportment," he risked expulsion—"if he persists contumacious." Finally, any student leaving town without the permission of the president or tutors could be fined, suspended, or, again, "if contumacious," expelled. "Obstinacy and perverseness in all cases," the college laws of 1763 summarily declared, "shall be punished by expulsion." The attitude in which a crime was committed, then, figured largely in the severity of the judgment rendered. Indeed, in the case of expulsion, it was decisive.[27]

This emphasis on demeanor heightened the college fathers' sensitivity to all slights. The indictment against Spaulding, Goodrich, and Wiggins, it will be recalled, carefully detailed their acts of contempt ("odd Bowing," "appearing without any Gown or Hat," "unseemly" gestures, "Stepping too & fro"). Along the same lines, President Clap in 1762, in the midst of a full-scale confrontation with the senior class over a new policy of examinations, was incensed not only by the contents of a student petition, but also by the manner in which the students had signed the document— "round the letter . . . in an odd and ludicrous manner." The stress on deportment made it unnecessary as well as unwise to engage in such open assaults on personal worth as David Brainerd's declaration in 1741 that one of his tutors had no more grace "than the chair I . . . leaned upon." More effective and more entertaining were the antics of Tertius White, who "stood up and profanely mimicked" President Clap during prayers.[28]

This thin-skinned sensitivity, however, was not restricted to the president and tutors. Students were caught up in the same system of status-oriented interaction. Punishments that affected a student's standing in the college also altered the nature of his relationship to the remainder of the community, and thus were especially effective. When sophomore James Douglass was convicted of stealing "8 sheets of Paper & a Pen-Knife" in 1772, King's College authorities reprimanded him "before all the Students." Douglass then had his "Gown stripped off by the Porter" and was forced to "kneel down & read a Paper containing an Acknowledgement of his Crime, expressing much Sorrow for it, & promising Amendment for the future." Finally, Douglass was "forbidden to wear his Gown or Cap for one Week." The importance of gown-wearing as a status marker and as a tool of discipline is dramatically illustrated in this little ritual of admonition. One senses that sophomore Douglass, publicly stripped of the accoutrements of superiority and reduced to the level of the freshmen for one week, felt sorely chastised.[29]

The custom of fagging was likewise a formidable disciplinary lever because its privileges could be withheld or its indignities prolonged. In 1755 the Yale Corporation, in an attempt to suppress the tumultuous activities that attended commencements, ruled "that if any Freshman should be any way accessary to the fireing [of] the great Guns att the Commencement their Freshmanship shall be continued one Quarter of a Year longer and during that Time they shall be obliged to go on Errands and not have the liberty to send a Freshman on any Errands nor to wear a Gown." Five years later, in 1760, the corporation punished several members of the freshman class for their role in a raucous commencement eve display by depriving them of the "Privilege of Sending Freshmen on any Errand for the space of fourteen Days."[30] Yale's laws warned: "If any Scholar Shall behave himself obstinately, refractorily or Contemtionally toward the President or either of the Tutors," he will be fined and admonished, or "Deprived of the Liberty of Sending Freshmen for a certain Time." Hence in 1752 President Clap ruled that one student, "Porter," for his "contemptuous Behavior towards the Tutors," was to be "deprived of the Liberty of sending Freshmen, 'till the Spring Vacation: and all Freshmen are hereby prohibited from going [on] any Errands for him, & from treating him with any more than civil Respect."[31] It is not surprising, then, that the custom of fagging was so resolutely defended. Clap suspended freshman Samuel Cary because the youth had refused to wait upon a group of abusive sophomores. In 1795 Professor Josiah Meigs and three tutors recorded a vigorous protest against a proposal for omitting the fagging custom from the college regulations. Their protest was effective; the threatened custom remained in force until 1804.[32]

These observations on punishments lead to a consideration of the second point raised in conjunction with the 1752 account of the Spaulding-Goodrich-Wiggins incident—namely, the college authorities' reluctance to use their powers of suspension and expulsion—and what this reveals about the nature of collegiate society. We begin with the statement made by Charles Thompson, the first valedictorian of the College of Rhode Island, that students lived under a system of "paternal inspection." The most obvious manifestation of this system of supervision was the official practice of regularly visiting the students' chambers. The Yale Corporation was not alone in its belief, expressed in 1761, that if the officers of the college would be "strict in visiting," then "this Society" might "always be kept pure."[33] The College of Rhode Island specified the manner in which these visits were to be performed: let "no student refuse to open his door when he shall hear the stamp of the foot or staff at his door in the entry, which shall be a token that some officer of instruction desires admission." In order to maintain the gravity of this "token" performance, the college laws warned that "every student is forbid to counterfeit or imitate [it] under any pretence whatever." In the event that admission was refused, the president or tutors had the right, according to the regulations of Yale and King's College, to "Break open any College Door." [34] This close and constant surveillance of student activities was in accordance with Locke's contention that during his "Nonage," the individual had to depend upon the will and understanding of his guardian. Yale's laws further stipulated that "no Scholar Shall undertake to Do or Transact any Matters or Affairs of Difficulty and Importance, or which are any ways new or beside the common & approved Customs & Practices of the College, without first Consulting with the President and Obtaining his Consent." [35]

If students were thus constrained in the exercise of discretion, then schoolmasters, as Eliphalet Pearson observed in 1789, had to be vested with *"discretionary"* powers and *"parental"* authority. College fathers were expected to be flexible in enforcing written codes and, where no such codes existed, to be guided by the prescriptions for well-affected rulers. At Yale the president was empowered to govern "according to Such Laws and Rules & Orders as are made by the President and Fellows & in Defect of them according to the Established Customs of the College, and where there are no Such then according to the best of his Judgment and Discretion." More specifically, in the area of penal laws, it was clear that "particular Laws cannot be made for all Emergent Affairs and Cases that may occur"; therefore, the president "Shall have Power to Give Such particular Direction, Orders and Rules from Time to Time as he shall think proper, agreable to the Nature and Tenour of the Laws." The president also had the authority to "inflict any reasonable Punishment agreable to the Tenour of these herein Mentioned." The College of Rhode Island likewise ruled that "whereas the Statutes are few & general, there must necessarily be lodged with the President & Tutors a discretional, or parental Authority." In dealing with infractions for which no specific provision existed, the officers of the college were to "exercise this discretionary authority according to the known customs of similar institutions, & the plain, general rules of the moral law." [36]

An examination of the "Tenour" of the laws further supports the contention that the social environment of the college was an intimate world of mutual dependence. Interaction was maintained by a regular exchange of recognized signals. Social reality was thus largely dependent upon reciprocals. As the College of New Jersey specified, students were "divided into four distinct classes," with the members of each class "giving and receiving in their turns those tokens of respect and subjection which belong to their standings, in order to preserve a due subordination." An individual's failure to participate in this give-and-take would undermine the social places of others and, consequently, disrupt the syntax of conduct. Given this rather fragile situation, all forms of discipline presupposed a great deal of self-submission.[37]

The collegiate penal system, then, had to be stout enough to discourage deviance, and yet flexible enough to encourage voluntary submission to communal values. Penalties must be geared, the laws of the College of Rhode Island proclaimed, to be "at once expressive of compassion to the offender & indignation at the offence." Only by maintaining this dual focus would disciplinary proceedings be truly educative, for they would then "move the more honourable Springs of good Order" and gain cheerful "submission to Government." Ezra Stiles was greatly concerned with the tension inherent in the balance between compassion and indignation. On 26 March 1782, Stiles reported that "this Even[in]g about 20 or 25 Scholars went into a great Tumult & Riot, in Contempt of a public Judgment & Punishment inflicted in the Chapel for Damages done to the Hall & Buttery." At evening prayers on the twenty-seventh, "in a very full Chapel," three of the offending scholars were expelled. Two days later, another was expelled and twelve others rusticated, admonished, or "otherwise settled." "It has been a very distress[in]g affair to me," Stiles lamented. After the judgment had been rendered, Stiles continued to be troubled. "College settled," he recorded in his *Diary*, "but not quite to my Mind. I think we were not quite severe eno'." The students were prepared for "great Punishment," and "Our great Mildness towards the last I fear has disserved Government." If he had been more unsparing, Stiles thought, perhaps "this would have given Scholars a Conviction of resolute & firm Discipline." President James Manning of the College of Rhode Island, according to one of his scholars, Jonathan Maxcy, succeeded in preserving the delicate balance "which secures obedience while it conciliates esteem."[38]

David James Dove, the mid-eighteenth-century Philadelphia schoolmaster, seems to have practiced less formally the principles adopted by the affectionate collegiate fathers. Alexander Graydon, who was Dove's pupil in 1760, recalled that Dove substituted "disgrace for corporal punishment." The rod was rarely used to inflict physical pain; rather it was "generally stuck into the back part of the collar of the unfortunate culprit, who, with this badge of disgrace towering from his nape . . . was compelled to take his stand upon the top of the form, for such a period of time, as his offence was thought to deserve." For students who were tardy in their morning attendance, Dove had another equally effective method of correction. He would "despatch a committee of five or six scholars for them, with a bell and lighted lantern, and in this 'odd equipage,' in broad day light, the bell all the while tingling, were they escorted through the streets to school." Graydon once was unfortunate enough to be so attended, and, he testified, it "was to me a serious punishment." [39]

Similarly, Benjamin Rush remembered the Reverend Samuel Finley as a model of paternal affection. Rush, who attended Finley's West Nottingham Academy as a youngster, described the schoolmaster as "strict but never severe." Finley managed expertly to convert disciplinary proceedings into additional occasions for instruction. Thus he always prefaced his punishment with a "discourse upon the nature, hainousness [sic], or tendency of the offence." Finley even encouraged his charges to "give their opinions upon the nature of an offence, before he gave his own, and now and then he obliged them to pronounce sentence of punishment, before he inflicted it." The instrument of correction was a "small switch," which Finley used to strike the palm of the offender "never more than three times." In truth, Rush declared, the "solemn forms connected with this punishment were more terrible and distressing than the punishment itself." In one case, these "solemn" proceedings continued for half an hour, until the culprit, "trembling and weeping" in filial fear, was finally consoled by a fatherly Finley with the remark, "I mean shame, and not pain [to] be your punishment." [40]

Rush provided the reasons for this substitution of shame for corporal punishment. He was convinced that beatings and blows were "altogether unnecessary in schools," for they were simply the residue of more "barbarous ages." Besides the bodily injuries and the "spirit of violence" and "hatred to instruction" that the rod induced, there was a more compelling reason for doing away with corporal punishment. Drawing upon his principles of medicine, Rush said that the "fear of corporal punishments, by debilitating the body, produces a corresponding debility in the mind." Not only were the intellectual faculties of the mind depleted, but the "moral faculty," which was seated in the brain, was also "weakened." "Where there is *shame* . . . there may be *virtue*. But corporal punishments . . . have a tendency to destroy the sense of shame, and thereby to destroy all moral sensibility." As a general rule, "sensibility is the avenue to the moral faculty"; therefore "everything which tends to diminish it tends to injure morals." By destroying the sense of shame, then, we destroy "one of the strongest outposts of virtue." [41]

Rather than employing a "barbarous" form of discipline, Rush suggested a system based on "*private* admonition," confinement, or small signs of disgrace administered "in the presence of a whole school." If such penalties failed to reclaim the offender, "he should be dismissed from school, to prevent his corrupting his schoolmates." Yale's penal laws, often more explicit but otherwise unexceptional, embodied the spirit of these suggestions.[42] Yale prescribed fines, admonition (private and public), degradation, rustication (being exiled to study under a minister outside of New Haven), suspension, and finally expulsion, as the "Case may Require." Only such "Great and Atrocious" crimes as physical assaults upon the president or tutors or fornication justified immediate expulsion. For the more "ordinary and common Crimes & Misdemeanours"—and there were many, including swearing, cursing, irreverence, drunkenness, quarreling, idleness, and, somewhat surprising, "wearing woman's Apparel"—the penalties varied. A student could be fined or privately admonished or both for a first offense; fined at a higher rate, publicly admonished, degraded, rusticated, or suspended for recurrences of the offense; and finally, expelled, if he continued to be "obstinate." [43]

The penalties enumerated served two immediately different educative purposes. Fines, private and public admonition, and degradation were primarily intended for the reformation of the individual offender. Samuel Blair remarked in his *Account of the College of New Jersey* that during the administration of such penalties, the "president or tutors, separately or in conjunction, privately reason with the offender, in order to make him sensible of his ill conduct." As college fathers they attempted to convince the offender that they were "actuated from motives of sincere regard to his own welfare." To be sure, public admonition and degradation stigmatized the culprit, made an example of him. But this took place while the offender remained within, or after he had been readmitted to, the community as a participating member, hence his affections might be engaged. But if the criminal's actions were so heinous or obstinate as to endanger the orderly arrangement of the college, then the defense and reaffirmation of communal values took precedence over the correction of individual misbehavior, and the suspension or expulsion of the criminal was not only justified but indeed mandatory. The laws of the College of Rhode Island summarized this idea. "After private admonition the pecuniary penalties shall be from two pence . . . to . . . six shillings, or a dollar, after which they [the offenders] shall be publicly admonished before the College and Corporation, which proving ineffectual, the offenders shall be rusticated, or suspended, from all connection with the College, after which degraded, if judged necessary. For the last and concluding punishment they shall be totally and forever expelled from the College." [44]

College fathers, of course, were concerned because their powers were limited in time and place. They insisted that scholars observe established rules of conduct even while away from college. In addition, at Yale students were warned that "if any Graduate Shall behave himself Scandalously to the Dishonour of the College, The President and Fellows may . . . recall or take his degree from him & Declare it to be Null and Void and Fix up Such a Sentence in the College-Hall, and may Order his Name to be razed out of the Catalogue, or continued with the word *Degradatus.*" This kind of concern over the transience of their power meant that the established officers would be disinclined to inflict any penalties that would remove some scholars even further from their control.[45]

But the reluctance to suspend an offender, and the more pronounced reluctance to expel him, was also the product of a more fundamental concern, one that was a characteristic of all affectionate commonwealths: the necessity to secure a compounded balance of compassion and indignation, individual correction and communal affirmation. For if social reality needed to be ongoingly reaffirmed through recognized forms of affectionate interaction, then frequent suspensions and expulsions would inevitably undermine the social order by alienating the affections. The need for constant social reinforcement was only intensified by the fact that the college was a more conspicuously artificial social environment than the truly domestic albeit status-conscious family.

In 1774 President Manning, while publicly admonishing four scholars, recapitulated the logic of the collegiate system of punishment: "When every method for the Reformation of Delinquents, in a private way, has been used to no Purpose, the Good of Society and the Honor of Government, as well as the Interest of the Delinquents, require those more public and mortifying Exertions of Authority which must either reclaim, or prove, that obstinate Offenders must be cut off as Pests to the Body."[46] Indictments thus had to provide detailed clues to an offender's attitude because this was a principal way of identifying the temporary deviator and the persistent deviant. Public confessions figured largely in the decision to reclaim offenders or to cut them off as "Pests to the Body" because throughout these little ceremonies private attitudes were on display. Yale's laws specified that "when any Scholar is Ordered to make a public Confession for any Crime or Breach of the Laws of this College, and he refuse after admonition, he Shall be Expelled: and no Scholar Shall be Readmitted or admitted to a Degree unless he first make a public Confession in the Hall or Meeting-House." College fathers wanted an open and frank acknowledgment of wrongdoing by the offender, Samuel Blair explained; consequently, "lying and wilful equivocation, are resented as the highest aggravations." In 1786 Ezra Stiles recorded that he had expelled "Butler," a sophomore. Rather than meekly submitting to the penalty or showing any signs of contrition, however, the "profane Butler damned the Authority & left the Chapel." Butler's deportment proved that he was incorrigible, and Stiles celebrated the loss of this obstinate student: "Happy Purgation!" [47]

By the same token, if an offender made a humble public confession, the severity of his penalty was often mitigated. In any event, collegiate society displayed a readiness to readmit the contrite deviator. In 1729 the Yale trustees ruled on the "Miscarriages Delinquencies & Crimes of Mix," a student accused of "striking . . . several Students & after that running away without the leave of ye Rector or Tutor near forty miles distant from ye College & not long after that striking & fighting with a man of this Town." When confronted with these charges, Mix confessed without equivocation. The trustees ordered him suspended for a year. If at the end of that time Mix appeared "reformed in his manners and is become a diligent improver of his Time & Studies his Suspension may be removed[,] he making an Acknowledgement of his Faults publickly in the Hall." A year later, Mix humbled himself publicly, and the trustees voted to accept his confession and to restore him to his "former Place & privileges in the College." [48] Ebenezer Baldwin in 1762 recounted a similar incident. "Bull," a student convicted for "going to Milford without liberty" and for general misconduct, "was ordered to depart from College and to live under the care of some minister at a distance till he should show signs of reformation and be fit to take a degree." However, "not liking to suffer ye penance inflicted," namely rustication, Bull "travelled off on foot to the westward," again without official leave. It was supposed, said Baldwin, that "he intends to go on board of a Privateer." A week after the initial judgment had been rendered, Bull returned, "having gone no further than Milford." He offered a suitable public confession of his misconduct, "Particularly going out of town and refusing to go to ye President when sent for, and so was restored to ye same standing as before his punishment." [49]

Such leniency, Edmund Morgan has argued, reflected the realization by the "Puritan community" that the "flesh was weak" and, therefore, that once the offender had shown remorse, his crimes must be forgiven. [50] But the phenomenon was not restricted to Puritan communities; rather, it seemed to be a characteristic of the affectionate world of the school. Public confessions and readmissions were components of the ceremonial idiom by which the social equilibrium of that world was sustained and reaffirmed. Moreover, college officials realized that maintaining the syntax of the ceremonial idiom required a resistance to external interference.

Thus the regulations of the University of Pennsylvania warned that no student "shall . . . neglect any business, task or duty prescribed to him; nor shall any Note or Apology from a Parent or Guardian be admitted in excuse for neglect of duty . . . or the breach of any Law which respects the decent behavior & good conduct of the student towards their instructors or one another." The laws of Yale cautioned the student against filing a "Suit or Complaint whatever against any other Member or Officer of this College for any Supposed Injury or Defect to or before Authority or Judges whatsoever besides the Authority of this College." Should any student register such a complaint and thus expose the internal affairs of the college to an external arbitrator, he "Shall be forthwith Expell'd." [51] In 1782 Ezra Stiles recalled an appropriate incident. "A great Contest has arisen between the young Sirs and Collegians on one side and Gentlemen in Town . . . on the other" concerning arrangements for the commencement ball, Stiles observed. "Half a dozen Bachelors of Arts residing in Town chiefly & not in College, joyned in a separation from their College Brethren," but one in particular "spoke with less Delicacy than was prudent [Stiles had first written "aspersed and vilified" but then settled for this polite rendition] upon the Candidates & their Company." The actions of this imprudent and disloyal graduate "excited the Resentment of all [in the] College"; subsequently, "the Undergraduates in disguise took him under the College Pump—an high Indignity to any & especially towards a Graduate." It was clear, however, that Stiles was not protesting this "high Indignity" and obvious breach of the rules regarding deference and demeanor. The apostasy of the victim was complete: "He, instead of entering a Complaint to the College Authority, complained to the Grand Jury & obtained a Presentment; & also brot an Action at common Law for £1000. Damages." [52] In this situation, communal ties took precedence over the rules governing demeanor; indeed, the latter could function only if the former were sustained.

As Stiles's entry suggests, the communal ties of collegiate life would not survive the full impact of the Revolution. The school, as a face-to-face society designed "not only for the instruction & advancement of youth in learning; but also for the preservation and improvement of their Morals, together with a decent & respectful deportment towards their instructors, & a suitable & becoming conduct towards each other," was perforce an exclusive institution. The Revolutionary commitment to republicanism, however, required a comprehensive and inclusive educational system. Every citizen of the republic needed to be prepared to participate in the affairs of the state and in the protection of the constitution. As the numerical base of the college was broadened, the institutional arrangements that supported its affectionate order began to lose their original significance. Under the impact of demographic changes in the student community and perceptual changes in the Revolutionary population, the ceremonial idiom of the familial colleges eventually deteriorated into an ungrammatical compendium.[53]

III

DISAFFECTION

The American Revolution was not a common Event. It's Effects and Consequences have already been Awful over a great Part of the Globe. And when and where are they to cease?

But what do We mean by the American Revolution? Do we mean the American War? The Revolution was effected before the War commenced. The Revolution was in the Minds and Hearts of the People. A Change in their Religious Sentiments of their Duties and Obligations. While the King, and all in Authority under him, were believed to govern, in Justice and Mercy according to the Laws and Constitutions derived to them from the God of Nature, and transmitted to them by their Ancestors: they thought themselves bound to pray for the King and Queen and all the Royal Family, and all the Authority under them, as Ministers ordained of God for their good. But when they saw those Powers renouncing all the Principles of Authority, and bent upon the destruction of all the Securities of their Lives, Liberties and Properties, they thought it their Duty to pray for the Continental Congress and all the thirteen State Congresses, &c.

There might be, and there were others, who thought less about Religion and Conscience, but had certain habitual Sentiments of Allegiance and Loyalty derived from their Education; but believing Allegiance and Protection to be reciprocal, when Protection was withdrawn, they thought Allegiance was dissolved.

Another Alteration was common to all. The People of America had been educated in an habitual Affection for England as their Mother-Country; and while they thought her a kind and tender Parent (erroneously enough, however, for she never was such a Mother,) no Affection could be more sincere. But when they found her a cruel Beldam, willing, like Lady Macbeth, to 'dash their Brains out,' it is no Wonder if their fillial Affections ceased and were changed into Indignation and horror.

This radi[c]al Change in the Principles, Opinions, Sentiments and Affections of the People, was the real American Revolution.

John Adams to Hezekiah Niles
13 February 1818

5

Revolution:

The Alienation

of Affection

The familial paradigm, so pervasive in the life and thought of colonial Americans, supported and was supported by the situation of the colonies in the British empire. The most common perception of the empire was distinctly familial. Indeed, the notion that colonies were properly the "children" of an imperial "mother" had been an essential part of the English rationale for colonization from the very outset. In his *Plain Pathway to Plantations*—according to Louis B. Wright, "the most carefully reasoned of the Jacobean treatises on colonization"—Richard Eburne described the establishment and growth of colonies as a natural phenomenon, comparing them to "children," "born and bred up in their father's house," who eventually leave home for new "habitations." Similarly, Francis Bacon observed in his 1625 analysis of the first years of the Virginia colony, "I may justly account new plantations to be the children of former kingdoms." And John White in 1630 warned "that a Colonie denying due respect to the State from whose bowels it issued, is as great a monster, as an unnaturall childe." [1]

That the parent-child analogy was no mere decorative metaphor, but rather the paradigmatic basis for, and thus preceded, an understanding of the imperial union, was made evident in the nature of the colonists' expectations and in the form of their protests. If the colonies were children, and by implication unable to fend for themselves, then protection must be provided, as Robert Beverley said in 1701, "by their lawful Mother *England.*" The most explicit denunciation of imperial policy prior to the Revolutionary era was founded on this Fifth Commandment imperative. In the *Groans of the Plantations* (1689), Edward Littleton, a Barbadian planter who had recently settled in England, protested the efforts of the mother country to disturb the economic and political well-being of her colonies. The projectors of imperial policy, knowing that "we poor *English Forrainers* are compell'd" to ship all of our commodities to the mother country, have imposed heavy duties upon sugar and other goods.

What could account for their wanting to "hold Our Noses to the Grind stone, and make us pay what they pleased"? "What have we done, or wherein have we offended, that we should be used in this manner? Or what strange Crime have we committed, to make us the Object of so great Severities? And how have we incurred the displeasure of *England,* our great and dear Mother?" [2]

Despite her inexplicable policies, however, Littleton explained, the colonies were steadfastly devoted to England. Grotius might have argued that colonies owed merely an observance rather than an obedience to their mother country, but we renounce that doctrine, Littleton continued. "It is an Obedience as well as Observance that we owe eternally to *England;* and though our dear Mother prove never so unkind, we cannot throw off our Affection and Duty to her." Prolonged subjection under the present "sad condition" was preferable to separation; therefore, the originators of the revenue schemes, whatever their motives, will find that we shall bear the current burdens with the "most submissive patience."

Littleton thus assumed a characteristically humble posture of filial dependence. And yet, he confessed, the actions of the mother country were especially mortifying. If our avowed enemies were controlling our affairs and attempting to crush us, such policies might be understood; we could expect no better. "But to be ruin'd by those, by whom we hoped to be cherish't and protected, is wholly unsupportable." Arguments had been advanced that such deplorable treatment was justified because the colonies were injurious to the mother country. If this was true, Littleton said forebodingly, then despite the sentiment against separation and independence, "we shall compose our Minds to bear it. And like Children truly dutiful, we shall be content to part with our dearest Mother, rather than be a burden to her." [3]

The familial perception of the imperial order identified problems worthy of attention, determined the scope and language of ensuing appeals, and proposed the methods by which crises might be resolved. During the years preceding 1776, this same familial model, compounded by the complex of ideas associated with the English "country" ideology, continued to serve as the starting point for political dialogue. As the Revolutionaries proceeded to "desacralize" the moral authority of the British, they extended the line of reasoning Littleton had employed more than a half century earlier. [4]

Joseph Reed, in 1766, described the filial nature of American dependence upon England: "we stand in need of her protection, nurture and care. Exposed by our situation . . . and yet in a state of infancy, it would be extremely difficult, if not impossible, to form any Union among ourselves that would be sufficient to repel the attacks of a formidable invader. In this weak, this defenceless, state, therefore, we must look up to our indulgent parent, whose vigorous, salutary aid we have so often already experienced. Upon her we must rely for support, and under her wing shelter ourselves." [5] Reed's description highlighted the bases of the familial image of the empire. In this arrangement, England was, or ought to be, a kind, tender, indulgent, and sometimes chastising parent; a sympathetic and faithful guardian; a legitimate and, most important, affectionate nursing mother. The colonies, in return, were, or ought to be, obedient, dutiful, grateful, and properly subservient; attitudinal postures befitting the legitimate offspring of Mother England. Contrary behavior would make them disrespectful, insolent, or petulant children. These adjectives were common currency among writers of diverse persuasions. "Colonies, my lord Bacon observes, are the children of more ancient nations," wrote Isaac Hunt in a 1775 paraphrase of Bacon's 1625 statement. In the aftermath of the Stamp Act crisis Richard Bland argued that it would be useless "to search the civil Constitution of *England* for Directions in fixing the proper Connexion between the Colonies and the Mother Kingdom; I mean what their reciprocal Duties to each other are, and what Obedience is due from the Children to the general Parent." Instead, the Fifth Commandment might be a more appropriate guideline, for, as Oxenbridge Thacher pointed out, "filial" and "parental affections" constituted the bond between England and her American colonies, and these affections determined the extent of their reciprocal duties as well as the nature of colonial obedience. The imperial union must be understood, Joseph Reed concluded, as a "grand FAMILY COMPACT, which must be cemented by every tie of duty, loyalty and affection from the Provinces, and every mark of kind protecting tenderness from the mother country." [6]

The affective bond of the familial paradigm magnified the difficulty of desacralizing British moral authority; however, it contributed at the same time toward making the "country" ideology more compelling. If, as the paradigm implied, the colonies were in a state of infantile incompetence, then separation surely was dreadful to contemplate. It is true that the paradigm provided for the eventuality of a child maturing to a stage of self-sufficiency, but, as Henry Barry cautioned in 1775, "in the political as well as natural body, the progressions to independence are gradual and imperceptible, and all uncommon attempts to force either, are usually destructive of their end; time should therefore accomplish that which human endeavours cannot precipitate, though too often destroy." Time and timing were critical considerations. And the decision for independence was delayed by the lingering suspicion that the time was not right;

that, as Isaac Hunt said, the colonists still needed to be shielded against the advances of those "aspiring states" that were awaiting an opportunity, "like vultures hovering o'er their prey," to violate American liberty and property. Because it was "scarcely probable" that they could survive without the aid of some protective superordinate authority, "to whom . . . but *Great Britain*" could Americans "go for succour?" "Unconnected and divided" as the colonies were, Joseph Reed added, "how difficult, and next to impossible, would it be to rescue them from a state of anarchy." James Otis, in 1765, believed that "none but rebels, fools, or madmen" would contend for separation from the mother country. Independence would be the "beginning of a terrible scene" of "blood and confusion." James Mitchell Varnum warned, in 1769, "we are not yet arrived to maturity. We are infants and stand in the greatest necessity of dandling on the knees of an indulgent parent." [7]

Self-preservation, the "first principle of nature," thus seemed to dictate that the colonies preserve their bond with England. But there was more involved, for England was not merely a protector, she was a true "nursing mother of her Colonies." The arts and sciences, agriculture and commerce, were "planted, cherished and encouraged" by this affectionate parent. Budding genius had been taken by the hand and led "in the paths of industry and useful improvements." Precisely because England had been "an indulgent and kind mother" as well as a "powerful protectress," the colonists felt compelled to respect and obey her with filial fear. During the crises of the 1760s and less frequently during the 1770s, colonial spokesmen continued to allude to the familial model of affectionate obligations. Only after they were convinced that England was purposefully rather than unintentionally violating the moral codes of union, were they able to renounce their filial attachment and opt for revolution. The process, as might be expected, was slow and often psychologically painful. [8]

The distress of the Revolutionary generation was nowhere more poignantly revealed than in the transforming radicalism of Abigail Adams. As late as the spring of 1771, after the furor of the Stamp Act and Townshend Acts and shortly after the first anniversary of the Boston Massacre, Abigail still confessed to a "great inclination" nurtured since "my Infancy . . . to visit the Mother Country as tis call'd." Although the desire to do this was "greatly diminished" as a result of the "unnatural treatment which . . . our poor America has received from her," Abigail told her cousin Isaac Smith, Jr., "I yet retain a curiosity to know what ever is valuable in her." [9]

The accumulation of grievances in the next few years managed to sour Abigail's curiosity. In 1774 she complained to Catharine Macaulay about the "complicated misiries [sic] and distresses" brought on by the "inhumane acts" of Parliament. The Coercive Acts were so oppressive, so destructive to commerce and justice, that the colonists were virtually being forced to choose between the "Horrours of a civil war" and the "chains of Slavery." Abigail went on to describe the "firmness" and "fortitude" exhibited by the majority of Americans, an "undaunted resolution" inspired, no doubt, by the knowledge that they were the "injured not the *injurer*." And yet, there was a plaintive, almost apologetic, tone to Abigail's epistolary account of the imperial crisis. She felt compelled to mention in her letter to Macaulay, for example, that despite the "Eneffi-cacy" of past appeals the colonists were continuing to offer "united Supplications" for relief with "anxious Hearts and eager expectations." Even Abigail's thinly veiled threat, a reference to "redress by the Sword," must be read in conjunction with her description of the "three fold cord of Duty, interest and filial affection" binding the colonists to their king, a cord so strong and tightly laced that it could not be snapped or untied but "like the Gordean knot" would yield only to the blade.[10]

By mid-1775 Abigail was certain that the "sword" had been drawn against the "Gordean knot" of filial affection. Apologetics gave way to exasperation and anger. Earlier the colonists had hoped for reconciliation, but the indignities endured by them at the hands of the king's minions, "every indignity that it was possible for humane nature to endure," had made a mockery of the situation. Then on the "terrible 19 of April" the king's troops, "once the pride and Glory of Europe" but of late better known for their mobbish outrages, "premeditately went forth and secretly fell upon our people and like savage furies sheath'd their Breasts with Steal [sic]." The action at Lexington and Concord proved that earnest supplications fell on deaf ears. All hopes for a peaceful and honorable settlement were dashed when England "plunged her Sword into our Bosoms and laid 40 of our Breathren in the Dust." From that moment on it was clear that "Tyranny, oppression and Murder" were to be the only "reward of all the affection, the veneration and the loyalty which has heretofore distinguished Americans."[11]

Abigail Adams made no effort to conceal her emotional investment in the developing crisis of the empire. She long bemoaned the disrepair into which the colonists' relationship with England had fallen, and blamed this unfortunate state of affairs on the "Dark designs" of artful men. Prior to 1775, her complaints evinced a kind of embarrassed consternation that "those men . . . whose contagious Ambition" was so patently self-serving could have succeeded in swaying the actions of the home government. "We Blush when we recollect from whence these woes arise," Abigail remarked in her 1774 letter to Macaulay. Repeated attempts to effect the "most wicked and hostile measures," however, and the king's reluctance even to grant the colonists "an opportunity to be heard in [their] defence," finally convinced her that the roots of the current crisis reached much deeper than she first surmised. England, once the "envy of nations," must have succumbed to the "Arbitrary Will of the worst of her own citizens." Americans, therefore, had to take up the sword of war, that "dreadful alternative" to "beggary and Slavery." It was, as Mercy Otis Warren testified, "with a heart trembling" that Abigail conveyed all of this to her most cherished correspondents. But because her decision had not been arrived at lightly, Abigail would remain firm in her resolve. By the time she wrote to her "dearest Friend" on 12 November 1775, Abigail's transformation was already completed. She had that day refused to sign a petition for reconciliation initiated by "our worthy parson," Abigail told John. The time for "supplications" was past. "Let us seperate [sic] . . . Let us renounce them." Instead of behaving as "formorly [sic] for their prosperity and happiness, Let us beseach [sic] the almighty to blast their counsels and bring to Nought all their devices." Her refusal to sign the parson's conciliatory petition flowed from the conviction that England was "no longer [a] parent State, but [a] tyrant State." [12]

Because Abigail was informed by John and intimately involved in his political maturation her changing outlook was understandably reflective of the changes occurring in the larger resistance movement itself. Colonial polemicists, operating under a familial perception of the imperial order, were, like Abigail, self-consciously humble in their initial reaction to English measures. During the Stamp Act crisis John Dickinson wrote that British policies were driving the mother country and her colonies apart, but, he added, if the final break ever came, it must be "when the present generation and the present set of sentiments are extinct." Property rights were being violated, legislative assemblies suppressed, trial by jury ignored, and standing armies placed in their midst. Moreover, these arbitrary actions of the mother country came at a time when, following the defeat of France and the contributions of the colonies in that effort, Americans were "expecting, not unreasonably perhaps, some mark of tenderness in return." Nevertheless, Dickinson said, colonial resentment was "but the resentment of dutiful children who have received unmerited blows from a beloved parent." An obediential carriage, coupled with "seasonable" pleas for relief in the case of unwarranted chastisement, were the marks of true filial affection. Supporters of royal policy disagreed with Dickinson's depiction of colonial circumstances, but their operating premises were identical. The mother country, Martin Howard declared, had spent immense sums for the security of the colonies, but when she sought to draw upon the wealth of the colonies they responded "with all the petulance of children, who, by long indulgence, become impatient of the smallest restraints." [13]

After the repeal of the Stamp Act, Jonathan Mayhew cautioned the colonists against appearing "insolent and assuming" lest they should seem "ungrateful and indecent" children. John Joachim Zubly voiced a similar sentiment when he advised a return of "filial respect to the indulgence and tenderness of an affectionate parent." The bonds of affection had been renewed by the repeal and, it seemed, the old moral order was left intact. "We have seen our mother-country act the part of a tender parent," Zubly advised, therefore, "let us never fail to act the part of truly dutiful children." [14]

The imperatives of the familial paradigm continued to be influential in succeeding crises. In 1774, Richard Wells called for a general nonimportation of British goods in order to pressure the ministry into rescinding all of its arbitrary measures. Nonimportation, Wells explained, was a highly proper way of resisting the policies of the mother country, for it allowed the colonies "sensibly [to] wound" without delivering a "mortal blow." "Far be it from the heart of a child essentially to injure a parent," Wells remarked. Instead, "let our incisions be no deeper than are just necessary to discharge the corrupted mass that collects about her vitals." [15]

Objections to the parent-child analogy only testified to its prevalence. George Mason spurned the use of the metaphor, and yet, he confessed, the "epithets of parent and child have been so long applied to Great Britain and her colonies" that royal instructions were routinely couched in the "authoritative style of a master to a schoolboy." Although a moment's reflection would reveal the epithets to be "a little ridiculous," individuals on both sides of the Atlantic "have adopted them." Silas Downer was similarly convinced that "if this doctrine of the maternal authority of one country over another be a little examined, it will be found to be the greatest absurdity that ever entered into the head of a politican." Subordination could not be inherent in the process of emigration, for otherwise sovereignty and superiority would properly belong only to the original cradle of all mankind, the ultimate maternal authority. Downer, however, could only conclude in hopeful protest that "in the future the words *Mother Country* will not be so frequently in our mouths, as they are only sounds without meaning." [16]

If the affective familial model of the empire retarded the movement toward independence, it simultaneously enhanced the potential impact of the "country" ideology. As Abigail Adams's transformation indicated, ideologically charged assumptions heightened the moral indignation of the Revolutionaries and eventually helped to make independence a categorical imperative. The "country" ideology, we know, was founded upon the belief that man, an imperfect being likely to succumb to temptations, existed in a world in which he was constantly tempted by the forces of vice and corruption. In the realm of politics, where some men were necessarily entrusted with public authority, there was a continuing danger of self-aggrandizement on the part of the few at the expense of the many. The people-at-large, therefore, had to ensure that the powers delegated were not abused, and this depended first upon their vigilance in resisting the snares of luxury and indolence, and second upon their ability to detect the initial signs of corruption in public life.[17]

For a populace schooled in this tradition, wary of any deviation from the norm among civic leaders, what could be a surer sign of corruption than the repeated attempts of the ministers of the mother country to "murder and butcher" its "children . . . that have been so obedient, useful and affectionate"? What could be more alarming than "unnatural Encroachments, from a haughty Parent Country, that should treat them affectionately, even with a tender Guardian Friendship"? Samuel Langdon concluded that the imperial mother must have been impelled by her public vices "to wage a cruel war with its own children in these colonies, only to gratify the lust of power, and the demands of extravagance!" To be sure, added Stephen Hopkins, "natural parents, thro' human frailty, and mistakes about facts and circumstances, sometimes *provoke their children to wrath,* tho' they tenderly love them, and sincerely desire their good." But repeated encroachments forming a pattern of provocation, regardless of their causes, indicated that the moral order of the imperial family was "unhappily changing." The colonial situation could only be attributed, explained an anonymous writer, to "our Mother's slumbering Delusions," or to her desire to "gratify imperious Lust very wantonly, impoliticly, and even very unnaturally in her advanced years, at the Expence or Ruin of her legitimate Offspring, and hitherto dutiful Children." The colonists had hoped that the grievous imperial situation was caused by the former, but they came increasingly to fear that it proceeded from the latter. Otherwise, how could one account for the persistence of the imperial mother in enforcing her arbitrary impositions "after our importunate Clamours awake her, and excite her to ponder maturely!" Some "enchanting Fiend" or "malevolent Seducer" had to be directing imperial policy, thus transforming "our Unity to Discord, our Glory to Ridicule."[18]

The "monstrous" actions of England subverted the familial order and, consequently, encouraged the colonists to question their filial obligations. The paradigmatic understanding of the imperial union made it a very special relationship. Founded upon mutual affection, it was a relationship that was distinct from other forms of authority and subordination. Parents were "not *tyrants,* or even *masters,*" Jonathan Mayhew explained, and children were "not *slaves,* or even *servants.*" In this scheme of things, the colonies could be "humble and respectful" like children, but must not be "abject and servile" like slaves or servants. Imperial policies, insufficiently motivated by parental affection, were straining the colonists' assumption that England was attached to them "by the natural ties of a mother country." The irregular restraints placed upon them would inevitably reduce the colonies to slavery, Maurice Moore said, and this was "a situation in which it is very unnatural to think a Mother can take pleasure in viewing her Children." [19]

Were the colonies "Legitimate Children"? The allegation that Stephen Watts had dismissed in 1766 became more credible as England began to appear in the role of a "cruel Step-mother." The logic of the parent-child paradigm thus had a compelling simplicity for the Revolutionaries: "if they are not considered as Children, their Treatment is that of Slaves, and therefore, if oppressed, they must unite," as Nicholas Ray put it. The imperial mother, deranged by vice and corruption, could no longer remember the distinction between legitimate children and slaves; therefore, exclaimed an exasperated colonist, if this state of subserviency was truly a filial condition, "what is Vassalage!" [20]

The Revolutionaries realized that, as Isaac Hunt said, colonies, like children, "receive nourishment from the milk of their mothers, till they are capable of digesting other food." Whether Americans were ready to be weaned, whether they were capable of surviving without imperial protection, was uncertain. But abject servitude under a decrepit and rapidly decaying mother country, one that could no longer recognize its legitimate offspring, was no alternative. The imperial mother no longer provided succor, and, as Alexander Graydon recalled, "when the nurturing season is past, the young of all kinds are left to act for themselves." In addition, the decade of crises, which entailed a close examination of the parent-child model, led to a reevaluation of the gap between theory and reality. By the mid-eighteenth century most of the colonies had developed sufficient social and political competence for self-government. This experiential background, plus their work on the extralegal associations of resistance, contrasted sharply with the suggestion that the colonies were mere infants. The crises of the 1760s and 1770s confirmed the suspicion that the mother country had aged beyond her prime years, and that the colonies had entered the stage "when youth shall no longer be subject to the controul of age." It was in this spirit that Richard Wells proudly proclaimed: "We look to manhood." [21]

II

Although the process had been emotionally stressful, the Revolutionaries were singularly optimistic once the separation from England had been formalized. Independence was indeed a "cathartic" experience. If initially they were compelled to opt for independence by a demented imperial mother who had forgotten or chosen to ignore the distinction between slaves and children, Americans were soon convinced that the Revolution had actually "restored the order of nature." England, certainly, had behaved unnaturally as a cruel stepmother after the mid-1760s. But no less unnatural, the Revolutionaries were telling themselves after 1776, was their unnecessarily prolonged nursing period. "To know whether it be the interest of this continent to be independent," declared Thomas Paine, "we need only to ask this easy simple question: Is it the interest of a man to be a boy all his life?" Americans had been such "dutiful children" filially adopting the prejudices of a parent they considered, as Joseph Buckminster put it, "superior in every respect, to all others on earth," that they had failed to notice their own potential. That realization came with independence, and thus, David Ramsay said, the "separation which the Colonists at first dreaded as an evil, they soon gloried in as a national blessing." [22]

It appeared as though the American genius had lain dormant until the bonds of affection with England were broken. Only after Americans had dissociated themselves from the imperial mother and the constraints imposed by the familial posture of humility were they able to perceive the latent promise of their condition. While in a state of filial dependence, Jefferson noted, "our minds were circumscribed within narrow limits, by an habitual belief that it was our duty to be subordinate to the mother country in all matters of government, to direct all our labors in subservience to her interests." Jefferson almost surely would have found congenial John Brooks's declaration that independence "awakened all the active powers of the human mind, and seemed to add fresh vigour to its native elasticity." A considerable "advantage derived from our independence consists in the expansion it has given the human mind," James Campbell agreed, "and the new fields it has opened for enquiry." It was clear, David Daggett added, that "a nation, like an individual, while dependent, will forever be confined in its operations." Because they met with "no real incentives to great exertions," the colonists, like indolent children, had tended to "drag heavily along, contented with a state of mediocrity." Only after their state of filial dependency was ended could Americans change "their mode of thinking and acting." They began to "feel an importance" in themselves and to call upon hitherto inert powers. Benjamin

Rush was "satisfied," following a strict examination of the "state of the mind," that the "ratio of intellect is as twenty are to one, and of knowledge, as an hundred are to one, in these states, compared with what they were before the American revolution." [23]

Rush's friend David Ramsay provided a clear statement of these ideas celebrating the end of the "unnatural union" in his 1778 *Oration on the Advantages of American Independence*. The arts and sciences would flourish in the new nation "till they have reached the remotest parts of this untutored continent," Ramsay predicted, because independence had removed Americans from that cramped "state of minority" during which they had merely followed the "leading strings of a parent country." While under the "guardianship" of England, Americans were occupied with "trifling" matters and "benumbed with ease and indolence . . . sloth and effeminacy." "Cramped and restrained by the limited views of dependence," the whole circle of arts and sciences would have dwindled and decayed. In contrast, independence effected that "elevation of soul" that was the foundation of "true genuis." Every circumstance now contributed toward the probability of the arts and sciences being "cultivated, extended, and improved, in Independent America." The natural environment of the vast "untrod" country gave "ample scope for the improvement of mechanicks, mathematicks, and natural philosophy." At the same time, "our free governments are the proper nurseries of rhetoric, criticism, and the arts which are founded on the philosophy of the human mind." The opportunities in commerce and manufacturing, the rapid growth of the population, and the separation from the turbulence of European politics all combined to encourage independent Americans to such exertions "as cannot fail of making many of them despise the syren call of luxury and mirth." Whenever he contemplated the future glory of the new nation, Ramsay confided, "my heart distends with generous pride for being an American." "What a substratum for empire!" [24]

The breakup of the imperial family was thought to have inaugurated a new era, immediately in America and indirectly in the rest of the world. This new era, according to Rush, would be characterized by "freedom . . . without licentiousness, government without tyranny, and religion without superstition, bigotry, or enthusiasm." To William King Atkinson, the Revolution marked a "distinguished period in the annals of mankind . . . which will be remembered with reverential awe and gratitude." Its effects "have not been confined to America alone; like that of the electric fluid, the mighty shock has pervaded the whole earth." Grandiose visions of an independent "empire" were legion, whether from the pen of David Ramsay, Joel Barlow, David Humphreys, Jedidiah Morse, Noah Webster, or a host of other writers and artists. It was a time, said

Charles Backus, when the "imagination of the Poet knew no bounds, in describing what America *would* be. The Philosopher became a Rhapsodist, in contemplating the importance of the American Revolution." [25]

The vision was so engaging that it reduced all sacrifices to comparative insignificance. The war itself, David Ramsay believed, was a "glorious exploit." Independence was of such consequence that, he explained to Rush in 1776, "forty thousand lives would *be* cheaply thrown away to effect our continental government." Rush needed little encouragement to rhapsodize about the Revolution. The "inestimable blessings" of independence could not "be too joyfully received, nor purchased at too high a price," he declared. Certainly, they would be "cheaply bought at the loss of all the towns & of every fourth, or even third man in America." Even after the war the losses seemed dwarfed by the promise. The losses in "both blood and treasure," John Rodgers observed in 1784, "are less, much less than we had a right to expect." The "calamaties" of the war, agreed John Lathrop, amounted to a "price, though dear, yet not too dear for the blessings secured." According to George Duffield, the accomplishing of "an event of such magnitude and importance . . . in so short a space of time, and with so small a share of difficulty . . . is one of those occurences . . . that command the admiration of every observer." [26]

More specifically, what made the sacrifices worthwhile was the nature of the empire the Revolutionaries envisioned. Independent America was to be a republic even though the received wisdom of the eighteenth century offered little in the way of encouragement for such a system. Fundamental axioms, acknowledged truths in the mainstream of the political thought of the period, argued against the American position. First, as Montesquieu had pointed out, republican systems were viable only for states of very limited size. Second, the history of past republics, a history familiar to Americans, revealed them to be fragile, unstable, and short-lived. Finally, republican institutions required more self-sacrifice for their upkeep than was consistent with human nature. Indeed, much of the antirepublican sentiment of the pre-Independence years stemmed from the belief that a republic was an ideal rather than a real form of government for men. Rousseau explained that a democratic republic in particular presupposed too many things that were "difficult to have at the same time." Extending the ideas of Montesquieu, he argued that the demands of simplicity, equality, frugality, and virtue were befitting a "nation of Gods," for surely a "government so perfect is not suited to men." [27]

The American commitment to republicanism, therefore, epitomized the changes in the "mode of thinking and acting" that David Daggett said invariably occurred the moment people begin to "assume a character for themselves." The Revolutionaries treated conventional antirepublican arguments as potentially irrelevant. In the first place, whenever they contemplated the future of America they were enormously impressed by what they perceived to be the significance of their historical moment. "Experience proves," David Tappan said, "that political bodies, like the animal economy, have periods of infancy, youth, maturity, decay, and dissolution." The American body politic, only recently weaned from the imperial mother, was entering the promising stage of youth. During this time, said Tappan, people were "usually industrious and frugal, simple in their manners, just and kind in their intercourse, active and hardy, united and brave." These admirable qualities, complemented by a spirit of sacrifice for the common good, were natural responses to the "feeble, exposed, and necessitous condition" of the body politic. In time, the practice of these genuinely republican virtues would lead to maturity and prosperity, and eventually to infection and decline. But this deterioration of the state, in natural sequence, would come after a "certain point of greatness" had been achieved and the simple ways of the founders had given way to pride, avarice, luxury, and idleness. Thus, a "hundred years hence, absolute monarchy will probably be rendered necessary in our country by the corruption of our people," Benjamin Rush wrote to John Adams. "But why should we precipitate an event for which we are not yet prepared? Shall I at five-and-twenty years of age, because I expect to be an old man, draw my teeth, put on artificial gray hairs, and bend my back over a cane? No, I will enjoy the health and vigor of youth and manhood, and leave old age to take care of itself." The imperatives of nature, then, directed the attention of the Revolutionaries toward republicanism.[28]

Other characteristics of youthful independence were equally encouraging. "Countries, like individuals, commonly enjoy most quiet when they are young," Charles Backus declared. Having freed themselves from the unyielding prejudices of a deteriorating mother country, there was little chance of Americans suffering from deep-seated tensions. Everything in the young body politic, Rush insisted, was in a "plastic-state." Whereas rigid modes of thinking and acting confounded all attempts at reform and improvement in old states, such as those of Europe, the situation in America was quite different. Here, Rush told William Peterkin, "everything is new & yielding." To John Howard, Rush repeated, "Remember, my dear sir, that we are at present in a *forming* state." Because the American mind was "like soft clay," he reasoned, "much good may be done by individuals, and that too in a *short* time." Indeed, it was an "important era" for Americans precisely because it was a time to "form the fashion of thinking of a whole country." The rubbish of ignorance and prejudice would be removed—the separation from a corrupt England had already removed a major source of error—and good habits cultivated.[29]

There was, however, a special sense of urgency inherent in the image of society as a natural body with distinct stages of growth. Americans were convinced that, as David Tappan observed, "childhood and youth are the seed-time of life, yea, in some important sense the seed-time for eternity." "*Now* is the time to sow the seeds" of a glorious future, Rush advised. The basis for this conviction was the realization that the flexibility and plasticity of youth would pass with the aging of society. The body politic would not be as ready or willing to receive new impressions "five or even three years hence." Therefore, Rush cautioned, although error and deception might now be supplanted without much difficulty, "our state may assume a new complexion" within a few years.[30] This conception of the ossification of the body politic left no time for indolence in the season of youth. "Those habits that are formed & those propensities that are discovered in youth," Charles Nisbet said, "ordinarily prevail through the whole of life." David McClure agreed, "those impressions which are made upon the mind in childhood and youth are most lasting." Simeon Doggett believed that the turn that the young mind received was "very stubborn and probably will in a measure continue until and—awful thought!—beyond death."[31]

According to this perception of societal maturation, then, the years immediately following the separation from England were "teeming with the happiness or wretchedness of millions yet unborn." Alexander Contee Hanson reminded the Revolutionaries to "reflect on the situation of your country, like an ardent youth just rising to manhood, whose conduct, at that critical period, must fix his character for life." "'Tis with governments as with individuals," Alexander Hamilton concurred, "first impressions and early habits give a lasting bias to the temper and character." Republican habits might be instilled, Rush explained, because the young body politic had as yet "few habits of any kind, and *good* ones may be acquired and fixed by good example and proper instruction as easily as *bad* ones without the benefit of either."[32]

Clearly, as Rush's statement indicates, if a conscientious effort was not made to "turn the mind right," then "bad example and indulgence [would] turn it wrong." "The young mind cannot be stationary," Simeon Doggett said. Jeremy Belknap was sure that "if good principles are not early implanted . . . bad ones will assume their place like noxious weeds in a neglected garden."[33] The new and yielding state of things in independent America presented extraordinary opportunities for the advancement of virtue or, failing that, for the growth of bad habits. The alternatives stood out in sharp relief. And while good habits required careful cultivation, "assiduous care," bad ones, "like rank and poisonous weeds spontaneously shoot forth their baneful influence." Youth, therefore, was a time of simplicity and hardy virtue, a period "full of hope" and lively employment, but it was also, and perhaps more importantly, a "season of danger." [34]

Alone, the qualities associated with youthful independence could not have precipitated the Revolutionaries' ready acceptance of republican doctrine. What made the traditionally fragile and unstable system of government attractive to them was their additional belief in the conjunction of providential and historical currents in the new nation. Not only was the American polity in its forming stage, but it had entered that stage at an especially propitious moment. Divine favor had been manifest in the soil, climate, productivity, and exemption from pestilence and natural disasters from the outset of colonization in America. [35] And during the late war for independence providential dispensations had been so numerous that to "enter into a particular consideration of each," John Rodgers said, would be "as vain as an attempt to count the stars in the firmament, or number the sands on the sea shore." The stage had thus been set for the rise of a celebrated "new born" empire. The past was merely prologue to the glorious present, and the present probably prologue to an even more glorious future. [36]

The disruption of the imperial family was seemingly a fitting culmination to the advances made under special circumstances and a proper beginning of a new era in the history of mankind. In the newly invigorated Revolutionary imagination, American independence followed a long-established pattern in the evolution of society and civilization. From time immemorial, Timothy Dwight pointed out to the Yale class of 1776, the "progress of Liberty, of Science and of Empire has been . . . from east to west." The idea of such a transit of civilization was, of course, widely accepted in the eighteenth century, and nowhere more so than among independent Americans. There was welcomed reassurance in the thought that "true Religion, Literature, Arts, Empire and Riches" were, as David Ramsay said, "now about fixing their long and favorite abode in this new western world." Equally encouraging was the knowledge that the "glory of empire has been progressive, the last constantly outshining those which were before." By this reckoning, the British empire was superior to its predecessors, and the new American empire likely to surpass the British. [37]

Implicit in the celebration of the westward trek of civilization was the assumption that all knowledge was cumulative and, therefore, that current generations know more about themselves and the universe around them than their forefathers knew. "This empire is commencing," Timothy Dwight observed, "at a period when every species of knowledge, natural and moral, is arrived at a state of perfection, which the world never before saw." The theories and principles of past generations need no longer be humbly accepted. Rather, it was incumbent upon Americans freely to examine such ideas and to improve them "by experiment" or to expose them as absurdities.[38]

This advancement in knowledge made the Revolution in America both unique and promising. The revolutions of other countries in other times had generally been products of accident or chance; hence the destruction of one tyrant was followed by the inauguration of another. More could not have been expected, Noah Webster concluded, for those nations had existed "in rude times of ignorance and savage ferocity." Men were then largely "without science and without experience." The American Revolution, in contrast, was the product of an enlightened age of reason and science. The separation from England came "at a period when the principles of society and the nature of government were better understood than at any former existence of the World," declared William Pierce. In starting out on their independent course, therefore, Americans need not be bound by the prescriptions of the past, Joel Barlow believed, because American statesmen proceeded upon principles "totally unknown to the legislators of other nations." The superiority of their situation was so obvious to the Revolutionaries that they could only marvel at the chaos that lay at the foundations of other states. The fates of those nations were often determined by "trifles that ridicule belief," an incredulous Pierce exclaimed. "A circumstance as light as air has been the cause of a people's ruin, or a country's glory." How different it was in America, Pierce boasted, "with what contempt does an American look back and trace over such scenes of past folly!"[39]

The assumed superiority of the American present, complemented by the idea of the plasticity of the body politic in its forming stage, contributed directly to the Revolutionaries' conversion to republicanism. Americans had, David Osgood reported, the "wisdom and experience of all former ages together with the discoveries of the present" to direct their course of action. This meant that the historical record of past republican failures might be safely ignored because no previous nation "was ever in a situation to make the experiment," Noah Webster said. Even the Greeks and Romans had been handicapped by their relatively crude knowledge of the essentials of republicanism, David Ramsay declared; thus the principles of republican government had "never yet been fairly tried." As one Pennsylvanian put it, "such a favourable combination of circumstances" as Americans "are blessed with at this important juncture, never did take place among any people with whom history has made us acquainted." [40]

Their minds no longer circumscribed within the narrow limits of filial dependency, the new-generation republicans concluded that the advantages they enjoyed were unsurpassed, indeed unequaled, in the entire course of history. The fortune in accumulated knowledge, the natural advantages, the westward transit of civilization, and the ennobling nature of the Revolution itself all seemed to indicate that Americans, in their formative years, might establish the foundations and prolong the tenure of those hardy domestic virtues that were characteristic of the early years of all nations. If they succeeded in doing this, the Revolutionary republic would be more durable than any in the past.

Nothing better illustrates the impact of these assumptions than the Revolutionary generation's preoccupation with the specter of failure. The coincidence of so many favorable currents, natural as well as historical, at this critical juncture of the nation's development encouraged republican aspirations but, at the same time, placed the burden of failure squarely on the shoulders of Americans. The warning, often repeated, took on a familiar ring: "Circumstanced as we at present are, it would be unpardonable" if we should fail "daily [to] increase and improve in arts, manufactures, and literature." That past nations had failed to make such distinctive advances was understandable and, indeed, predetermined by their handicaps. Their predicament has "partly been owing to their want of skill, and partly to their want of opportunity, under favorable circumstances, like those which fell to us," Edward Bangs explained. Independent Americans, it followed, must realize that failure would have to be attributed primarily to personal and national shortcomings. Moreover, their unprecedented advantages altered the very definition of success. Americans were expected to surpass, not merely to match, the achievements of previous generations. They were, after all, said Jonathan Jackson, within reach of honors "no nation had ever so great a prospect of, with the practice of half the industry and frugality, which other nations have been obliged to use." [41]

By dwelling on the consequences of failure, the Revolutionaries intensified their sense of urgency. If Americans did not "establish and perpetuate the best systems of government on earth," Noah Webster warned, "it will be their own fault, for nature has given them every advantage they could desire." Zabdiel Adams agreed that "if it be not our own fault, we may *now* be the happiest people upon the face of the globe!" With the "experience of a long succession of ages to direct us," and the counsel of the "best political writers to assist us," another observer noted, if we "neglect this opportunity . . . we shall of all nations be the most foolish." Joseph Buckminster believed that the foundations of a "superb political edifice" already existed and that "Heaven" had presented Americans "with a fair opportunity for advancing the honor, dignity, and happiness of civil society." Therefore, if they fell into a "state of supineness," if they succumbed to the "charms of luxury, venality and extravagance," then the "fair foundation that is laid for our future greatness must remain without the superstructure, and we become as much the object of derision, as we at present are of admiration to the nations of the earth." Josiah Bridge summarized contemporary thought on the subject with a harsh projection: "With all these advantages, greater perhaps than providence has ever committed to any one people 'since the transgression of the first pair'; with all our own raised expectations, and that of others, should we through our folly and perverseness, miscarry, alas how contemptible shall we appear!" Indeed, "how criminal and wretched shall we be!" Without a doubt, Americans would be, said John Murray, the "most inexcusable among nations, generations and worlds." [42]

These warnings were reminders that their advantages notwithstanding, the essential catalyst in the formula for republican grandeur was the moral character of the American people. The Revolution promised to turn the new nation into a "new theatre admirably calculated for the display of every thing great, of which men are capable in civil society." Yet Americans had to be careful not to assume too much, lest they stifle all that the event portended. What the various writers were describing, Joseph Buckminster said, were "important events" and their "probable consequences." However, these "consequences are not so indissolubly connected with these events, that they must inevitably follow without any reference to the temper with which we receive them, or the manner in which we improve them." Actually, one contributor observed, "our situation is unparalleled, if we comprehend our political and local advantages." Americans would be a happy people, another prophesied, if they made a "wise improvement" of that which they had inherited. The proposition amounted to a hypothetical imperative. We must first "*wisely improve*" our current situation, John Rodgers remarked, in order to "render it a fruitful source of happiness to ourselves and millions yet unborn." "In a word," Samuel Stillman concluded, "God hath put into our hands a prize of the most inestimable value: it lies with us to improve it." [43]

In the *Dangers of Our National Prosperity; and the Way to Avoid Them,* Samuel Wales reviewed the promise of America by way of a cautionary note. "In the midst of all our present publick happiness," Wales warned, "dangers surround us and evils hang over our heads." So much remained to be done that Americans ought not to flatter themselves. While all were anticipating future greatness, "we are in danger of expecting the end without a proper attention to those means which are absolutely necessary in order to obtain it." Wales saw the problem as one rooted in the universal enthusiasm of youth. "Young States," liberated from the control of a mother country, were "like young men; exceedingly apt, in imagination, to anticipate and magnify future scenes of happiness and grandeur, which perhaps they will never enjoy." It was "fashionable to prophesy" the rise of a new generation of "*Lockes* and *Newtons,* of poets, philosophers and divines greater than have ever yet lived; of towering spires, and spacious domes, of populous towns and cities rising thick throughout an empire greater than the world has ever seen," but these visions, while "beautiful in poetry," should not distort "serious and didactic prose." That providence had laid the foundations of a "very flourishing and mighty empire" was beyond question. What ought to be equally obvious, but what Americans were in danger of forgetting, was that the "superstructure is not yet finished, nor ever will be unless we use the proper means" to effect its completion. "And whether we shall use such means or not," declared Wales, "is a matter of very great uncertainty."[44]

The unparalleled advantages of the "young" republic also meant that its fate would be characterized not only by "misery" or "happiness," but also, as John Rodgers said, by misery or happiness "in the extreme." There was no middle ground. The Revolution, Silas Deane emphasized, would prove to be either a great "blessing" or a great "curse." Because providence had been especially generous to Americans, John Adams explained, "if they betray their trust, their guilt will merit even greater punishment than other nations have suffered." The Revolutionaries were thus obliged to prove themselves worthy of their special inheritance. Robert Livingston beseeched his audience to "rejoice with Roman pride, that those you love have done their duty," and through strenuous effort to "crown the glorious work which they have begun." Jonathan Loring Austin, aware of the lasting impact of youthful habits, added that "now, if ever, is the time to keep a more than ordinary watch over our manners; to encourage industry, frugality and economy." John Rodgers was even more emphatic. "The sons of profaneness cannot now sin at the cheap rate . . . they were wont to do," he said. "Your guilt is greater . . . than in years past, in proportion to the great things God has done for us, as a people." In short, the Revolutionaries believed, as David Tappan put it, that they must succeed in establishing a durable republic or their extraordinary advantages would lead to "exemplary ruin."[45]

Assumptions such as these elevated the stature of the Revolution from a colonial war for independence to an event of significance for all mankind. The shock of the "electric fluid" of the Revolution, as William King Atkinson said, was felt throughout the world. Americans would be contemptible and criminal if they failed because their example would transcend the borders of the new nation; it would determine the limits of human aspiration. Because the American situation was superior to all that had gone before, and, as many asserted, was likely to remain unsurpassed in the future, the present was a moment of final reckoning. "I have always thought," Aedanus Burke confessed, "that the revolution in America would reduce to a certainty, whether mankind was destined by nature for liberty or slavery; for a republican government never before has had what we call fair play in any part of the globe." Revolutionary America had become a symbol of human liberty; thus it was incumbent upon its inhabitants to prove that the republican model was workable. "Otherwise," John Taylor warned, "she betrays mankind." [46]

This sense of certainty and finality led John Rodgers to exclaim "How dignified, how interesting the situation!" "The eyes of the nations of the earth . . . are upon these States, to see what they will make of these great things God has done for us." The larger audience and larger purposes were never submerged or obscured in the American mind. "I should do little justice to the motives that induced you to brave the dangers and hardships of a ten years war," Robert Livingston stated, "if I supposed you had nothing more in view, than humble peace and ignominious obscurity." Such limited designs were characteristic of a dependent people, and thus hardly appropriate among independent Americans. With providential favors and divine retribution introduced into the equation, the American experiment was of cosmic dimensions: "Heaven and earth are looking [on] with eager expectation." To Levi Hart, the "events connected with the present day" were so "great" that together they constituted an "era pregnant with the fate of the world!" Elias Boudinot, believing that the "hopes of men" rested on the fate of America, confessed, "I tremble for the event, while I glory in the subject." [47]

It is important to remember the tension incorporated into the Revolutionaries' conception of their historical moment in order to explain their sometimes frenetic efforts in shaping the American body politic. The advantages that put greatness within reach removed at the same time the possibilities of rationalizing failure. No petty accident or trivial incident, no ingrained habits or imposed customs, no "Fortunate Usurpers," to use Charles Backus's term, had circumscribed the activities of the Revolutionaries. Deliberate action rather than crude necessity would shape the American future. But because the issue of whether independent Americans would complete the superstructure was in doubt, Robert

Livingston's lament accurately expressed a common sentiment: "Reflection on the past brings to memory a variety of tender and interesting events, while hope and fear, anxiety and pleasure, alternatively possess me, when I endeavor to pierce the veil of futurity." [48]

This ideological tension was aggravated by what seemed to be the actual disposition of many of the fledgling republicans. Through ignorance or carelessness, the American public appeared to be following a course of action that could lead only to disaster. They were, Josiah Bridge thought, on the verge of giving a "loose reign to the vices too apparent in the present day." If this propensity continued, "Have we not every reason to expect, that our most pleasing prospects will be soon closed, and succeeded by the deepest gloom?" Americans ought to remember, Alexander Contee Hanson asserted, that "to realize those flattering prospects which presented themselves . . . will require more wisdom and political virtue, than have been manifested since the earliest periods of the contest." Thomas Day remarked that it was the "duty" of the people "as citizens, to remember . . . that the preservation of our government requires no less exertions, than were required to establish it." [49]

Yet an abundance of evidence indicated that Americans were disregarding these warnings. "I feel with you," Ramsay confided to John Eliot in 1785, "the declension of our public virtue. Liberty which ought to produce every generous principle has not in our republics been attended with its usual concomitants." Instead, "Pride, Luxury, dissipation & a long train of unsuitable vices have overwhelmed our country." In 1786, Ramsay confessed to Rush that he was "ashamed" to have to admit that the "morals of the people are so depreciated that legal honesty is all that is aimed at by most people." The Revolution did not seem to have effected any improvement in the moral disposition of the people. It must be conceded, David Daggett said, that "before the revolution, our circumstances were in various respects preferable to what they are at the present. Our public character was much less tarnished." [50]

A major cause of this disturbing state of affairs, ironically, could be traced back to the special favors Americans had experienced, particularly during the war with England. In general, such conflicts could have distinctly paradoxical effects on the morals of a nation. To be sure, as Rush said, "war tends to loosen the bonds of morality and government in every country." Ramsay agreed: "war never fails to injure the morals of the people engaged in it." But the hardships of war could also decidedly benefit a nation. Thus Ramsay wrote in 1779 that "King George for once in his life is promoting the grand cause of American liberty & republicanism." The people's manners ought to correspond to their form of government, and the British were promoting the welfare of Americans by making it "necessary for [them] to live in a more plain simple republican manner." Hence, "we promise fairer for the simplicity of republicans than if the enemy had not visited us." In 1781, Ramsay repeated these observations to Benjamin Lincoln. The "invasion will leave the people of Carolina most excellent republican materials." Because of these beneficial consequences, Ramsay hoped that the other states would receive "their quota of continental sufferings." [51]

Rush enthusiastically shared these views. In 1777, while France hesitated in recognizing American independence, and the future of the patriots' cause appeared rather dismal, Rush nevertheless found solace. He was "pleased" that France was so reluctant to join the Americans, for "I have long thought that we were in a great danger of being ruined by a too speedy rupture between France and England." Rush's explanation was simple: "we are not ripe for being delivered." One or two more campaigns, he thought, would be needed to "purge away the monarchical impurity we contracted by laying so long upon the lap of Great Britain." With France joining in the effort, the war would end prematurely, Rush cautioned, and that "would be the greatest curse that could befall us." [52]

The deterioration of American morals, then, was thought to stem in part from the advantages of the American situation. These advantages had allowed victory to be too "cheaply bought," before the people could be adequately prepared for republican independence. Such easy successes, the Revolutionaries believed, tended to place the political body in a precarious state, for "like the human frame," it could become "corpulent." The body politic could "arrive at such a degree of health, as will border upon disease," William Jones explained. This diagnosis was applied to the American polity. "Elated with success and blinded by prosperity, we too soon began to relax in our *manners,* and to adopt the luxury, the follies, the fashions of that nation which so lately we had every reason to detest," scolded John Gardiner. The American people, "elated with success," had plunged into "habits of expence and idle speculation," echoed William Pierce. The readers of the *Columbian Magazine* were warned that "We have departed from those plain and simple manners, and that frugal mode of living which are absolutely indispensable in the infant state of our country, and best suited to our Republican form of government." Consequently, despite our enormous potential, "we have, by our own misconduct, tarnished the rising glory of our country." [53]

In describing their predicament, the Revolutionaries recalled once again their recent status as a filial dependent. Rush had prophesied in 1778 that an early end to the war "would leave us in the puny condition of a seven-months child." David Daggett could think of no analogy more fitting to explain the errors of the new republicans than to liken them to "many a giddy youth" who had "embarked too early in life, and taken the helm before his prudence was sufficient to guide him." Elbridge Gerry affirmed that "since their dismemberment from the British empire, America has . . . resembled the conduct of a restless, vigorous, luxurious youth, prematurely emancipated from the authority of a parent." The analytical context of these complaints, of course, differed from what had existed earlier. These admonitions were directed at the wayward "child" for failing to realize his potential and not, as it were, for being insolent or disaffected. Self-fulfillment rather than filial fear or deference was at issue here.[54]

By the time David Ramsay began writing the *History of the American Revolution,* he had absorbed enough of the postwar experience to reflect a change from the attitude embodied in his oration on independence. The war had not fostered a "plain simple republican manner" or left the people as "excellent republican materials." Instead, it now appeared as though the war had sadly injured the moral fiber of Americans. It was still true that "on the whole, the literary, political, and military talents of the citizens" had been improved by the Revolution, but it was now equally appparent that "their moral character is inferior to what it formerly was." "So great is the change for the worse, that the friends of public order" must exert "their utmost abilities in extirpating the vicious principles and habits which have taken deep root during the late convulsions."[55] Ramsay thus identified one of the principal motives behind the reform efforts of the Revolutionary generation. At the very moment when the promise of independence should have been progressing toward full realization, it was in danger of being squandered away. The predicament was a matter of some astonishment: "Could anyone have conceived that a people who had given such signal displays of fortitude and patriotism," asked John Brooks, would "soon, very soon, so far forget their own dignity and interest, as to abuse their liberty, and prostitute it to the vile purposes of licentiousness?" Since considerable sacrifices had already been made in order to achieve independence, Joseph Lathrop pleaded, "let us submit to some self-denial, that we may secure it."[56]

The Revolutionaries, well-versed in the cyclical implications of the organic model, knew that old age and decline inevitably followed the years of maturity. "As man himself must soon fall into the earth, and give way to succeeding generations," Edward Bangs said, "so all, even the most lasting, things on earth are still liable to decay and change." They knew and could accept the idea that there was never "a rising or meridian, without a setting sun," and that it was "certain that a chilling winter will, finally, close the scene." What they understood as a basic premise, however, was that this evolution would be gradual. The seeds of empire would "probably require centuries to grow, in order to be centuries in flourishing and centuries in decaying," James Campbell observed. Revolutionary writers were not directing their complaints at the organic process itself, but rather at the subversion of it. The advantages of America, compounded by an emulation of European practices among its inhabitants, were interfering with the sequences of growth so that, as David Rittenhouse noted, "we have made most surprising, I had almost said unnatural, advances towards the meridian of glory." These unnatural advances meant that "in all probability our fall will be premature." [57]

While the advantages arising out of the progress of knowledge and providential favor heightened the Revolutionaries' sensitivity to failure, the apparent decline of public virtue in the postwar years made those apprehensions even more foreboding. David Daggett's judgment in 1787 summed up these fears. The people of Europe, with their eyes "fixed upon us . . . respect us for what we have been—admire us for what we might be, but despise us for what we are." It is important to bear in mind, however, that despite such disparagement, the promise embodied in an independent America was never thought to be lost. Indeed, as Daggett's statement makes clear, the burden was great and Americans despised because the opportunity to fulfill the expectations engendered by the Revolution seemed to persist. This persistence, in turn, sustained the admiration "for what we might be." If the future of the rising empire was threatened, it was because Americans were drifting away from the natural order of things. "Alas!" Thomas Dawes lamented, "it is because we have not lived up to the first principles of our Independence . . . that we have suffered at all." [58] The propitious concurrence of the progressive forces of history in the young and yielding body politic not only encouraged but also obligated Americans to expend themselves in an effort to effect a successful republican system or to suffer the lasting condemnation of mankind.

6

Depersonalization:
The Law Is King

It was a truism among the early domestic counselors that the fate of the colony and the fate of the family were inextricably intertwined. The convergence of events in the mid-eighteenth century provided at least an oblique endorsement of their faith, for the erosion of paternal authority in the colonial family dovetailed nicely with the dissolution of the imperial family. Recent studies have shown that by the middle decades of the eighteenth century American society had undergone some fundamental changes. Demographic conditions, in particular, seemed to have diminished the social space occupied by the family and reduced the scope of paternal authority. The way men perceived themselves and the world around them, however, lagged behind this societal transformation. Thus an ever-widening gap between the way men were and the way they thought they ought to be produced anxieties and some tension. Whether this situation was translated into political radicalism and channeled into the imperial crisis itself remains a matter of much scholarly controversy, but need not detain us here. It is enough for us to note the existence of the tension between the real world and the ideal, and to recognize the coincidence of the various domestic and civil changes in mid-century America. It then becomes possible to suggest that under the combined impact of social evolution and political revolution, the explanatory power of the familial paradigm was severely curtailed. In the first place, the withdrawal of the family in the social arena rendered it a more distinctive social unit whose imperatives, of necessity, became less applicable to the wider society outside of the home. Second, the withdrawal of the colonies from the imperial family made the language of filial humility in politics appear anachronistic. What was needed was a new mode of perceiving civil relationships, cne not so dependent upon the familial model.[1]

The alternative was revealed during the Revolution as Americans committed themselves to republican principles. Indeed, a large part of the appeal of republicanism—which for most of the eighteenth-century world was a historically discredited doctrine—was that for the Revolutionaries it helped to explain their past as well as to express their hopes for the future. As a result of this commitment, the Revolutionary generation was able to bridge the gap between ideals and reality. Americans, as colonists, had never been at ease with their departure from acknowledged standards of metropolitan excellence. But Americans, as independent Revolutionaries, viewed such departures as milestones in the progression toward republican perfection. The gap, which earlier had served as evidence of unfortunate behavior, was now indicative of erroneous standards. The commitment to republicanism entailed nothing less than the forming of a new identity. The Revolution, as Benjamin Franklin said, forced men to break the bonds of dependence and, consequently, to "comprehend the character they had assumed." [2]

The new republican character was no longer bound by the prescriptions of affection so central to the familial paradigm. Republicanism instead seemed to require a depersonalization of authority. Monarchical rule, as John Locke pointed out, was so preeminently personal that it was often and understandably confused with paternal authority. In the "Original of Commonwealths," nature and necessity conspired to lodge the reins of government in the hands of the father. And this was only proper, for "Paternal affection" rendered him the "fittest to be trusted" and hence the easiest "to submit to." With the passage of time, the "natural *Fathers of Families,* by an insensible change, became the *politick Monarchs* of them too." In a republican polity, however, with all semblance of paternal continuity ended, political authority was less personal and less affectionate. The exercise of discretion in civil or judicial matters, especially, smacked too much of a paternalistic monarchy and seemed too dangerously close to ruling by arbitrary will to be condoned. [3]

In *Common Sense* Thomas Paine indicated the direction in which American republicanism was headed. Paine did this by posing a rhetorical question and, in the process, issuing a ringing proclamation. Some people may be tempted to ask, he said, "But where . . . is the king in America?" Paine's answer is noteworthy because he did not simply contend that in a purified America there was no king and, furthermore, no need of one. Instead, he responded by declaring that "in America THE LAW IS KING." Paine was not content, nor were his contemporaries satisfied, merely with a symbolic killing of the king. They proceeded in the aftermath of Independence to crown a successor, impartial law, and thereby signified the transference of authority from the grasp of the personal to the realm of the impersonal. [4]

The process by which authority was depersonalized was best illustrated in the evolution of American constitutional thought. The "law" that would be "king" was fundamental law. It would sit in judgment of the actions of all citizens and their governments. This law, however, unlike the English constitution, was not a living and growing body of customs, statutes, and institutions. Rather, the American Revolutionaries conceived their constitutions to be solemn embodiments of the sovereign will of the people. This was the logic behind the innovation of constitution-making through conventions. The sovereign people convened to draw up the fundamental law, then adjourned to place themselves under that institutionalized authority.[5]

Even more revealing of the process of depersonalization than this procedural innovation was the transformation in the doctrine of constitutionalism itself after Independence. In order to appreciate the full measure of the Revolutionary generation's rejection of the personal-affective sources of authority, we must understand the problems encountered and the solutions proffered by American constitutional theorists as they adapted the axioms they had inherited to the social perceptions prevalent in the new republic.

By the time of the imperial crisis the vast majority of American political observers had grown accustomed to the boast that the English constitution, rooted in the classical theory of mixed government and incorporating the seventeeth-century version of the separation of powers, was the finest fruit of human wisdom. The "Compound of Monarchy, Aristocracy and Democracy, such as is the English Constitution," William Livingston declared, "is infinitely the best." John Adams was so bold as to declare that although Polybius had praised the balanced constitutions of the Greek and Roman republics, "we may be convinced that the constitution of England, if its balance is seen to play, in practice, according to the principles of its theory . . . is a system much more perfect." Quite simply, the English constitution was the "most stupendous fabric of human invention."[6]

Beyond such celebration, the colonists had also grown accustomed to the practice of identifying their provincial governments with the mixed monarchy of the mother country. Joseph Warren, in his orations on the Boston Massacre—the best of the numerous orations commemorating that event, David Ramsay and John Eliot agreed—referred to the basics of the balanced government concept in criticizing the attempts of Parliament to tax the colonies. "The British constitution (of which ours is a copy) is a happy compound of the three forms (under some of which all governments must be ranged) viz., monarchy, aristocracy, and democracy; of these three the British legislature is composed, and without the consent of each branch, nothing can carry with it the force of a law." The actions of Parliament were without constitutional sanction because they failed to meet a fundamental requirement: money bills must originate with the democratic branch and be approved by the aristocratic branch of the legislature. Warren went on to describe the existence of parallel institutions in America: "the democratic branch, which is the house of commons in Britain, and the house of representatives here . . . the aristocratic branch, which, in Britain, is the house of lords, and in this province, the council . . . the monarchic branch, which in Britain is the king, and with us, either the king in person, or the governor whom he shall be pleased to appoint to act in his stead." [7]

The celebration of and close identification with the classical theory of the English constitution posed some vexing conceptual problems for the Revolutionary generation. That the mixed monarchy had degenerated into tyranny was unsettling enough, for it seemed to confirm the charge that the balanced constitution was more susceptible to corruption than any other form; therefore, that the esteem in which it was held was misplaced. The more classically oriented polemicists, however, could offset such an indictment by arguing that the process of constitutional degeneration was circumstantial. It merely confirmed the contention that even the most admired political forms were not self-sustaining. Differences among governments, they argued, did not always arise from disparate constitutions; they frequently resulted from the ways in which magistrates used or abused their delegated powers. As William Livingston explained, the "very Notion of Government, supposed in some Person or other, a Right to decree and execute Justice; and therefore this power may be well or ill applied." The duty of the people, after delegating power, was thus to keep a proper watch against its abuse. The people of England, unfortunately, had not been sufficiently alert; hence the influence of the crown eventually subverted the balance built into their constitution. The English experience, then, did not invalidate the classical principles of their fundamental law, for, as William Hooper told the members of the Provincial Congress at Halifax, "what is at present stiled the British Constitution is an apostate." The Maryland convention agreed with this assessment and informed its delegates to the Continental Congress in 1776 that despite the apostasy of the English, "we are attached" to the English constitution, "not only by habit but by principle, being . . . persuaded it is, of all human systems, best calculated to secure the liberty of the subject, to guard against despotism on the one hand, and licentiousness on the other." [8]

A more profound conceptual problem was posed by the social assumptions inherent in the classical theory of the English constitution. In England the association of King, Lords, and Commons with the classical orders of society—one, few, and many—strengthened the appeal of the balanced constitution. Political equilibrium was a social phenomenon in the sense that it was identified with and attributed to the personal authority residing, usually by birthright, in different orders of men. The arrangement of three estates, each one controlling and controlled by the others, presumably preserved the liberty of the whole.[9]

In the new republic, neither the natural rights argument for independence nor the structure of society allowed much room for justifying such a mixed system. The dimensions of the task facing American constitutionalists were reflected in the thoughts of David Ramsay. The rejection of the British monarchy, Ramsay said, "drew after it the necessity of fixing on some other principle of government." What would this other principle be? "The genius of the Americans, their republican habits and sentiments, naturally led them to substitute the majesty of the people, in lieu of discarded royalty." In spite of this substitution, "in most of the subordinate departments of government, ancient forms and names were retained." This circumstance, plus the fact that under the old system "a portion of power had at all times been exercised by the people and their representatives," made the change in sovereignty "hardly perceptible, and the revolution took place without violence or convulsion." Ramsay, however, had understated the difficulty of the intellectual transition, for the very imperceptibility of the change in sovereignty fueled the theoretical debate. The retention of old forms and names, and the recognition of the role of the "many" in the classical doctrine of the mixed state, confounded more than a few of those who attempted to construct a constitutional system based on the majesty of the people. Ramsay himself recognized the problem. "The checks and balances which restrained the popular assemblies under the royal government, were partly dropped and partly retained, by substituting something of the same kind." Yet, because "no distinction of ranks existed in the Colonies, and none were entitled to any rights, but such as were common to all," creating a substitute system of checks and balances "was a matter of difficulty." Out of a "homogeneous mass of people," how were Americans to establish the necessary political divisions?[10]

The incongruity of classical constitutionalism and Revolutionary social perceptions forced American republicans to refashion their theoretical inheritance. At its most basic level, the problem was one of securing stability in a society with "no distinction of ranks," where the predominant model was the mixed and balanced English constitution, which presupposed the existence of hereditary distinctions. In the course of grappling with this problem, republican constitutionalists initially rallied around two sets of principles apparently at odds with each other. Out of this confrontation came a revolutionary synthesis that replaced the interpersonal safeguards of the classical orders in counterpoise with a multitude of institutional safeguards appropriate to a one-class commonwealth.

II

The first group of constitutional polemicists drew their inspiration from the champions of the seventeenth-century version of the separation of powers doctrine. In its pristine form, this doctrine was rooted in an examination of the functions of government and guaranteed the stability of the body politic irrespective of the presence or absence of different orders of men. According to such early proponents of this scheme as the Leveller writers John Lilburne, Richard Overton, and William Walwyn, the propensities toward abuse in all governments could be checked by carefully separating and placing in different hands the powers of the state, principally the powers of law-making and law-administering. The concentration of these powers in any one agency was an open invitation to abuse because accountability then became highly problematic. As Lilburne explained, if Parliament was entrusted with the power not only to make the law but also to administer it, the people would be robbed of the benefit of appeal, "for in such cases they must appeale to Parliament either against it self, or part of it self; and can it ever be imagined they [members of Parliament] will ever condemne themselves, or punish themselves?" A century later, Montesquieu was thinking in these terms when he warned that no political liberty could possibly exist under a system in which legislative and executive powers were lodged in a single body because that body might then "enact tyrannical laws . . . [and] execute them in a tyrannical manner." [11]

The separation of powers doctrine found a loyal following among republican Americans. Men such as John Taylor and Thomas Paine, the intellectual heirs of Lilburne and Overton, dismissed as absurd the idea that political stability was dependent upon the sharing of governmental powers among the variously conceived social orders. In effect, they believed that Americans had abolished the ranks of King and Lords as the Rump had done in 1649, and they saw no need to replace these discarded orders. Indeed, it was argued, the existence of different classes of men was productive not of harmony but of unceasing civil strife. "It was so in *Rome;* it has been so in *Great Britain;* and has been remarkably so in these Provinces in times past." The experiences of all former republics demonstrated, wrote "Salus Populi," that disparate interests inevitably attempt to subjugate one another and, therefore, that "two or more interests can never exist in a society, without finally destroying the liberties of the people." Some nations had tried to reconcile the clashing interests of the different orders, but to no avail. Even the English at the height of their wisdom and virtue had failed to perfect an arrangement in which the rights of the "three distinct classes" were secured. General John Sullivan thus charged that those who revered the English constitution actually understood "nothing of it." [12]

For these polemicists, an important aspect of the new republic's unparalleled advantages was its seamless social structure. To be sure, the Revolutionaries, as E. S. Corwin has noted, celebrated their "sense of command over the resources of political wisdom." They believed that America was perhaps the "only country in the world free from all political impediments, at the very time they are under the necessity of framing a civil Constitution." But unsurpassed in its potential was the singular advantage of beginning with "no rank above that of freemen." In forming their governments, Americans had "but one interest to consult." Why, then, adhere to the conventional scheme of constitutional balances predicated on the presence of the hereditary orders of the "one" and the "few"? The adoption of such a system might in time cause the American polity to "degenerate" and thus to resemble the English "or something like that." One of the gravest fears of these constitutional theorists was that the republic's great advantage—the absence of established orders—would be squandered away by a foolish regard for the old provincial forms. There was "no need of a representative of a King, for we have none; nor can there be need of a Council to represent the House of Lords, for we have not . . . a hereditary nobility," but, one observer warned, if a mixed political system was adopted "there is danger that there may be in time." [13]

The rejection of the mixed system and the social equilibrium it portended meant that the objects to be regulated by the constitution were solely the powers of government. Of these, as the Levellers had already explained, two were paramount: "first the making and secondly the executing of the laws." The rights of the people depended on the disposition of these functions, not on the political give-and-take of the three classical estates. The "liberties of a people," declared the anonymous author of *The People the Best Governors,* "are chiefly, I may say entirely guarded by having the controul of these two branches in their own hands," that is, in a democracy, where every freeman participated in the framing and administering of the laws. But a country with a relatively large and widely dispersed population, like America, must establish "some mode of governing by a representative body." Once power was so committed, several precautions were necessary to protect against its abuse. First, the people must carefully surrender "just so much of their natural right as they find absolutely convenient, on account of the disadvantages in their personal acting." Second, executive and legislative operations must be kept distinct, as prescribed in the seventeenth-century separation of powers doctrine. Thus the plan outlined in *The People the Best Governors* proscribed the practice of plural officeholding and called for a strict separation between a legislature, whose powers "ought never to extend any further than barely the making of laws," and an executive, who must be "without any concern in the legislature." If such a separation was not effected, then, reiterating the logic of the seventeenth-century proponents of separated powers, "should there be in some important affairs very unjust decisions, where could the injury gain redress?" The final safeguard in this proposal centered on the frequency of elections. By regularly and routinely returning all officers to a level with their neighbors, the temptation to abuse delegated powers would be held in check because rulers would come to realize that they might soon be out of office and subject to the consequences of their misconduct. Since all three of these mandatory precautions required neither a "body different from the plebeians" nor a balancing of the authority associated with the classical social orders, the system they constituted seemed admirably suited to a nation with but one interest to consult.[14]

Thomas Paine further popularized the notion that a constitutional scheme established without regard to the personal authority ordinarily possessed by the traditional orders of men was best for America. It was best because of the one-class structure of the republic, Paine said, and because it was in accordance with the principles of nature which recognized as arbitrary the division of society into the one, few, and many. Arguments for a mixed polity were merely reminders of an unfortunate habit cultivated during America's years of unnatural attachment to a false mother country. Paine was in full agreement with the author of the "Interest of America": having severed the constricting bonds of dependence, Americans were now blessed with an opportunity deliberately to assume a new mode of governing, and "it ought properly to be new."[15]

According to Paine, the classically balanced government, which he derisively labeled a "government of *this, that,* and *t'other,*" tended to encourage corruption rather than to keep it under control. The system was so "exceedingly complex" that even if the people suffered abuses, the roots of their suffering would remain hidden. Some would say the fault was in one part of the government, some in another, until eventually "the parts cover each other" and all sense of "responsibility is lost." A well-constituted republic had no need for such social ordering of discordant parts. Stability would be achieved through an arrangement of governmental functions. The division of power, executive and legislative, and its distribution to separate agencies within the state, rendered irrelevant the arbitrary social distinctions incorporated into the classical theory of the English constitution. All that was needed to complete this scheme was to ensure magisterial accountability, and, Paine argued, this was easily accomplished by mandating frequent elections. The dynamics of the electoral process reminded magistrates that they might be removed from power; therefore, they would be inspired to avoid making a "rod" that might be used against them in their private stations.[16]

It was left to John Taylor to present the most detailed case for the application of the strict separation of powers doctrine in America, and thus to indicate the limits of its usefulness. Taylor, like the others, scoffed at the suggestion that political stability could in any way be attributed to the existence of three contending social orders. He dismissed as "fanciful" the idea of mixing the interests of king, lords, and commons in precise equipoise. Such a mixture would invariably be subject to wild fluctuations, resulting not in harmony and stability but in "continual political fermentation." [17]

In his *Inquiry into the Principles and Policy of the Government of the United States,* which was published in 1814 but had occupied his "occasional spare time" in the preceding two decades, Taylor offered his program for rendering power safe and the republic stable, while minding the "deep rooted contrariety" between the fundamentals of the American and English constitutions. Rather than relying on the mutual exchanges that formed the substratum of the "balancing whim," Taylor proposed an arrangement in which magistrates were held to their trust as they were "awed by the social jurisdiction" of the people-at-large. At the core of this system of "social jurisdiction" was the belief that power must be divided before it can be rendered responsive and responsible, and that the most important division of power was between the "government and the people." Furthermore, for the system to work, the people must retain a share of the available political power vastly greater than the "dividend allotted to the government." The portion of power committed to the government, in turn, had to be subjected to a "multitude of other divisions." Taylor insisted, however, that these secondary divisions were not intended to constitute a balance of interests within the realm of government; instead, they were merely aimed at preventing "such an accumulation as to awaken ambition." Despite the persistence of the old categories of power—legislative, executive, and judicial—it was important to remember that these allotments were "subordinate to a division of power between the people and the government." [18]

A veritable fragmentation of the powers of government kept magistrates keenly aware of their impotence in the presence of the people and thus encouraged their good behavior. As Taylor put it, "power having been first sparingly bestowed on the government, is minutely divided, and then bound in the chains of responsibility." In a vivid phrase, Taylor captured the essence of his program: "to place every publick officer, isolated in the midst of the publick will." Indeed, pushed to their logical extreme, Taylor's arguments amounted to a refutation of the conventional definition of tyranny. The separation of powers doctrine postulated that a concentration of the executive, legislative, and judicial functions of the state in a single governmental agency "would be an end of everything." In Taylor's case, however, the powers assigned to the government were so minuscule in comparison to the powers still in the hands of the people that even if one body acquired control over all of the delegated functions there would be little danger of tyranny. The people in that event would simply impose their sovereign will on their errant representatives and frustrate any unconstitutional design.[19]

In Taylor's analysis, divisions within government were divorced from any connection with hereditary social authority. Ultimately, he rejected the entire classical inheritance pertaining to political categories. The one, few, and many, "singly or collectively," have never been capable of describing a system founded on "good moral principles," Taylor asserted. The "opinion which supposes monarchy, aristocracy and democracy, or mixtures of them, to constitute all the elements of government, is an error." Taylor's wholesale rejection caused the classically oriented John Adams to protest, "What government, then, ever was deduced from good moral principles? Certainly none. For simple, mixed, or complicated with a balance, surely comprehend every species of government that ever had a being, or that ever will exist." In the science of politics, said Adams, these comprised all the possible variations, just as "in a right-angled triangle, the hypotenuse and the two legs comprehend the whole diagram." [20]

Taylor's rejection of the traditional definition of tyranny and the classical taxonomy of the forms of government invited opposition. But few of his colleagues ventured to that logical extreme. More decisive, therefore, in thwarting attempts to implement the strict separation of powers doctrine in the decade after Independence were two additional considerations. First, constitutional checks established solely on the basis of the separation doctrine seemed to depend too heavily on intellectual distinctions for their perpetuation. The opportunity for encroachment by one branch of the government was greater than in the case of a mixed system of countervailing self-interested parts. In the new states, this fragile system was rendered precarious because the effective distribution of power tended to favor the legislatures. Combined with a tradition of legislative assertiveness, a tradition nurtured by the colonial assemblies' struggles against provincial governors, this meant that the new legislatures possessed the means as well as the inclination to usurp the privileges formally reserved for the other branches. The minute dispensations of power, the "diminution of the booty to be divided," did not curb this inclination as Taylor had hoped it might. In 1784 the Pennsylvania Constitutionalists, supporters of the radical 1776 state constitution, claimed that the violations committed by the legislature resulted from the actions of unprincipled men who had served as legislators. The men in power, rather than the form of government, needed to be replaced. But such an explanation ran contrary to the reason for establishing constitutional government in the first place. Political and institutional arrangements, whether the powers were mixed or separated, were supposed to guarantee the rule of law in spite of, or indeed, because of the sad truth that men were unprincipled, self-serving, and easily tempted by the perquisites of power.[21]

The second difficulty with the separation of powers doctrine in the American setting was that it relied on the ambiguous idea of the accountability of public officers to the electorate, a problem of no mean proportions considering Taylor's formulation of "social jurisdiction." Was accountability restricted, for example, to the electoral process or was it an ongoing proposition? This ambiguity was intertwined with the problem of determining the force of constituent instructions in the ordinary operations of government. Were such instructions binding on the representatives of the people? The prevailing concept of popular sovereignty would seem to suggest that they were, but such notions were not easily reconciled with the deferential expectations incorporated into eighteenth-century politics or with the premises of contractual government. Moreover, there was a considerable chasm separating the rather clinical observation that the people ought to be sovereign from the unsettling realization that the voice of the people could be, as Douglass Adair put it, "singularly unattractive."[22]

The strict separation of powers doctrine, in other words, although free of the personal sources of authority contained in the classical English constitution and apparently fit for a society with no distinction of ranks, could not long maintain the constitutional structure of the republic. Barriers built into the frame of government in the form of checks and balances were needed to complement the theoretical separation of executive, legislative, and judicial functions, if the impartial rule of law and the good of the whole were to be preserved and promoted.

III

In his autobiography, John Adams recalled that in 1775 some members of the Continental Congress approached him for advice on a plan of government. Adams, always mindful of tradition, recommended a "Plan as nearly resembling the Governments under which We were born and have lived as the Circumstances of the Country will admit." The circumstances to which Adams alluded were primarily social. "Kings We never had among Us, Nobles We never had. Nothing hereditary ever existed in the Country: Nor will the Country require or admit of any such Thing." Without these social orders it was impossible to re-create the English constitution in America. Nevertheless, it was clear to Adams that a "Legislature in three Branches ought to be preserved." Contrary to the assertions of Paine, whose constitutional ideas, Adams said, flowed from "simple Ignorance," this tri-partitioned institutional arrangement was "founded in nature and reason." Deprived of a balance of some sort built into the frame of government the body politic "must be destined to frequent unavoidable revolutions." [23]

Because Adams was the most forceful spokesman for the balanced government theory in opposition to the proponents of the strict separation of powers doctrine, his political tribulations are especially revealing of the problems confronting the classically oriented constitutional polemicists. Adams realized, of course, that the social situation in America distinguished it from England and from all of the mixed republics he described in the *Defence of the Constitutions*. In Harringtonian terms, because the people "have the whole property of land," they alone were "undoubtedly sovereign." Even in such an essentially undifferentiated polity, however, the exercise of sovereignty, the "annual administration" of power, must be committed to a relatively few representatives of the people. As such, the "great question" remained "what combination of powers in society . . . will compel the formation, impartial execution, and faithful interpretations of good and equal laws. . . ?" One thing was certain: all men, Americans included, were moved by "self-interest, private avidity, ambition, and avarice." To expect self-denial from persons who had the "power to gratify themselves, is to disbelieve all history and universal experience." Although the majesty of the people in the new republic had replaced a discarded royalty, the requirements of a system ruled by law, not by the arbitrary wills of men, were unchanged.[24]

Adams's fascination with the universality of human passions led him to conclude that "all nations, under all governments, must have parties." Differences, however generated, abounded in every state, city, village, and family, and these differences were the stuff of partisan contests. The "great secret" sought by rational men in all epochs was a method of controlling the effects of these contending groups. According to Adams, the lessons of history demonstrated that there were only two ways of doing this: first, by the force of a monarch and a standing army; second, by a balanced constitution. Since the former must be anathema to genuine republicans everywhere, the remedy had to be found in the latter.[25]

Adams's ideas stimulated a lively opposition largely because his version of the balanced constitution fell squarely within the mainstream of eighteenth-century thought on the subject and thus evoked visions of the personalized authority of the classical estates. Like Bolingbroke and Montesquieu, the chief expositors of the classical theory of the English constitution in the eighteenth century, Adams subordinated the separation of powers idea to the notion of mixed orders. This was evident in his classification of types of government. To Roger Sherman, Adams explained that all governments were either despotic, monarchic, or republican. In despotic states, all power was concentrated in a single body; in monarchies, legislative and executive powers were so concentrated, but judicial authority resided in a separate entity. Thus far, Adams was subscribing to the logic of the separation of powers doctrine. In his definition of republican systems, Adams deviated from this pattern. The state characterized by a distribution of the three functions of government to separate civil agencies was not a republic but merely a transitory state descending into arbitrary rule. What was needed, what constituted the essence of a republican form, was a mixture of the "powers of the one, the few, and the many, in equal proportions, in the legislature." Whenever any one body in the state, whether king, nobles, plebeians, or "human nature in every shape and combination," came to possess legislative power in its entirety, that body eventually became tyrannical, "and so it ever will." The balance Adams sought, then, was not of executive, legislative, and judicial operations, but rather of different orders incorporated into the legislative branch. The *sine qua non* of a republic was that "legislative [power] is always vested in more than one." [26]

The problem with Adams's mixed theory in America was obvious: how would the different orders be identified? It was one thing for Adams to assert that the "greatest writers" on government had demonstrated the "utility and necessity of different *orders* of men, and of an *equilibrium* of powers and privileges," but it was an entirely different matter for him to justify any distinctions to a citizenry already sensitive to the social implications of the balanced-government concept. What the sovereign people of the republic, the "fountain and original of all power," needed to do was to "appoint different orders to watch one another," but, as Adams acknowledged, this was a difficult requirement to meet in a country with "no nobles or patricians" and where "all are equal by law and by birth."[27]

In arriving at a solution to this predicament, Adams, like the separation of powers advocates, tried to dissociate the notion of constitutional checks from the idea of social equilibrium. He did this not by repudiating the mixed government component of the English constitution, but by attempting to redefine the bases of the traditional orders. In the American version of the balanced constitution, Adams said, there must be "different orders of *offices,* but none of men." Although a few select citizens might be placed in offices of elevated importance, and the legislature balanced along the lines of the classical English model, "out of office, all men are of the same species, and of one blood." Distinctions established in nature would be accommodated in this political structure, but there was room for "neither a greater nor a lesser nobility." Hence, while an aristocracy of sorts would gain public recognition and acceptance through the several orders of offices, it would be founded on merit and remain fluid enough continually to assimilate new talent. Properly understood, Adams's plan for a mixed legislature called for an institutional equilibrium in place of the traditional social balance.[28]

Despite the best efforts of Adams, the concept of balanced orders, even orders of offices, suffered from its ready identification with the English constitution. The persistence of old names, a circumstance that Ramsay claimed had eased the transition from colony to commonwealth, served instead to increase the probability of theoretical confusion. Of all the arts and sciences, Adams complained, the study of politics was burdened most by a "confusion of languages." For an advocate of a mixed system of balanced offices, semantic precision was paramount in garnering popular support. "Terms must be defined before we can reason," Adams reminded his intellectual adversary John Taylor. But near the end of the third volume of the *Defence of the Constitutions,* after his most extended effort at explaining the principles of mixed republicanism, Adams was forced to confess, "I am not without apprehensions that I have not made myself fully understood." His suspicions were well placed. Although Adams had no intention of reconstructing the traditional balance of social orders, his efforts at distinguishing the natural aristocracy aroused anxieties. The labels "gentlemen" and "simplemen," along with untimely references to parties of the "poor and rich, patricians and plebeians, nobles and commons, senate and people"—"call them by what names you will"—breached the semantic and contextual confines Adams had established. Indeed, Adams himself while denying that "gentlemen" and "simplemen" identified social classes, "high-born" or "low-born," admitted that the force of circumstance generally dictated that the first come from the "more noted families" and the second from among the "husbandmen, merchants, mechanics, and laborers" of America. Adams's version of a balanced constitution for the republic was insufficiently depersonalized. Because it too closely resembled the classical formulation, his plan of government could not escape the suggestion that the powers it sought to regulate were manifestations of the authority commanded by different orders of men. Adams's presentation failed to quiet the lingering fear that by adopting a mixed arrangement Americans would unwisely "erect different orders of men" in a society originally free of them.[29]

IV

The process of successfully depersonalizing the authority of the balanced constitution began with Adams's ideas concerning the salutary effects of mixed orders of offices but subordinated them to the separation of powers doctrine. Even more important, however, the logic of the separation doctrine itself was extended to include not only the various agencies of the state but also, in keeping with the ideology of republicanism, independent citizens actively engaged in defending the constitution. The culmination of this extended arrangement was the conception of a system of fundamental balances structured after patterns revealed in the natural world.

Elements of the emerging Revolutionary synthesis may be seen in the *Essex Result,* written by Theophilus Parsons in response to the proposed 1778 Massachusetts constitution. In this influential essay, Parsons objected to the proposed plan of government because it failed to maintain a proper separation of legislative, executive, and judicial powers, and also because it did not provide the executive with a veto as a means of resisting legislative aggrandizement. Parsons, like Adams and Montesquieu, understood political stability to be dependent upon two complementary sets of constitutional checks. Unlike Adams, however, Parsons deduced the elements of his mixed and balanced government from a functional analysis of the American polity rather than from a review of the nature of social categories. He did not, for example, envision a restless scramble for dominion between the few and the many; thus his argument for a bicameral legislature emphasized efficiency over equilibrium. The division within the legislature tended to promote operational efficiency by tempering the political probity of the bulk of the citizenry with the wisdom of "some of their fellow subjects." Because "wisdom and firmness are not sufficient without good intentions nor the latter without the former . . . let the legislative body unite them all." This coordinate assembly would be the perfect complement, Parsons thought, to a single executive whose functional advantages were vigor, secrecy, and unity.[30]

The Massachusetts constitution of 1780 incorporated many of the changes suggested in the *Essex Result*. Shortly after its adoption in June 1780, Adams declared that he had been the "principal engineer" of the new frame of government; that although the other members of the committee assigned to draw up the plan, and later the whole convention, had made some alterations, the "frame and essence and substance" of the original had been left intact. Adams's declaration notwithstanding, the convention did make two telling changes that reversed the order of priorities contained in the Adams draft. Adams, it will be recalled, placed greater emphasis on the mixed government aspect of the balanced constitution than on the separation of powers doctrine. It seemed to him that political stability and the welfare of the republic would be better served if legislative power was shared equally by the one, few, and many, than if the executive, legislative, and judicial functions of government were rigorously separated and assigned to discrete agencies. In Article 31 of his Declaration of Rights, Adams stated that the "Judicial department of the state ought to be separate from, and independent of, the legislative and executive powers." For Adams, this was the substance of the separation of powers doctrine. The executive and legislative departments, embodying the one, few, and many, were not separated in this article because they were the components of a more important safeguard, a balanced legislature. Accordingly, in Article I of his Frame of Government, Adams empowered the executive with an absolute veto, "a negative upon all the laws" comparable to the negative that the Senate and House of Representatives possessed in the General Court.[31]

By altering both provisions, the convention established the primacy of the separation of powers doctrine. The Declaration of Rights in the 1780 constitution dropped Adams's Article 31 and specified that in the government of the Commonwealth of Massachusetts, the "legislative department shall never exercise the executive and judicial powers, or either of them: The executive shall never exercise the legislative and judicial powers, or either of them: The judicial shall never exercise the legislative and executive powers, or either of them: To the end it may be a government of laws and not of men." Having first asserted in no uncertain terms the full application of the separation doctrine, the 1780 document then proceeded to balance the branches and to promote their independence. The governor, under the new frame of government, possessed a legislative lever but, unlike Adams's executive, was limited to a qualified negative on all bills. Empowered only to check the excesses of the legislature, the governor was not a third partner in that branch.[32]

The Massachusetts convention attached a lengthy address to the proposed constitution when it was submitted to the towns for ratification. In their explanation of the "Reasons upon which we have formed our Plan," the delegates employed the logic of the classical republicans but again subordinated the idea of mixed orders to the separation of powers. The confusion and tyranny that must accompany the "overbearing of any one of its Parts on the rest" would be avoided in the new constitution by giving a "due Proportion of Weight . . . to each of the Powers of Government." It was clear that "when the same Man or Body of Men enact, interpret and execute the Laws," the rights of the people were in jeopardy. Checks and balances, by maintaining the distinction between law-makers and law-administrators, formed the surest guarantee of responsible rule.[33]

The efforts to establish a new state constitution in New Hampshire registered some of the same priorities set forth in the *Essex Result* and the Massachusetts constitution. In a protracted struggle over ratification, which lasted from 1779 to 1783, New Hampshire constitution makers never wavered in their commitment to the separation of powers. A review of the assorted theories of government, coupled with provincial political experience, had convinced the members of the New Hampshire convention that executive, legislative, and judicial powers must be kept "as separate and distinct as possible." If these powers were ever united under a single authority, the form of government would devolve into a "complete system of tyranny." However, the New Hampshire constitutionalists did not believe that a strict separation of powers alone was sufficient to ensure that impartial laws would prevail over the arbitrary wills of men. They agreed with Parsons that the separation doctrine had to be supported by the creation of such balanced offices "as the nature of a free government will admit." Also, like Parsons, they offered a functional explanation of the institutional orders. The American republic contained no rank above freeman, but a stable polity still required civil officers capable of operating as checks on one another. A particular concern of the New Hampshire delegates was the establishment of an active single executive. It was best to have such an executive because of the functional advantages of the "one," namely "secrecy, vigour, and dispatch." And while election to this office might "set him on high" above the rest of the citizenry, it was important to remember that the governor was merely a conduit, "only the right hand of *your* power, and the mirror of *your* majesty."[34]

The concept of the balanced constitution gradually emerging out of these political contests was spared most of the challenges that plagued Adams's program. By emphasizing the separation of powers doctrine over the socially grounded mixed-government theory, and by stressing the operational characteristics of the various orders of offices—each a reflection of the sovereign will of an undifferentiated populace—over the distinctions that stigmatized the English model, state constitution makers adapted the classical tradition to a revolutionary situation. However, the process of depersonalizing the authority of the balanced constitution required more than this for completion. It required a conceptualization of the polity in which individuals, as citizens and not as members of an hereditary social order, preserved the equilibrium vital to the survival of the state.

As in so much else pertaining to the nature of fundamental laws, James Madison summarized and clarified the basic arguments on the constitutional role of the individual in a republic. The instability and oppression too often attendant upon republican governments could be traced back to two sources, Madison said. The first and "more fatal" source "lies among the people themselves." Because the founding principle of a republic was that the "majority however composed" must "ultimately give the law," what would keep an impassioned majority from committing "unjust violations of the rights and interests of the minority, or of individuals?" Restraints arising from a concern for the welfare of the whole or from the influence of religion were ineffectual at best. A "respect for character"—that is, self-esteem and a jealous regard for one's civic reputation—might curb some excesses, but the force of this restraint "diminished in proportion to the number which is to share the praise or the blame"; hence, it was not likely to exert much influence on the actions of a majority faction. Madison's solution for this problem is well known: minority and individual rights would be secured by the heterogeneity of interests encompassed in a large republic. Madison stood Montesquieu's conventional argument for a small republic on its head. The disarray of contending interests, "creditors or debtors— rich or poor—husbandmen or manufacturers—members of different religious sects—followers of different political leaders—inhabitants of different districts—owners of different kinds of property &c &c." protected private rights because out of this multiplicity "a common interest or passion is less apt to be felt and the requisite combinations less easy to be formed." The variety of competing "pursuits of passions" effectively checked factional appetites "whilst those who may feel a common sentiment [toward abuse] have less opportunity of communication and concert." "If this is not the language of reason," Madison apologized, "it is that of republicanism." [35]

The second, and more frequent if less fatal, source of republican vices was not brought under control by the remedy offered for the first. Indeed, the operation of countervailing passions had the potential of increasing the absolutist propensities of the government. As Caesar Rodney, the Delaware Revolutionary, explained, the "very act of committing the government to a less number than the whole, divides the society into two distinct parts, the *rulers* and the *ruled*. And these distinct parts are hence forward controuled by distinct interests and obligations." Curbing the passions of the ruled, therefore, did nothing in the way of mitigating the appetites of the rulers. It followed that, as Madison put it, the "great desideratum" in politics was such a "modification of the sovereignty as will render it sufficiently neutral between the different interests and factions," not only by keeping "one part of the society from invading the rights of another," but also by ensuring that the government "at the same time sufficiently controuled itself, from setting up an interest adverse to that of the whole Society." "Exterior provisions," such as Taylor's idea of "social jurisdiction," were inadequate to the task of rendering government impartial. "A dependence on the people is, no doubt, the primary control on the government," Madison conceded, "but experience has taught mankind the necessity of auxiliary precautions." Popular supervision, control by the people out of government, would fail for two reasons. The first was inherent in the nature of things. "Whatever respect may be due to the rights of private judgment, and no man feels more of it than I do," Madison wrote Edmund Randolph, "there can be no doubt that there are subjects to which the capabilities of the bulk of mankind are unequal." Most people, unorganized and uninformed, simply did not possess the capacity to supervise those whom they had appointed to manage the esoteric affairs of government. The clever manipulator could overcome the defenses of the masses. Even annual elections were no guarantee. "How easily are base and selfish measures masked by pretexts of public good and apparent expediency?" "How frequently will a repetition of the same arts and industry which succeeded in the first instance, again prevail on the unwary to misplace their confidence?" Moreover, whenever the people were engaged in a debate over statecraft their *"passions"* and not their *"reason"* determined the outcome. This amounted to a solecism in politics, for governments were instituted to regulate the passions of men rather than to be regulated by them.[36]

The second reason for rejecting popular supervision was linked directly to Madison's vision of contending interests in an extended republic. The variety that curbed the ill-effects of factions by making difficult any sort of concerted action by a self-interested majority or sizeable minority, likewise diminished any influence the people might have in relation to their government. The people, after discovering the "impossibility of acting together," would realize also the "inefficacy of partial expressions of the public mind." Eventually, in despair, they would succumb to a "universal silence and insensibility, leaving the whole government to that *self-directed course,* which, it must be owned, is the natural propensity of every government." Madison, in effect, revived a version of the conventional argument that a large republic might be handicapped by its size. The "more extensive a country, the more insignificant is each individual in his own eyes—This may be unfavorable to liberty." [37]

The "auxiliary precautions" Madison envisioned constituted an extension of the checks and balances included in the separation of powers doctrine in America. The accumulation of executive, legislative, and judicial powers "in the same hands, whether of one, a few, or many, and whether hereditary, self-appointed, or elective" was the "very definition of tyranny." But the "celebrated Montesquieu," the "oracle" of this doctrine, did not favor a strict separation; "he did not mean that these departments ought to have no *partial agency* in, or no *control* over, the acts of each other." Only where the "*whole* power" of two or more departments were exercised by the same hands were the fundamental principles of a free constitution subverted. Given the "encroaching nature" of power, the only effective means of restraining it within the limits established for the various branches of government was by creating "practical" supports for the distinctions outlined in "theory." In a rebuke aimed at the strict separationists, Madison contended that the "compilers of most of the American constitutions" had frequently slighted the necessity of these practical supports, and instead had relied on "parchment barriers against the encroaching spirit of power." Subsequent experience had proven the inadequacy of such barriers as the legislative department was everywhere enlarging its sphere of influence and "drawing all power into its impetuous vortex." [38]

Madison applied the idea of institutional checks and balances to the paradox of the extended republic: the possibility that the same variety of interests that controlled the effects of factions might also render all concerted action by the citizenry so difficult and the individual so insignificant as to threaten the foundations of liberty. Unlike Taylor, Madison thought that the people had delegated the bulk of their political power, under conditions specified in their constitutions and according to the natural rights of men, to the different institutional orders of the government. These orders, however, were not confined to the bureaucratic structure of a single level of jurisdiction; on the contrary, they were distributed among the multiple levels of the extended state. The arrangement of these "subordinate distributions" enabled each of the several institutional orders to be a check on the others. [39]

An understanding of this multiple distribution of power was at the heart of Madison's distinction between a "single republic" and a "compound republic." In the former, the power surrendered by the people was administered by a "single government; and the usurpations are guarded against by a division of the government into distinct and separate departments." In the latter, the power surrendered was "first divided between two distinct governments, and then the portion allotted to each subdivided among distinct and separate departments." The different levels of government in the compound republic controlled one another, while their internal dynamics forced them to control themselves. Thus there was at the very least a double security on the rights of the people. Additional partitions among the jurisdictional levels could be justified in similar terms. "If a security against power lies in the division of it into parts mutually controuling each other, the security must increase with the increase of the parts into which the whole can be conveniently formed." The eventual end of these successive reductions was an enhancement of the role of the individual. Through local agencies the will of an autonomous citizenry might still be ascertained, even if the people were "spread through so many latitudes as are comprehended within the United States." Rather than becoming silent and insensible, the "private interest of every individual may be a sentinel over the public rights." [40]

The concept of the individual as constitutional sentinel was an arresting one, ideally suited to a republic in which the people, undifferentiated, were sovereign. Requiring none of the higher orders of men to make it work, the system proportionately increased the burden of responsibilities assumed by ordinary citizens. The assemblage of checks and balances in the compound republic obliged every citizen to be knowledgeable enough to recognize his role "in so vast a plot," and upon such recognition, to possess the wherewithal to fill that role, which was "perhaps a capital one." It was therefore fitting for Jefferson to present a terse review of the principles of the compound republic in his discussion of a general system of American education. [41]

Writing to Joseph Cabell, one of his principal correspondents on this subject, Jefferson explained that the "way to have good and safe government is not to trust all to one; but to divide it among the many, distributing to every one exactly the functions he is competent to." Power must be divided within and among the several orders of the national, state, and ward governments. By "dividing and subdividing these republics from the great national one down through all its subordinations," the whole system was rendered more stable and the individual citizen converted into a participant because these reductions progressed until they ended "in the administration of every man's farm and affairs by himself." The "secret" thus revealed in the American republic was that the stability and security of a state were not dependent upon the actions and authority of its orders of faithful superiors; rather they were extensions of a "synthetical process" whereby the sovereign people delegated power successively to "higher and higher orders of functionaries." Furthermore, in contrast to the colonial reliance on discretionary authority founded on paternal affection, Jefferson's synthetical process ensured a "trust [of] fewer and fewer powers, in proportion as the trustees become more and more oligarchical." [42]

Jefferson's reasoning must not be confused with the traditional arguments in favor of a territorially restricted republic. Indeed, Jefferson predicted "that the doctrine, that small states alone are fitted to be republics, will be exploded by experience, with some other brilliant fallacies accredited by Montesquieu." It seemed far more plausible that in order "to obtain a just republic" the state must be "so extensive as that local egoisms may never reach its greater part." Under such conditions, factions will be forced to give up their pursuit of "particular interests" and to promote instead common "principles of justice." Later, in a note to Robert Williams, Governor of the Mississippi territory, Jefferson repeated these observations. Experience confirmed the supposition that the "smaller the society the bitterer the dissentions into which it breaks." The American commonwealth, in all probability, owed "its permanence to its great extent, and the smaller position comparatively which can ever be convulsed at one time by local passions." [43]

What Jefferson had in mind, then, when he confessed that the "pure and elementary republics" of the wards are "nearest my heart," was the concept of a constitutional order in which individual citizens would never slip into silence and insensibility amidst the galaxy of countervailing interests because they filled specific institutional roles. Every citizen became a "sharer in the direction of his ward republic, or of some higher ones." The potentially bewildering hierarchy of orders of offices became a prerequisite to the rule of law, for it "cemented" diverse interests "by giving to every citizen, personally, a part in the administration of the public affairs." And, because he was a "participator," the citizen-sentinel in turn became a more responsible person. He experienced that regard to reputation, arising from a direct sharing in the praise or blame affixed to certain public measures, which, in other systems, might apply only to specific magistrates occupying select offices. Thus ennobled, citizens collectively might curb governmental excesses by operating in a manner reminiscent of the procedure outlined in John Taylor's notion of "social jurisdiction." Whenever their functionaries in high offices became "corrupt and perverted, the division into wards constituting the people . . . [into] a regularly organized power, enables them by that organization to crush, regularly and peaceably, the usurpations of their unfaithful agents." [44]

In this constitutional scheme, the will of the sovereign people, institutionalized through a complex network of offices, replaced the personal authority of the classical social orders and, as Jefferson said, comprised "truly a system of fundamental balances and checks for the government." Equally important, the "gradation of authorities" was especially felicitous because, as was earlier indicated, it tended distinctly to enhance the political trustworthiness of the average citizen. If in a republic it was true that much was demanded of the individual, it was also true that the system itself seemed to engender the very qualities of public spiritedness that Montesquieu had identified as "virtue." Even John Adams, whose faith in the moral condition of the American people had waned precipitously in the years after Independence, believed in the efficacy of organizationally induced virtue. The "best republics will be virtuous, and have been so," Adams observed, "but we may hazard a conjecture, that the virtues have been the effect of the well ordered constitution, rather than the cause." Adams's continued commitment to a republican form of government in the face of his disillusionment with the American character must be attributed at least in part to this belief. In a world where prejudices, passions, and selfish interests predominated, it appeared as though "neither religion . . . nor anything, but a well-ordered and well-balanced government" could encourage men to be just. In his *Defence of the Constitutions,* Adams reiterated his conviction that a proper arrangement of the institutions of government would "always produce" those treasured republican characteristics: patriotism, bravery, simplicity, reason, and tranquillity. To Samuel Adams, he expressed doubts whether "men should ever be greatly improved in knowledge or benevolence, without assistance from the principles and systems of government." Indeed, Adams explained to Henry Marchant, the moral deterioration they both abhorred in Americans might accurately be traced to the carelessly assembled constitutions under which the people lived.[45]

The perceived impact of the inanimate world of things upon the moral behavior obtaining in the animate world of beings was a perception grounded in the corpus of ideas associated with Newtonian mechanics. The specific implications of this supposed interaction between the physical and moral condition of man, and its contribution to the evolution of American republicanism, will be examined in the next chapter. For the moment, we can gauge the broadest constitutional outlines of this moral perception in George Logan's revealing discourse on the natural and social order of the world. In this piece, Logan, a prominent Philadelphia physician, altered the traditional imagery of social integration by coupling bodily analogies with those drawn from the physical universe. In the realm of animal and vegetable matter, "from the most

stupendous immensity to the minutest particles that can be conceived,—
order, proportion, fitness and congruity in the relation and government
of all things universally prevail." Individual components, "though infinitely varied among themselves," ultimately conspired to promote the
good of the whole. This was possible because "eternal" principles succeeded in establishing the "natural order of things in the moral and
physical world." [46]

Logan's prescription for social harmony was not deduced solely, or
even primarily, from the constitution of the human body. Rather, the
"luminous Bodies" of the universe provided him with the most appropriate models. Society ought to be organized after the example of "our solar
system [which] has its several orbs, each of which is another system of
itself." As this reference to discrete "orbs" suggests, there was in Logan's
presentation more than a hint of the strength of autonomous participation
in the composition of the whole. Thus it was only "highly probable that
all and every one" of the heavenly bodies contributed "to the support
and carrying on the work of each other." Thus, too, it was crucial for
these bodies to be "exactly proportioned and fitted each to the others'
operations" lest they become "destructive one to the other, and produce
the utmost confusion." Above all, it was this capacity for autonomy that
made the laws of nature more remarkable and meaningful. Under their
superintending influences "even the smallest particles of matter are so
uniform in their operations that the effects which they will produce
under particular circumstances" can be predicted with mechanical precision; the results of their actions, Logan declared, can be "known *a
priori.*" [47]

Viewed in this context, the concept of a constitution stripped of the
classical estates, but balanced nevertheless through a compound network
of discrete offices, appeared to be an expression of the eternal order of
nature. That the individual citizen, upon whom the stability of the
republic depended, experienced an improvement in his moral and
political capacities was not unexpected. It was proof that the American
system of constitutional balances was true to the universal principles of
nature, for the "beauty of all complex objects" in the natural world consisted of a combination of gradation and proportion that, as Levi Hart
noted, heightened the "perfection of the whole" while it ensured that the
beauty of each part was not merely "preserved, but exhibited, with
superior advantage." [48]

In the final analysis, the rejection of once-hallowed constitutional
assumptions, a development presumed to have been instigated by advances in knowledge and civilization, legitimated the existing social order
and further encouraged bold projections concerning the perfectibility of

the individual. Such projections, to be sure, intimated a seemingly contradictory blend of individual responsibility and predictable uniformity. However, as we shall see, these were complementary attributes of republican citizenship. If the most insignificant particles of the universe exhibited the "wonderful regularity" that Logan said characterized the natural order of the world, then, surely, it was "impossible to believe for a moment that Man, designed the brightest ornament of the creation," would fail to achieve a corresponding regularity in his own affairs. Better than any other, the American constitutional system promised to perpetuate the new order of the ages inaugurated by the commitment to republicanism.[49]

IV

REPUBLICANISM

London, 1768

My whole time is now employed in attending lectures and hospitals and in visiting places in London which are most worthy the notice of a stranger. I went a few days ago in company with a Danish physician to visit the House of Lords and the House of Commons. When I went into the first, I felt as if I walked on sacred ground. I gazed for some time at the Throne with emotions that I cannot describe. I asked our guide if it was common for strangers to set down upon it. He told me no, but upon my importuning him a good deal I prevailed upon him to allow me the liberty. I accordingly advanced towards it and sat in it for a considerable time. When I first got into it, I was seized with a kind of horror which for some time interrupted my ordinary train of thinking. "This," said I (in the words of Dr. Young), "is the golden period of the worldly man's wishes. His passions conceive, his hopes aspire after nothing beyond this Throne." *I endeavored to arrange my thoughts into some order, but such a crowd of ideas poured in upon my mind that I can scarcely recollect one of them.*

Benjamin Rush to Ebenezer Hazard
22 October 1768

[Philadelphia, ca. 1800]

I mentioned a little while ago the name of Mr. Bostock. I delivered the letter his aunt gave me in Liverpoole to him, and soon afterwards breakfasted with him. He was well informed upon all subjects, particularly upon history, geography and belles lettres. In the course of our acquaintance he informed me that his father commanded a company under Oliver Cromwell. I told him that my first American ancestor held the same rank in Cromwell's army. This was like a discovery of relationship between persons who had previously behaved as strangers to each other. He now opened his mind fully to me, and declared himself to be an advocate for the Republican principles for which our ancestors had fought. He spoke in raptures of the character of Sidney, and said that he once got out of his carriage in passing by Sidney's country house, and spent several hours in walking in the wood[s] in which he was accustomed to meditate when he composed his famous treatise upon government [Discourses Concerning Government]. *Never before had I heard the authority of Kings called in question. I had been taught to consider them nearly as essential to political order as the Sun is to the order of our Solar System. For the first moment in my life I now exercised my reason upon the subject of government. I renounced the prejudices of my education upon it; and from that time to the present all my reading, observations and reflexions have tended more and more to shew the absurdity of hereditary power, and to prove that no form of government can be rational but that which is derived from the Suffrages of the people who are the subjects of it. This great and active truth became a ferment in my mind. I now suspected error in every thing I had been taught, or believed, and as far as I was able began to try the foundations of my opinions upon many other subjects.*

Rush recounting his 1766 meeting
with John Bostock, in *Autobiography
of Benjamin Rush*

7

Republican Machines

The familial commonwealth placed a premium on the intricacies of mutual dependence. A "Mutual good Affection" founded on the social imperatives of the Fifth Commandment was the desired basis of order and stability. Authority, in all of its various manifestations—civil, ecclesiastical, and parental—was a "sacred Thing" and, therefore, to be "reverenc'd accordingly." Society as a whole was so organized as to instill the necessary lessons of cheerful obedience on the one hand and judicious discretion on the other. The commitment to republicanism, however, undermined the social significance of the bonds of affection. In a republic, citizens by definition ought to be autonomous in their personal bearing and independent in the exercise of their wills. Dependence of any kind supposedly rendered one susceptible to all sorts of temptations and impositions. Thus dependence was despised by republicans, and dependent persons became objects of suspicion because they were seen as easy targets of corruption.[1]

The Revolutionary catharsis evident in the American republican commitment thus entailed a change in social perceptions. The full extent of this change is best illustrated in Benjamin Rush's voluminous reflections on the educational imperatives of the new American order, on the proper mode of preparing fledgling republicans to assume the responsibilities of citizenship. The institutions of the old familial commonwealth had sought to nurture a sense of affectionate interdependence among the people, but, Rush noted, the "business of education has acquired a new complexion by the independence of our country." By the very nature of the Revolution, it was now necessary to "examine our former habits" in education as in everything else, and to "adapt our modes of teaching to the peculiar form of our government."[2]

The "peculiar form" to which Rush referred was the compound republic of countervailing orders of offices. Based in large part on his experiences in Pennsylvania, where an unconventional combination of a strong unicameral legislature and weak executive was productive of much turmoil in the decade after 1776, Rush was a confirmed traditionalist. He admired the classical theory of the English constitution, even though he, like Adams, realized that in America there could be no order of men above the rank of freeman. The American republic would prove durable, more long-lived than history had led men to expect, only if civil powers were analyzed and combined to promote durability in the same way that "matter of a perishable nature [was] rendered durable by certain chemical operations."[3]

That Rush was confident this could be done is evidence of his faith in the progress of knowledge and the perfectibility of mankind. Government, "like all other sciences, is of a progressive nature," said Rush. The intellectual ferment generated by the spirit of independence had uncovered this truth and "happily unloosed" the "chains" that had long "bound this science in Europe." Consequently, Americans, by drawing upon their accumulated advantages in science and experience, might incorporate into their forms of government combinations that were unknown to earlier generations of republicans. Circumstantial advantages thus seemed to bode well for the American experiment.[4]

Structural improvements in the frame of government, however, did not obviate the need for a virtuous and, by extension, educated citizenry. The American Revolutionaries continued to believe that virtue was the bedrock of the ideal commonwealth. Advances in statecraft, especially the depersonalization of authority through a constitutional arrangement of the powers of government that tended institutionally to promote stability, could not displace virtue from its central location in the traditional republican equation. But if "virtue" was still on the minds of most Americans, the context in which the concept was understood had changed. In the familial state, virtue was defined socially in terms of interpersonal relations founded on mutual affection. Virtuous persons, as Winthrop put it, mindful of the bonds of affection, "doe mutually participate with eache other, both in strengthe and infirmity in pleasure and paine," to effect the good of the whole. Winthrop went on to describe the social virtues needed to sustain the ideal of communal harmony. "Wee must be knitt together in this worke [of establishing a Christian utopia] as one man," he declared.

> Wee must entertaine each other in brotherly Affection, wee must be willing to abridge our selves of our superfluities, for the supply of others necessities, wee must uphold a familiar Commerce together in all meekeness, gentlenes, patience and liberality, we must delight in eache other, make others Condicions our owne rejoyce together, mourne together, labour, and suffer together, allwayes haveing before our eyes our Commission and Community in this worke, our Community as members of the same body, soe shall wee keepe the unitie of the spirit in the bond of peace.

Deviations from this ideal of public virtue was, as noted earlier, the cause of considerable tension in the colonial temperament.[5]

In the republic, the ideal itself had been altered. Under the influence of classical republicanism and civic humanism, the Revolutionary understanding of virtue was at once less communal and more conspicuously political. Informed as they were by Montesquieu's popular *Spirit of the Laws,* the Revolutionaries knew that in a republic politics and morality were inseparable. But virtue came to be defined in individual rather than interpersonal terms. We need only to compare Winthrop's well-known communal imperatives with Rush's treatment of republican duties to begin to grasp the extent of the change. Rush, in *Thoughts upon the Mode of Education Proper in a Republic,* described the essence of civic virtue. The "form of government we have assumed," Rush noted, "has created a new class of duties to every American." Republican citizens must be attached not to each other primarily, but to the republic itself. "Our country includes family, friends and property, and should be preferred to them all," Rush declared. Therefore,

> let our pupil be taught that he does not belong to himself, but that he is public property. Let him be taught to love his family, but let him be taught, at the same time, that he must forsake, even forget them, when the welfare of his country requires it. He must watch for the state, as if its liberties depended upon his vigilance alone. . . . He must love private life, but he must decline no station, however public or responsible it may be, when called to it by the suffrages of his fellow citizens. He must love popularity, but he must despise it when set in competition with the dictates of his judgement, or the real interest of his country. He must love character, and have a due sense of injuries, but he must be taught to appeal only to the laws of the state, to defend the one, and punish the other. He must love family honor, but he must be taught that neither the rank nor antiquity of his ancestors, can command respect, without personal merit. . . . He must be taught to amass wealth, but it must be only to encrease his power of contributing to the wants and demands of the state. . . . Above all he must love life, and endeavor to acquire as many of its conveniences as possible by industry and economy, but he must be taught that this life "is not his own," when the safety of his country requires it.

That Rush used the third-person singular pronoun, whereas Winthrop had employed the first-person plural, is indicative of the transformation that had taken place. Rush's prescription was less personal and more individualistic. In addition, his message incorporated a clear appreciation of the potential for conflict between private and public interests; indeed, Rush seemed to anticipate such conflicts. Sacrifices still had to be made for the sake of the larger whole, but the work was no longer communal. Rather, each citizen was commissioned individually to fulfill his responsibilities. The virtuous republican had to look after the welfare of the state, "as if its liberties depended upon his vigilance *alone.*" Above all, he must be independent: loving popularity, but acting only in response to the "dictates of his judgement"; loving family honor, but commanding respect only through "personal merit." In short, the citizen was on his own.[6]

The concept of virtue thus underwent a modification corresponding to the depersonalization of authority in the commonwealth. The "new complexion" accorded to the business of education accommodated this new conceptual framework. As Rush saw it, the primary function of education must be to "convert men into republican machines." This conclusion, coupled with his reference to individuals as "public property," has led some twentieth-century critics to identify Rush as the archetype of the paradoxical American in whose mind freedom and uniformity are fused. Few things, it seems, could be more anomalous to the spirit of the Revolution than a mechanically fashioned polity.[7] Yet, even a cursory consideration of the Enlightenment's fascination with Newtonian mechanics should cause us to be skeptical about such pronouncements. A closer examination of the complex of ideas summarized in Rush's formula for republican citizenship would reveal that the connotations of the word *machine* for Rush were anything but menacing. Indeed, one of the first principles of his entire theory of medicine was that life itself was "truly mechanical." The phrase "republican machines," then, was drawn from Rush's medical doctrine, and only by placing it back into that context will we understand its meaning and thereby gain further insight into the Revolutionary perception of virtue.

II

Life, Rush contended, was mechanical because its motions were activated by "stimuli" in the same way that the "movements of a clock" resulted from the "pressure of its weights, or the passage of a ship in the water, from the impulse of winds and tide." Moreover, because he believed that the major part of these life-sustaining stimuli came from the environment, Rush was alive to the medical implications of man's surroundings. Following the lead of Montesquieu, he argued that "climates, weather, soils, and the local relations of different countries to rivers, seas, and mountains" all affected the human condition, and all were therefore properly within the province of medical studies. The "science of medicine," Rush said, was "related to every thing." A physician who claimed to know only those sciences "which are supposed to belong exclusively to his profession" was a "nonentity" undeserving of the "title [physician] in its extensive import." [8]

Even more decisive than such natural forces as climate and soil was the influence exerted upon the individual by the prevailing social environment. This was the message conveyed in the oration "Medicine Among the Indians of North America," which Rush delivered before the American Philosophical Society in 1774. On one level, the oration was a survey of the "natural history of medicine among the Indians . . . and a comparative view of their diseases and remedies with those of civilized nations." But there was a deeper significance to the oration. As Rush explained in a letter to Arthur Lee, "I have connected with the subject some political reflections which will tend to enlarge the ideas of the future populousness and grandeur of America." Indeed, the observations Rush made at the first level were intended to explicate the arguments he advanced in these "political reflections." His paramount concern was expressed in a terse passage that suggested a link between political and biological health. "Do the blessings of civilization," Rush inquired "compensate for the sacrifice we make of natural health, as well as natural liberty? This question must be answered under some limitations. When natural liberty is given up for laws which enslave instead of protecting us, we are immense losers by the exchange." Likewise, "if we arm the whole elements against our health, and render every pore in the body an avenue for a disease, we pay too high a price for the blessings of civilization." [9]

After reviewing those customs of the Indians "which we know influence diseases," namely, "facts" relating to childbirth and childrearing, diet, sex, and marriage, Rush concluded that their medical practices were rudimentary because "their diseases are simple and few in number." The frugal lifestyle of the Indian "excludes the influence of most of those passions which disorder the body." The "turbulent effects of anger" were reduced, while "envy and ambition are excluded by their equality of power and property." If, therefore, Indian remedies were simple and few in number, they were nevertheless "full of strength; . . . they are accommodated, as their languages are to their ideas, to the whole of their diseases." The "natural" remedies of the Indians were more effective than their "artificial" remedies; the latter, Rush remarked, often proceeded from ignorance and, at any rate, there was not a single "well attested case of their efficacy." But this was not unexpected. Given the state of Indian society, nature could be and was "active and successful in curing the diseases of the Indians." From this account of the "customs of the Indians," then, Rush observed, "we need not be surprised at the stateliness, regularity of features, and dignity of aspect by which they are characterized." These were the external signs of "health and a strong constitution." [10]

Turning his attention to the "civilized nations," Rush argued that the incidence and severity of diseases increased significantly. "The diseases introduced by civilization extend themselves through every class and profession among men." Nature was no longer the principal healer; "her strength, wisdom, or benignity" seemed unequal to the threats of civilization. The "Author of nature hath furnished the body with powers to preserve itself from its natural enemies; but when it is attacked by those civil foes which are bred by the peculiar customs of civilization, it resembles a company of Indians, armed with bows and arrows, against the complicated and deadly machinery of fire-arms." There were, of course, "cases in which nature is still successful in curing diseases," but more often the "efforts of nature are too feeble to do service." This situation prevailed because "fevers, the natural diseases of the human body," were "lost in an inundation of artificial diseases, brought on by the modish practices of civilization," diseases that were the "offspring of luxury." [11]

If diseases and their remedies were "so necessarily connected with the changes in the customs of civilized nations," it was incumbent upon physicians to be aware of these customs. The "state of a country in point of population, temperance, and industry" was a vital indicator of the biological health of its citizens. This did not mean, however, that the "blessings of literature, commerce, and religion" could be purchased only "at the expense of health." The "complete enjoyment of health is as compatible with civilization, as the enjoyment of civil liberty." The import of Rush's message was clear. He assured Americans that a country might be "rich in every thing that can form national happiness and national grandeur," and yet be faced with diseases "nearly as few and simple as those of the Indians." This was the crux of the "political reflections" Rush had incorporated into his oration. The blessings of civilization could be enjoyed in good health as long as people remained simple and restrained, temperate and frugal in their manners. The Jews and the Romans "in their simple ages" suffered little from diseases, and then only from those of the natural order. "In proportion as they receded from their simple customs, we find artificial diseases prevail among them. . . . In the time of our Saviour, we find an account of all those diseases in Judea, which mark the declension of a people." This example, Rush believed, revealed a general truth: as man receded from a simple existence "by the progress of the arts of civilized life, he has become subject to many new and artificial diseases." But it must be understood that moral declension, the "depravity of . . . manners," was the ultimate source of those diseases that appeared to be inherent in civilized countries.[12]

Rush further developed this theme in his lectures on the "state of animal life in the different inhabitants of our globe, as varied by the circumstances of civilization, diet, situation and climate." More specifically, he was interested in the impact of one variable in the social environment, the "influence of *government* upon health." Rush began with a threefold classification: "Governments are despotic—*half* despotic or *half* free—as in limited monarchies—and lastly *free*—as in pure Republics where all the power of a country is derived from the Suffrages of the people." Under the influence of despotic governments health was precarious. The Indians of North America, the inhabitants of the "torrid regions of Africa," and the people of Greenland all labored under hardships imposed upon them by their harsh natural environments. Yet, it was among the "miserable inhabitants of those eastern countries which compose the Ottoman empire" that "we behold life in its most feeble state." The people of Turkey suffered "not only from the absence of physical, but of other stimuli which operate upon the inhabitants of other parts of the world." Physical deficiencies could be remedied with relative ease compared to the "general deficiency" of a despotic government, which "weakens not only the understanding; but annihilates all that immense source of stimuli which arises from the exercise of the domestic and public affections." The severely reduced "Stimulus of the love of liberty" and the "feeble operation of the desire of life" made it inevitable that "animal life" would exist in a "feeble state," a state in which "instances of longevity" would be uncommon. On the other hand, because the "public passions are torpid" in despotic countries, "madness is a rare disease." Mental derangement was much more common in limited monarchies.[13]

"A mixed government or limited monarchy," the second type of government discussed by Rush, was characterized by "great activity of the passions." It appeared, therefore, that this form of government tended to "predispose to madness." Although certainly a more healthy environment than the despotic state, the "conflicting tides of the passions" in a limited monarchy, "by their operation upon the understanding, become . . . a cause of derangement." Unlike the subjects of a despotic state, the people of a limited monarchy or mixed government possessed "a just and exquisite sense of liberty, and of the evils of arbitrary power," and this passion contributed to the incidence of madness. The "excitability of the mind is often accumulated by occasional oppression and a constant fearful apprehension of the loss of liberty, hence the passions act in many cases with a force which weakens & wears out the body." The alternating influences of the passions in response to "liberty & slavery," "like a variable climate, produces a succession of extremes of excitement and debility which have an unfriendly influence on the body." Thus, while madness was a "rare disease" in such despotic countries as Turkey, Russia, and China, the mixed government of Great Britain alone produced "between 4,000 and 5,000" cases.[14]

It was only in "pure Republics," then, that animal life flourished. The logic for this situation was syllogistically simple: the state of animal life was determined by the "indissoluble union between moral, political and physical happiness"; a "republican government was most favourable" to "moral-political-and physical good"; therefore, it could be "inferred a priori that it must be most favourable to animal life." But this conclusion, said Rush, "does not rest upon an induction." It was supported by medical evidence. In free or Republican governments the love of liberty itself was healthy because it provided a "uniform and gentle Stimulus" for the faculties of man. Citizens of a republic were less disposed to madness than subjects of a limited monarchy, for the "general suffrage, and free presses, serve, like chimnies in a house, to conduct from the individual and public mind, all the discontent, vexation, and resentment, which have been generated in the passions, by real or supposed evils, and thus to prevent the understanding being injured by them." "The security of property moreover in a free country contributes to lessen the influence of the debilitating passion of fear" and, consequently, exerted a "friendly influence upon health and life."[15]

It was clear from a study of the countries of antiquity, Rush argued, that the simple customs cherished by all republicans were conducive to good health. But it was unnecessary to appeal to ancient or remote examples for substantiation. "Many facts prove, animal life to exist in a larger quantity and for a longer time, in the enlightened and happy state of Connecticut, in which republican liberty has existed above one hundred and fifty years, than in any other country upon the surface of the globe." The hardy citizens of Connecticut were able to enjoy the blessings of civilization, while remaining, like the Indians of North America, "strangers to artificial diseases." Thus the experiences of the inhabitants of that "ancient and happy Republic of Connecticut," and even the experiences of an earlier generation of Pennsylvanians, proved that republican and medical principles were complementary. "Not only moral and political, but physical happiness are all alike promoted by republican governments." There could be only one conclusion drawn from this review of the "effects of Republicanism upon health," Rush emphasized, "a physician who is not a Republican, holds principles, that call in question his knowledge of the principles of medicine." "A good Physician must be a republican." [16]

III

The close connection between government and medicine, between political and biological health, broadened the implications of the American Revolution. "We live, gentlemen, in a revolutionary age," Rush affirmed in 1791. "Our science has caught the spirit of the times, and more improvements have been made in all its branches, within the last twenty years, than had been made in a century before." Rush repeated this assertion to his students in 1795: "Medicine has caught the spirit of the times." The source of this new spirit was clear: "The superstition of medicine received a deadly blow in the American Revolution." Rush was determined to "expose the errors and to establish the truths" contained in the principles of medicine of the Edinburgh physicians, especially the "great" Dr. William Cullen, Rush's mentor, and the "ingenious" Dr. John Brown. The "reverence for British Physicians and universities fell" once the bonds of affection with mother England were severed. "After reposing for near two centuries upon the lap of Great Britain," Americans were finally able to recognize the differences "between the climate and seasons of that country and America, and between their and our manners and diet." Independence had awakened the American intellect, and the consequence of this fundamental change in perception was a "revolution in the principles and practice of medicine in every part of our country." A correspondent in New York absorbed these sentiments and responded to the spirit of the times by sending Rush "some small Specimens of the medical operations in our city not doubting but that as a Republican in medicine, thou wilt be pleased with the boldness of opinions advanced in some of them, should they not prove intirely well founded, or be even falacious, since it evinces such a freedom of Thought & truly republican Spirit of enquiry, upon a subject which perhaps has been too much fettered in the tyrannical trammels of great Authorities." [17]

Rush noted that the "only Physicians in the United States who have refused to accommodate to this revolution in medicine, are men or descendants of men who were opposed in principle or practice to the American Revolution." This circumstance was more than merely a "remarkable" coincidence. It demonstrated, Rush thought, the importance of political principles in the "Republic of medicine." His own conversion to republicanism had begun a "ferment in my mind. I now suspected error in every thing I had been taught, or believed, and as far as I was able began to try the foundations of my opinions upon many other subjects." The "sequel" to this political catharsis revealed itself in Rush's medical doctrine. "The leading principle of my System was obtruded upon me suddenly," said Rush. "It was like a ferment introduced into my mind. It produced in it a constant endless succession of decompositions and new arrangements of facts and ideas upon medical subjects." The link between the "adoption of republican principles" and the new medical arrangement was clear. "To the activity induced in my faculties by the evolution of my republican principles by the part I took in the American Revolution, I ascribe in a great measure the disorganization of my old principles in medicine," Rush acknowledged.[18]

This same "ferment," Rush thought, could be instilled in the American masses. "Truth is simple upon all subjects, but upon those which are essential to the general happiness of mankind, it is obvious to the meanest capacities." Republican principles in politics and medicine were simple and accessible to all. This did not mean that in politics the common folk were equal to the task of administering the abstruse affairs of the state. The Pennsylvania constitution of 1776 proved that although the humblest of men could understand the principles of liberty, which were largely matters of feeling, they could not apply these "principles to practice," for this required a mastery of forms.[19] Nor did it mean that in medicine, although the "essential principles" were "few" and "plain," and easily disseminated, the "regular profession" could be abolished. Surgery and the treatment of rare diseases "will always require professional aid." What the simplicity of truth indicated was the "goodness of the Supreme Being" and the "unity and system in all his works." "Happiness, like truth, is a unit," Rush explained. "While the world, from the progress of intellectual, moral and political truth, is becoming a more safe and agreeable abode for man, the votaries of medicine should not be idle." The Revolution had opened "all the doors and windows of the temple of nature" and thus made advances in medical as well as moral and political knowledge possible. "By the adoption of republican forms of government, political knowledge has become so universally diffused that our women and children now possess more of it than was possessed by many of our legislators before the revolution"; in order to reinforce this situation it was time to "accelerate" a corresponding "change equally favourable to human happiness in the state of medicine." Only when the citizens were generally enlightened would men of merit in politics and medicine receive their due. Until then "credulity and superstition" would reign, and the majority of men would display a "preference of quacks . . . to such as are candid, simple, and polite; and of pretensions to skill . . . to a conduct uniformly grave, decent, and sober, in regularly bred physicians." [20]

The importance of dispersing medical knowledge becomes even more obvious when it is recalled that Rush believed that the collision of truths would reveal further truths and advance the general state of mankind. Indeed, in Rush's view of the millennium, the revolution in medicine was as important as the revolution in politics or religion. "In that happy period, predicted in the Old and New Testaments . . . religion shall combine its influence upon the passions and conduct of men, with fresh discoveries in medicine," so that "Christian Missionaries shall procure the same credit, and kind reception among Pagan and Savage nations, by curing diseases by natural means, which the Apostles obtained by curing them by supernatural power." The "spirit" of the Revolution was "so auspicious to medicine" that Rush cherished "a hope that our globe is about to undergo those happy changes, which shall . . . prepare it to receive the blessing of universal health and longevity." [21]

The close association of politics and physical health was revealed in important ways during the Revolution. "The political events of the revolution," said Rush, "produced different effects upon the human body . . . as they acted upon the friends or enemies of the revolution." Among the "enemies" of the Revolution, a form of disease prevailed that was termed "Tory Rot" or "*Protection fever*" by the common people, and "*Revolutiana*" by Rush. This malady, "confined exclusively to those friends of Great Britain, and to those timid Americans, who took no public part in the war," was brought on by changes in politics and religion compounded by changes in the diet and manners of the people.[22]

In contrast, "an uncommon cheerfulness prevailed everywhere, among the friends of the Revolution. Defeats, and even the loss of relations and property, were soon forgotten in the great objects of the war." Possessed of an "exquisite" sense of the blessings of liberty, the Revolutionaries knew that the conflict involved "the very existence of *freedom* upon our globe." Thus, during the cold winter months, men accustomed to the luxuries of city life nevertheless displayed an "extraordinary healthiness" even though forced to sleep in tents or in the open. The "uncommon tone of mind excited by the love of liberty" enabled officers and soldiers to endure "hunger, cold, and nakedness" with "Patience, firmness, and magnanimity." The "frequent disease" of "*homesickness*" was often "suspended by the superior action of the mind under the influence of the principles which governed common soldiers in the American army." [23]

In addition, many friends of the Revolution who had formerly suffered from "infirm and delicate" constitutions were "restored to perfect health." And the growth of the population was "more rapid from births during the war, than it had ever been," in part because "a considerable number of unfruitful marriages became fruitful." In spite of the general good health of the Revolutionaries, however, there was a species of insanity that affected their understandings and morals, and left them "wholly unprepared" for self-government. "The excess of the passion for liberty, inflamed by the successful issue of the war, produced, in many people, opinions and conduct which could not be removed by reason nor restrained by government." Reflecting perhaps on his experiences with the Pennsylvania radicals of 1776, Rush declared that this excess passion, which he labeled *"Anarchia,"* had "threatened to render abortive the goodness of heaven to the United States." [24]

IV

Rush, along with the rest of the circle of Jeffersonian philosophers, subscribed to a holistic vision of man. "From this view," he explained, human life "appears to be an unit, or a simple and indivisible quality or substance." Impressions made upon one part of the body will "excite motion, or sensation, or both, in every other part." It was impossible to explain the functions or to cope with the disorders of either the mind or the body without an adequate understanding of both, and of the intimate connection between them, because the "mind and the body are so much alike in their nature, their operations and their diseases, that they appear to have been made after one pattern." [25]

What was the essence of this single pattern? The mind and the body, Rush said, were subject to the same physical laws. Both the movements of the body and the actions of the mind were "mechanical." Rush, as we have seen, believed that the "motions of life" were generated by stimuli; similarly, "all the operations in the mind are the effects of motions previously excited in the brain, and every idea and thought appears to depend upon a motion peculiar to itself." He went so far as to argue that if a microscope of sufficient magnitude could be focused on the "naked brain" a specific movement "would be observable in it for every operation of the mind, for every act of the will, memory, etc." To the question "What is thought?" Rush answered with a description of its mechanics: thought was a "motion in the brain from stimulus of internal or external nature operating by impression made by means as purely mechanical as sound is conveyed to the ear." [26]

Because they were both patterned mechanically, and because the "laws of the mind and the body correspond with each other," medical practitioners had to begin with the assumption that the "body acts upon the mind and the mind upon the body reciprocally." In his inquiry into the diseases of the mind, Rush grouped the remedies for the various manifestations of mental disorder according to: "I. Such as should be applied to the mind, through the medium of the body; and II. Such as should be applied to the body through the medium of the mind." He urged his students to "pry into the state of . . . [your] patient's mind, and so regulate his conduct and conversation, as to aid the operation of . . . physical remedies." Hypochondriasis, for example, might require the use of such physical remedies as bleeding, purges, emetics, warm and cold baths, exercise, pain, and salivation, as well as the employment of such mental prescriptions as terror, humor, ridicule, counter passions, and deception. Mania, or the "highest grade of general madness," likewise responded to treatment that induced debility in the body, thereby attracting the "morbid excitement from the brain" and consequently relieving the severity of the disorder. Mania could also be remedied by diverting the "ruling passion or subject which occupies the mind . . . and fix[ing] it upon some other." By doing this, the passions were "made to neutralize and decompose each other, and thus to lessen their influence upon the body." Finally, memory lapses, delirious dreams, grief, and abnormal fears could be cured by "corporeal and mental" remedies. Even such "baneful passions" as envy, malice, morbid sexual appetite, and hatred responded to "rational and physical" prescriptions.[27]

It was precisely this view of the reciprocal activity of the mind and the body that lay at the heart of Rush's understanding of the virtue of "republican machines." For the Edinburgh-educated physician embraced the idea, characteristic of the Scottish philosophers, that the brain was the seat not only of such intellectual faculties as memory, understanding, and imagination, but also of a moral faculty. And since this faculty determined a person's ethical posture in every instance, it followed that individual morality was but another product of motions stimulated in the brain. Furthermore, given their mechanical bases, "in a sound state . . . these motions are regular, and succeed impressions upon the brain with the same certainty and uniformity" as the movements of a sound body succeed the impressions made upon the senses. Regularity and uniformity, therefore, were characteristics of health; irregularity, unpredictability, and eccentricity were manifestations of disease. "Sanity," said Rush, was the "aptitude to judge of things like other men, and regular habits &c. Insanity a departure from this." It is not surprising that Rush emphasized consistency in describing his friends. Thomas Fitzsimmons was "steady, sincere, and disinterested"; John Dunlap was "uniformly my friend"; George Clymer was a "firm, consistent Republican"; and Roger Sherman, a worthy son of that "ancient" republic of Connecticut, was "so regular in business" that he was known as a "republican machine." [28]

Nowhere was the importance of steadiness and regularity more clearly revealed for Rush than in his encounter with Charles Nisbet. Indeed, the Nisbet affair provides us with the best functional definition of Rush's "republican machine." The episode itself opened on a bright note when Rush, acting on a recommendation made by John Witherspoon, succeeded in persuading Nisbet to leave Scotland and to accept the position as principal of the "new-born infant" college in Carlisle. Nisbet had been known for his support of the American cause during the war, and Rush in 1783 could barely contain himself. "Come, sir," he exhorted, "and share with us in that liberty and independence which you have loved." Rush invited Nisbet to take part in making the Pennsylvania school, Dickinson College, the "first in America" and the "key to our western world." In 1784 he assured Nisbet that the "public mind is more filled than ever with expectations from your character." Throughout May and June of 1785 Rush was preoccupied with the preparations for Nisbet's arrival in Philadelphia and Carlisle. An "agreeable impression" might be made, Rush suggested in a letter to John Montgomery, if the trustees and "as many of the inhabitants [of Carlisle] as you can get together" were to greet the new principal on his way to the college. In addition, a small-scale ceremony might be in order: "one of the best speakers in the College" could address Nisbet, and the "Court house bell should be rung as he enters the town." For his part, Rush told Montgomery that he would spare no effort "to show the Doctor [Nisbet] to advantage to our citizens." [29]

Upon his arrival in Philadelphia, Nisbet appeared to be all that had been expected. "I cannot tell you how many friends he has made in our city," exclaimed Rush. With his "sensible," "elegant," and "agreeable" manners Nisbet was "charm[ing] everybody." Rush himself was enchanted; "I am so chained down to his company that I regret leaving him for a moment to attend my business." The "more I see of him—the more I love & admire him." Clearly, Rush thought, the benevolence of God was responsible for Nisbet's coming, for with his arrival "a new sun is risen upon Pennsylvania." [30]

All too soon, however, Rush's enthusiasm began to wane. He discovered that illness and homesickness had given rise to an outpouring of complaints from the "new sun." The principal no longer seemed to be "set upon doing good"; instead, his complaints were hurting the infant institution in Carlisle. Nisbet was causing "more mischief—than can ever be atoned for by his greatest exertions." Rush was stunned and felt betrayed. During his visit to Dickinson College for a meeting of the board of trustees in August 1785, Rush refused to call on the bed-ridden principal. After his return to Philadelphia, however, he reported that he was "happy in being able to contradict the terrible reports of Dr. Nisbet's illness and the sickliness of Carlisle." To John Montgomery, Rush explained that although Nisbet complained constantly "of the *heat* and *sickliness* of our climate," "I have reason to think he is actuated by *other* reasons." After all, upon his arrival Nisbet "bore the hottest of our weather in Philadelphia" with "good humor and patience." More probably, the complaints originated with his family's disappointment with the principal's salary. Moreover, Rush was convinced, Mrs. Nisbet's "natural temper" was "to complain and find fault." "In short, my friend," Rush confided to Montgomery, "we have made an unfortunate speculation in our principal." [31]

Charles Nisbet reponded by saying that he had "come over with the best intentions to be Master of Dickinson College but having lost my health was obliged to return" to Scotland. Could there be "any thing improper or extraordinary in all this?" Rush was mistaken in thinking that he, Nisbet, was dissatisfied with the college. The health of his family was his only reason for seeking to escape from Carlisle. And contrary to Rush's belief, Nisbet claimed that "not one word of complaint" was ever uttered by his wife or children, even when "rain seeped through" the walls of the wooden house in which they resided. What, then, could Rush possibly want, "could you really wish me dead?" Nisbet's oldest son made this same point even more abrasively. Dr. Nisbet's "harsh and cruel note" was "nothing compared with a letter I received from his son Tom," Rush told Montgomery. In his letter, Tom Nisbet strongly objected to Rush's attitude, for his father had "done nothing to merit censure." "There are very few less given to complain, or concern themselves with things of this world than he is." But "when he sees his own life & that of his wife & family in danger, he surely" must tend to their welfare. That Rush was unable to sympathize with the principal's predicament, Tom Nisbet concluded, was proof that he was inclined "to consider my Father as a mere machine, not possessed of the Desires, & feelings of other men." [32]

Rush was not convinced by these arguments and appeals because he believed that the afflictions of the Nisbets were rooted in circumstances far more fundamental than the explanations provided by the family. First, the Nisbets' constant complaining was in part a cause of their illness. "Many people," according to Rush, "have been cured by ceasing to Complain. A Gentleman once promised a Lady a Dollar for every day as long as she ceased to Complain. The Lady was offended, ceased to Complain, and recovered." Second, homesickness was easily suspended by the action of the mind under the influence of superior principles. If, therefore,

Charles Nisbet and his family could not overcome this malady, then it was because they were simply not devoted to the task before them, namely, the development of Dickinson College and the advancement of the arts in America. Third, the fevers the family suffered from were usually easily remedied. Being a "disease to which all newcomers are more or less subject," it did not usually call forth such complaints as those of the Nisbets, and was "considered here as a trifling disorder." The conduct of the Nisbet family in this situation seemed to confirm Rush's suspicion that the moral character of the family was flawed, for "folly and wickedness" often rendered "curable diseases, incurable." [33]

That the Nisbets suffered at all seemed less important than the manner of their suffering. Indeed, Rush believed that the "physical influence of diseases" tended in many cases "to improve our virtues and to form in us habits of moral order and goodness." "Hundreds and thousands of people" had acquired a sort of "passive virtue" by suffering dangerous or chronic diseases with resignation and fortitude. The Nisbets, and particularly Charles Nisbet, apparently lacked this strength of conviction and passive virtue. Rush implied as much in his rather callous letters to Nisbet, wherein he not so subtly mentioned the fortitude of the Reverend Samuel Finley and John Witherspoon. In response, Nisbet protested: "I am surprised at you taking notice that Dr. Witherspoon & his family never complained, as if my complaints were feigned." Moreover, Nisbet charged, "you represent worthy Dr. Finley in a ridiculous light. . . . I would never think it Christianity to see my poor weeping Children . . . panting under Troubles, to which I was conscious I had subjected them." [34]

Such protests could hardly quiet Rush's apprehensions. Rush accepted these protests as further proof that the "Doctor (naturally timid) sunk under his fever," and that his wife and children, naturally contentious, "availed themselves of the debilitated tone of his mind and body" and succeeded in convincing him to return to Scotland. "There can be no doubt but his wife and children are at the bottom of this disgraceful business," and the "Doctor's eldest son," Tom, is its "principal agent." Thus, in spite of the harm his leaving would inflict upon the college, and regardless of the personal dishonor associated with such a "defection," Nisbet was determined to renege on his commitments. Rush was at a loss to explain the "meaning of this mysterious providence," whereby an initially promising selection had become so manifestly unfortunate, but he was certain that "we shall not only know it but rejoice in it hereafter." Therefore, even if Nisbet "should at a future day alter . . . [his] resolution" to leave the college, he ought to be released. "Let not a straw be thrown in his way to detain him . . . we never can be happy with him with his present family." [35]

It was with considerable distress, then, that Rush learned of Nisbet's changing attitude. By November 1785, only a month after the Dickinson College trustees had accepted his resignation, Nisbet, whose health had improved in the meantime, was indicating a willingness to remain in Carlisle as the principle of the college. Rush and another charter trustee of Dickinson, John King, were convinced that Nisbet's turnabout was "another instance of his instability." It could be attributed, Rush thought, to the fact that "Tom Nisbet has changed his mind." The decision to remain in Carlisle, like the earlier decision to leave for Scotland, proved that Charles Nisbet had given himself up to the "government of his wife & children." "I have taken great pains to make apologies for his madness in this city—by ascribing it to his fever & his wife & children," Rush wrote to Montgomery. But this new development only underscored the fundamental flaw in the principal's personality, what King referred to as his "unsteady" mind. Rush agreed, "I have constantly considered *him* [Charles Nisbet] as *insane,* his wife as *foolish,* and his son Tom as *worse* than both." [36]

Rush suggested to his fellow trustees that if Nisbet chose to stay in Carlisle, they would have to restore him to his former position in the college—"We cannot do otherwise without incurring the folly of instability and thereby of resembling himself"—but they could offer him a reduced salary "until the College and his reputation recover from the blow they have both received by his late conduct." This suggestion for Nisbet's reappointment, however, should not be confused to "suppose I can feel much regard for him or his family," Rush added. "I freely forgive them"—and "forgiveness," Rush commented elsewhere, was a "divine mode of curing moral evil"—"if they mend their manners and if the Doctor will do his duty and give over whining and complaining." [37]

Charles Nisbet could reasonably conclude that Rush's attempts in 1786 to lower the "promised salary," along with his self-righteous proclamations, when compared with the encouraging letters he had written to Nisbet in Scotland and his initially enthusiastic reception of the new principal in Philadelphia, appeared to be the actions of "two different Persons, of the most opposite Characters than can be conceived." The transformation of Rush's attitude, as we have seen, corresponded to his progressively tarnished image of Nisbet. Rather than being another Witherspoon, the principal of Dickinson was, according to Rush, a "timid" man dominated and driven to madness by his complaining wife and children. Tom Nisbet had charged that Rush considered the principal a "mere machine"; Rush found the description accurate, calling particular attention, however, to the adjective "mere." For Charles Nisbet, clearly, was not a "republican" machine—that is, an independent being responding naturally to moral and physical causes. Instead, he was a "mere machine in the hands of his wife and children." Indeed, this would account for the principal's prolonged bout with what should have been a "trifling disorder" that affected all newcomers. As Rush explained in his study of "derangement in the will," persons governed by friends or favorites are soon deprived of a will of their own. The will in this state of "debility and torpor" resembled a "paralytic limb." Those unfortunate enough to be so afflicted were not only unable to discover an independent course of action, they also tended to be less responsive to all forms of medication.[38]

But most important, the moral faculty—that "native principle" and "capacity in the human mind of distinguishing and choosing good and evil, or, in other words, virtue and vice"—was seated in the will.[39] Without an independent will, a person lost the capacity for truly virtuous behavior. The severest indictment of Nisbet, then, and one supported by examples of his "unsteadiness" and surrender to the "whining" of his family, was that his will was paralyzed and, by implication, his moral faculty debilitated. In the most general terms, the question of first importance was not whether one was a "machine," for all of the mental and physical operations of men were mechanical, but whether one was a "mere" machine as opposed to a "republican" one. And that question brings into focus the long-standing problem of virtue and vice in republican forms of government.

V

The Nisbet affair highlighted Rush's ideas on the unity of mental, physical, and moral disorders, as well as his mechanical perception of the operation of the human faculties. More important for Rush, it sharpened his understanding of these ideas. In the midst of his confrontation with Nisbet, Rush noted that he had been appointed to deliver the annual oration before the American Philosophical Society. The subject that he had chosen, Rush told John Montgomery, was "An Inquiry into the Influence of Physical Causes upon the Morals." According to Rush, the central tenet of the address, which L. H. Butterfield has said became Rush's "most important philosophical paper," dealt with "the moral education of youth upon new and mechanical principles."[40]

Rush began by distinguishing between the moral faculty and the conscience. The former was seated in the will, the latter in the understanding. Even more significant, the "state of the moral faculty is visible in actions, which affect the well-being of society," whereas the "state of the con-

science is invisible, and therefore removed beyond our investigation."
Thus "virtue and vice," the products of the moral faculty, "consist in *action, and not in opinion.*" By this standard, Charles Nisbet's behavior
seemed almost surely to be a manifestation of a disordered moral
faculty.[41]

The theme of Rush's oration was a familiar one: a restatement of the
idea that the whole human body was a "simple and indivisible quality or
substance." It was "immaterial," therefore, Rush argued, whether the
physical causes he described acted upon the moral faculty through the
medium of the senses or through the intellectual faculties of the mind.
"Their influence is equally certain." Rush went on to discuss the effects
that climate, diet, liquor, hunger, idleness, disease, sleep, bodily pain,
cleanliness, solitude, music, eloquence, odors, light and darkness, and
medicines had upon moral sensibility. A better understanding of his subject might be achieved, Rush said, if notice was taken "of the influence of
the different stages of society, of agriculture and commerce, of soil and
situation, of the different degrees of cultivation of taste, and of the intellectual powers, of the different forms of government, and lastly, of the
different professions and occupations of mankind." But, as they were not
strictly physical causes—that is, they depended upon the mediation of
causes "unconnected with matter"—they were not proper topics to be
covered under the heading that he had chosen for his oration. Besides, he
had already discussed the influence of these forces in other lectures. It is
important, nevertheless, that Rush thought it necessary to mention them;
it was a reminder of the wider implications of his subject.[42]

A belief in the unity of man's existence was the source of Rush's opti-
mism concerning the potential development of the moral faculty. "The
extent of the moral powers and habits in man is unknown," he declared,
because the subject had never been scientifically explored. Thus, it was
"not improbable, but the human mind contains principles of virtue,
which have never yet been excited into action." Examples could be
found of the human body exhibiting a surprising degree of versatility and
agility, and of the intellectual faculties of the mind displaying a
remarkable capacity for improvement. "And if the history of mankind
does not furnish similar instances of the versatility and perfection of our
species in virtue, it is because the moral faculty has been the subject of
less culture and fewer experiments than the body, and the intellectual
powers of the mind."[43]

The solution, Rush believed, lay in the realization that the moral faculty
of man was as responsive to physical causes as his physical being.
"Physical and moral evil began together. They have constantly kept pace
with each other, and they must decline and cease at the same time." The

diseases of the moral faculty should be made to yield to "physical as well as rational and moral remedies." The cultivation of the moral faculty was the business not only of parents and divines, it was also the responsibility of legislators, natural philosophers, and physicians. A "physical regimen" should accompany every "moral precept," in the same way that physical prescriptions accompanied the treatment of every bodily ailment. "Should the same industry and ingenuity" that allowed medicine to triumph over such diseases as smallpox and "intermitting fever," "be applied to the moral science, it is highly probable, that most of those baneful vices, which deform the human breast, and convulse the nations of the earth, might be banished from the world." This line of reasoning was the basis of Rush's belief in the efficacy of a comprehensive educational system. "Virtuous" and "moral" instruction had to be provided very early in the life of the child for the "same reason" that music and foreign languages were taught during "the early and yielding state of those organs which form the voice and speech." Although the moral faculty was a "native" capacity, it had to be excited into action and nourished. "It is with virtue as with fire," Rush explained. "It exists in the mind, as fire does in certain bodies, in a latent or quiescent state. As collision renders the one sensible, so education renders the other visible." Ultimately, the idea that the moral faculty was influenced by the same causes that affected the human body, encouraged the belief that virtue could be induced mechanically, and consequently, that Americans might "promote the duration of republican forms of government far beyond the terms limited for them by history or the common opinions of mankind." [44]

Rush further clarified these formulations in his writings on physiology and pathology. Because the body and mind—specifically, the moral faculty of the mind—were similarly ordered, they were similarly disordered. They were activated by stimuli, affected by disproportions, and predisposed to disease by debility. "Does bodily disease consist in morbid excitement, or irregular action? Vice consists in like manner in undue excitement of the passions and will, and in their irregular . . . actions." Vice, in short, was the effect of stimuli acting upon the moral faculty and "producing morbid or wrong actions there." Just as there were physiological explanations for bodily disease and mental disorders, there was a physiological foundation for "moral derangement." The conclusion was inescapable: "Vice is a disease" and it is "analogous to disease of the body." Furthermore, like "bodily disease," vice was a "unit"—its innumerable forms were simply variations of "inordinate self-love." [45]

Vice could be conquered because it was a "disease in that part of the Brain which is the seat of the Moral faculty," and because the "laws which govern the body and the moral faculties of man" were identical. Vice, in other words, could be treated and its progress arrested "in the same way as the diseases of the body." The cure could be effected by "rendering partial excitement general, by abstracting it from the excited or plus system, and adding it to the minus or debilitated one." [46] The intimate connection between the physical and moral faculties of man required that the rational and moral remedies for vice be complemented by such physical prescriptions as bleeding and purging. Indeed, Rush suggested, "it is perhaps only because the diseases of the moral faculty have not been traced to a connection with physical causes" that the treatment of moral derangement had not kept up with the remedies for bodily diseases. "Medical and moral truth mutually support each other." There was an "intimate and necessary . . . connexion of morals and medicine." Therefore, Rush had "no doubt" that all forms of vice could be cured by the application of "physical remedies combined with such as are moral." [47]

The "worst grade" of mental derangement consisted of false perceptions, which resulted from the inability of the mind to appreciate the divinely ordered universe. It was characterized by a "misplacement of the fitness of things and their relation to each other." This "departure" from the natural order was not the work of a "disorganizing principle" being introduced into the mind, rather it was the effect of a "cause purely *negative.*" Just as cold was the effect of an absence of heat, darkness an absence of light, and ignorance an absence of knowledge, mental and moral disease resulted from the absence of a proper environment in which the unity of "truth or the relation of things upon all subjects" could be displayed. The deranged mind was like an "elegant house filled with costly furniture arranged in different rooms in exact and natural order suddenly falling by the abstraction of its foundation. Everything now appears out of order, and the eye turns from it with disgust." The diseased mind contained all the necessary "furniture" and lacked only a natural organization. Specifically, it was the responsibility of the "will" to arrange the "furniture in such a manner as to combine elegance with convenience," and to enable a person to "choose that which is good, & refuse what is evil." It was essential, therefore, that the "will" was kept healthy. Just as important, however, these observations led to the conclusion that vice was nothing more than a "dislocated virtue or a virtue out of place." Self-love was a dislocated love of God, pride a dislocated sense of dignity, and envy a dislocated spirit of emulation. Consequently, vice, the bane of all republics, could be managed, if not eliminated, by the introduction and cultivation of "*positive* good principles." [48]

The logic of the disease prescribed the nature of the remedy, which in turn revealed the extent of Rush's dependence upon the Scottish Enlightenment, especially the associationist psychology of David Hartley. The effects of an absence of organizing principles in the mind could be moderated by an enforced juxtaposition and association of facts. Rush was encouraged in this belief by Hartley's *Observations on Man,* which, he said, "embraced and connected the whole globe of the mind," and provided the "germ of my system of Physiology." Like Hartley, Rush believed that moral character was the product of customary association. "We are subject, by a general law in our natures, to what is called habit." This observation applied to the physical as well as the mental faculties of man. "Are the motions of the body influenced by habit and association? So are most of the operations of the mind," explained Rush, thus revealing the central assumption of a physiological psychology.[49]

The potential of an habitual association, according to Rush, could be observed on a very rudimentary level in the training of animals. A horse, for example, would seldom be startled by the firing of a gun or the beating of a drum if it had been introduced to these sounds while being fed. And the "same law of association may be applied in a variety of instances to the human mind." Indeed, associations operated with greater intensity in the human mind because the habitual responses of men covered a broader spectrum of thought and action. Physically, even respiration, the force that moved the "first wheel in the machine of the human body," was initially the result of conscious effort on the part of the infant, rather than an automatic act. "From habit *only,* the lungs after a while" were made to move automatically or involuntarily. By extension, therefore, all "actions originally involuntary may become *voluntary* from the influence of the will, and . . . actions originally voluntary may become involuntary from habit." Thus, "lying, as a vice, is said to be incurable. The same thing may be said of it as a disease, when it appears in adult life." But lying was "generally the result of a defective education," Rush asserted. "It is voluntary in childhood, and becomes involuntary . . . from habit."[50]

In the realm of morality, the force of habit was pervasive and often decisive. Indeed, Rush contended, the "mechanical effects of habit upon virtue have not been sufficiently explored." Rush, as we have seen, believed that the laws that governed the body also governed the moral faculty. This enabled him to ennumerate the "principal causes which act mechanically upon the morals." Solitude and silence, music, and the "eloquence of the stage" when properly directed were some "mechanical means of promoting virtue." "Labor of all kinds," by combating that "parent of every vice," idleness, likewise facilitated the practice of virtue.

If the virtue acquired through these means "are purely mechanical," said Rush, "their effects are, nevertheless, the same upon the happiness of society, as if they flowed from principle."[51] Rush himself had witnessed the beneficence of men possessed of this kind of mechanical virtue. In September 1777, following the battle at Brandywine, Washington had sent Rush and several other physicians to the British camp to attend the wounded American prisoners. Rush, already disillusioned with the American medical corps, was impressed by the "utmost order and contentment in their hospitals." The wounded soldiers who were evacuated with the American army "were not half so well treated as those whom we left in General Howe's hands." And yet, Rush remarked in a letter to John Adams, "You must not attribute this to their humanity. They hate us in every shape we appear to them." Their care of the American wounded was "entirely the effect of the perfection of their medical establishment, which mechanically forced happiness and satisfaction upon our countrymen perhaps without a single wish in the officers of the hospital to make their situation comfortable."[52]

Mechanically contracted virtue depended particularly upon feelings of pleasure and pain. The former consisted of "certain vibrations of the nerves which are harmonious and regular"; the latter was a product of vibrations that were "unharmonious," or irregular and disproportionate. But more important, pleasure and pain could be associated with, and through prolonged association become an habitual and inseparable part of, the collection of ideas and sentiments that constituted the image of an object or institution. Because "most of our pleasures and pains are derived from association," Rush observed, even the "tyrannical governments of Europe" were able to gather a loyal following from among those who associated pleasure with the "gaudy trappings of royalty." The same principle operated in the process whereby "artificial objects of taste which are at first disagreeable . . . from habit take a stronger hold upon the appetite than such as are natural and agreeable." In both cases, because associations are affected by time, the initial sensations of pain were eventually converted to pleasure.[53] These examples supported a general rule: "Notwithstanding pain is our natural state . . . there is a great predominance of pleasure over pain in the course of our lives," for "certain sensations originally painful, or disagreeable, become pleasant or agreeable from habit." And it was important to remember, Rush advised, that "painful impressions upon the mind are upon a footing with painful impressions upon the body, in being converted by repetition into such as are of a pleasurable nature." Thus, when Rush commented in 1790 on the persistence of traditional errors, and wished for a course on the "*art of forgetting,"* he was simply applying the general principle for dealing with diseases of the mind, namely, the "DESTRUCTION of all old associations of ideas." 54

If the mechanical effect of association could produce a habitual attachment to tyrannical governments and evoke a pleasurable response to artificial objects, it should certainly be able, Rush reasoned, to promote habits of virtue and thus to prolong the duration of republican forms. The founders of a republic must first recognize that habitual associations were formed from very early in life, while the mind was in its "yielding" state, and therefore, that nurseries and schools often determined the fate of the commonwealth. By scientifically structuring the environments of infants and youths, they could mechanically form virtuous men. Self-love was the first impulse of the infant; all of his actions for "several years are selfish." As the child advanced in life, however, this stimulus, if properly cultivated, "associates itself by means of pleasure with domestic affection, with friendship and benevolence." Eventually, "from habit the impulse of self love like air in the lungs ceases to be felt and the will acts under the influence of the domestic, social and benevolent principles." The stimulus of self-love, which would otherwise be at the root of all moral derangement, was thus incorporated, "through successive associations," into the conceptualization of social welfare and was converted, "in an apparently mechanical manner," into an appropriate foundation of the republic.55

Associations might be disrupted and dissolved by sickness. Dementia, or, as Rush "preferred naming it, from its principal symptom, DISSOCIATION," in particular, was a form of madness in which the afflicted were able to make a "constant and quick succession of such perceptions as are true, but wholly unrelated to each other." But even dementia could be remedied in part by the "benefit of habit, which prevents fatigue to a certain extent, from all the exercises of the body and mind." Generally, therefore, once an association was completed, so intimate became the connection between the objects involved that they continued in tandem long after the original justification for the association had been forgotten. The concept of a mechanical process of association, of "one perception exciting other perceptions, thoughts, and ideas," thus supported the contention that "we are a thinking machine as incapable of stopping a train of thought as tis to stop the motion of the earth." 56

By linking government and medicine, political and biological order, Rush tried to show that republican principles were conducive not only to human happiness, but to human health as well. Furthermore, by conjoining the well-being of the physical and moral faculties of man, Rush was able to redefine the problem of vice in the republic. Since the body and

REPUBLICAN MACHINES

the mind were governed by the same laws, they responded to the same physical influences. And because the moral faculty was a part of the life of the mind, it too responded to physical causes. The conclusion was that vice was a disease that could be treated with science and sympathy, and virtue was a response that could be mechanically induced in a proper environment. The habits of virtue had to be established early, but once the moral faculty was "properly regulated and directed," it would "never partake of the decay of the intellectual faculties in old age, even in persons of uncultivated minds." Indeed, the moral faculty then appeared to be "placed beyond the influence, not only of time, but often of diseases and accidents." [57] These beliefs made virtue the surest safeguard and a practical quest for American republicans, and sustained their hope that the life of the new republic would exceed the limits set by history and the traditional opinions of mankind.

What we are left with, then, in the phrase "republican machines" is a shorthand account of the ultimate goals of education in America. The new citizens would be, in the first place, attached to the republic, for they would learn that "there can be no durable liberty but in a republic." They would also be "republican" in the sense that education would provide them with a foundation for personal independence, an essential component of the classical definition of republicanism. Finally, and in large measure because of their personal autonomy, the new republicans would become so consistent, so "regular," so responsible in their behavior, as to deserve the title "machine." Only then could these independent participants be depended upon "to perform their parts properly in the great machine of the government." [58]

[165]

8

The Bonds
of Patriotism

In the *Spirit of the Laws,* Montesquieu made famous the argument that the "laws of education ought to be in relation to the principles of government." Despotic states, for example, could survive only if the minds of the people were debased. Servile fear and blind obedience, two essential characteristics of the subjects of these states, presupposed a degree of ignorance that rendered "learning . . . dangerous, emulation fatal" to the despot and his domain. Monarchies often benefited from national systems of education, but the principal aim of these systems was the creation of "good subjects" and not "good men." Accomplishments were deemed honorable not according to how "virtuous," "just," or "reasonable" they were, but rather how "shining," "great," or "extraordinary" they seemed. Subjects learned to value selfishness over social worth because the "virtues we are here taught are less what we owe to others than to ourselves." It was left to republican governments, then, to invoke the "whole power of education" in an effort to form a majority of good men. In democratic republics, where sovereignty resided ultimately in the hands of the people, there was a special need for an extensive system of education, for individual citizens had to be inspired with a "preference of public to private interest," which was "ever arduous and painful." [1]

American republicans accepted the logic of Montesquieu's arguments. Noah Webster was appalled by the "most glaring solecism" in the new nation. The constitutions of the states "are *republican,*" he said, but the "laws of education are *monarchical.*" This inconsistency was clearly contrary to the best interests of America. If the dissemination of knowledge in "ethics and . . . the general principles of law, commerce, money, and government" did not keep pace with the extension of political rights, the majority of the people would be unable or unqualified to participate in the great machine of the state. Thomas Dawes agreed that the importance of education in the new republic "need not be laboured." "In *arbitrary* governments, where the people neither make the law nor choose who legislate, the more ignorance the more peace." But, Dawes continued, in a "government where the *people* fill all the branches of sovereignty, *Intelligence* is the life of liberty." David Osgood observed that a "moment's reflection will render it sufficiently obvious, that where all power is derived from the people, every thing must depend upon their knowledge and virtue." If the people prove to be "ignorant and vicious, abandoned to idleness, pride and extravagance; if they are selfish and fraudulent, disorderly and factious," then, Osgood reasoned, "all must be anarchy and confusion, riot and licentiousness." There was no monarchy in the world that would not be preferable to such a republic. Benjamin Rush posited an additional warning: when the ignorant are neglected, their vices "are not confined to themselves," but are dispersed to contaminate the whole of society. The ignorant, by assisting in "choosing the rulers who govern," would eventually "give a complexion to the morals and manners" of the nation. "In short, where the common people are ignorant and vicious," Rush concluded, "a nation, and above all a republican nation, can never be long free and happy." [2]

The Revolutionaries thus believed not only that educational systems ought to correspond to the principles of government, but also that they inevitably would. A nation's system of education determined as well as reflected its form of government. Simeon Doggett declared it to be an "eternal truth, that the mode of government in any nation will always be moulded by the state of education." Whereas ignorance and tyranny were complementary, "literature and liberty go hand in hand." Despots could survive only by maintaining a "dark cloud of ignorance" over the "inslaved nation." Therefore, Doggett contended, "let general information and a just knowledge of the rights of man be diffused through the great bulk of the people in any nation, and it will not be in the power of all the combined despots on earth to enslave them." "Enlighten mankind and you cannot enslave them," William Linn agreed. "Despotic government makes them ignorant and barbarous, and when thus reduced, they are neither able nor willing to break the yoke." Ignorance, Samuel Knox confirmed, "has ever been the parent and stupid nurse of civil slavery." Indeed, it was possible, Rush argued, to categorize the different forms of government by looking at their educational practices. "Without learning, men become savages or barbarians" suited only for despotic governments; "where learning is confined to a *few* people, we always find monarchy, aristocracy, and slavery." It followed that a "free government can only exist" where knowledge and the means of acquiring it were widely distributed. [3]

"Knowledge and virtue are the basis and life of a Republic," Samuel Stillman remarked, "therefore, the education of children and youth, should be the first object of the attention of government, and of every class of citizens." It was no mere coincidence that Stillman, like Osgood and the others mentioned above, coupled knowledge with virtue and ignorance with vice. Samuel Harrison Smith hinted that virtue and wisdom were joined in panegyrics from "time immemorial," and for good reason because they "possess an inseparable connection." There were some who doubted "whether wisdom and virtue are in any degree necessarily connected," Smith acknowledged. Such skeptics invariably pointed to those enigmatic examples of "men who, though possessed of comprehensive powers of mind, are not only deficient in the exercise of virtue but actually famed for the most profligate indulgence in vice." However, Smith contended that this condition was exceptional and brought about only by the unceasing calumny and detraction heaped upon some men of superior intellect by those who were envious of them. It could not prevail, the enigma would not exist, "if virtue and talents were as common as vice and ignorance." The conclusion that virtue and wisdom were somehow closely interrelated was therefore valid.[4]

Smith's conclusion was rendered even more significant by the realization that the "crude wisdom which nature bestows is unequal to the production and government of virtue such as man in his pursuit of happiness discovers it to be in his interest to practice." The "original faculties of the mind," in other words, had to be "vigorously exercised, extended, and strengthened" by education, before they could be counted on in the creation and support of free governments. Indeed, in social terms, wisdom and virtue were linked together as cause-and-effect. The "diffusion of knowledge actually produces some virtues, which without it would have no existence," Smith declared. These "virtues, which are the exclusive and appropriate offspring of an enlightened understanding," were not connected with "any particular time, person, or place." They led to a "spirit of universal philanthropy" and lifted the "mind to an elevation infinitely superior to the sensation of individual regard." "Learning expands the heart with universal philanthropy—stimulates the soul to a generous emulation," David McClure concurred. The "genial warmth of science" could soften even the "barbarous tempers" of savages. Education was thus essential in the process of transforming self-love into social benevolence. In addition, education tended to suppress a number of vices. "Once properly excited," the quest for knowledge "gradually gathers strength, and becomes a powerful principle of action," Charles Nisbet noted. It occupies the "human faculties" in a suitable activity "amidst the temptations of an evil world." In this way, the "love of knowledge often becomes a counterpoise to the love of vice." Noah Webster was somewhat more circumspect in his assessment. "Virtue and vice will not grow together in a great degree, but they will grow where they are planted," he explained, "and when one has taken root, it is not easily supplanted by the other."[5]

Knowledge, in short, must be widely disseminated in a republic because it tended to "form good citizens." According to Charles Nisbet, "Learning is certainly the surest and most direct way of being prepared for doing the duties of good citizens." The radical Whig principles of the Revolutionaries enhanced this belief. While it was true that an enlightened people could not be reduced to "civil or ecclesiastical tyranny," Webster warned, it was equally true that when people are deprived of knowledge "they sink almost insensibly in vassalage." Education might prevent this insensible slide because it encouraged popular surveillance of the activities of public officers. The people must be kept alert, Jefferson told Edward Carrington, for "once they become inattentive to the public affairs, you and I, and Congress, and Assemblies, judges and governors shall all become wolves." Even under the "best forms" of government, Jefferson said, "those entrusted with power have, in time, and by slow operations, perverted it into tyranny." The most effective way of preventing this was to "illuminate, as far as practicable, the minds of the people at large," so that "they may be enabled to know ambition under all its shapes, and prompt to exert their natural powers to defeat its purposes." While "Learning and Education qualify a people for the noble purposes of being happily governed," Samuel Whitwell confirmed, "ignorance renders them inattentive to their rights and prepares them for the chains of slavery, which ambition is ever ready to rivet."[6]

It would not do to reserve the benefits of education for the rich, for then "the rest being ignorant may be easily deceived. How favorable such a circumstance may prove to usurpation and tyranny, I dread to think!" Jeremy Belknap exclaimed. Knowledge widely disseminated offered the surest protection against any usurpation of the rights of the people. Samuel Harrison Smith, convinced of the necessity of a comprehensive system of republican education, argued that the "citizen, enlightened, will be a free man in its truest sense. He will know his rights, and he will understand the rights of others; discerning the connection of his interest with the preservation of these rights, he will as firmly support those of his fellow men as his own. Too well informed to be misled, too virtuous to be corrupted, we shall behold man consistent and inflexible." In a passage that harked back to Rush's description of the citizen as a "republican machine," Smith emphasized that the enlightened American would be "in principle forever the same."[7]

As Smith's summary indicates, in a republic ordinary men were expected to act in a rather extraordinary manner, a manner traditionally required only of the "few." While in a "Monarchy or Aristocracy, only a few of the people are permitted to think or judge for themselves, and the great body of the people must follow the privileged orders in every[thing]," observed a Pennsylvanian, the common citizens in a "republican government . . . should be very intelligent and well informed in every thing wherein their welfare or interest is concerned." In terms of the duties it prescribed for every member of the body politic, this line of reasoning was in accord with the classical Aristotelian conception of the citizen as one "who shares in the administration of justice and in the holding of office." Additionally, it was influenced by the formulations of the civic humanists of the Italian Renaissance who identified the loss of one's share of authority, and subsequent dependence upon others, as a loss of virtue. The virtuous citizen, in this ideological scheme, must be, as J.G.A. Pocock has said, a "conscious and autonomous participant in an autonomous decision-taking political community." [8]

The ultimate "design of education," therefore, David McClure noted, was to "qualify youth for an active, *useful* and *virtuous life.*" Every citizen of the republic, Benjamin Hichborn said, must be a "*Soldier, Politician* and *Patriot*"; these would be the "cardinal characteristics of an American." Smith strengthened the appeal of this contention by referring to the long-standing tradition wherein virtue was opposed by fortune. The unenlightened inhabitant could never be truly independent and could never act as a virtuous citizen in the classical and civic humanistic sense because he remained the "sport of casualty and accident. He would nominally be his own master, but really a slave to some unknown power," that is, to fortune. But the educated citizen possessed the fortitude to withstand and the capacity to refashion ill-fortune. "He will look upon danger without dismay, so he will feel within himself the power of averting or the faculty of disarming it." [9]

These observations on autonomy and virtue illuminate an important axiom of American republican thought, and indicate the special context in which the Revolutionaries interpreted the Baconian equation that "knowledge is power." In what Pocock has labeled the "Anglo-American brand of civic humanism," property, especially an inheritable freehold in land, was the ideal measure of individual autonomy. A freehold was the best foundation for political independence and, consequently, for civic virtue, because it was the most permanent form of property. American republicans, however, were equally enthusiastic about the link between education and autonomy. To be sure, few would have disagreed with Noah Webster's declaration that "*property* is the basis of power." In America, Webster was convinced, a wide distribution of landed property, hence a dispersion of power among the people, was a "singular advantage, as being the foundation of republican governments and the security of freedom." He even insisted that the "system of the great Montesquieu will ever be erroneous, till the words *property or lands in fee simple* are substituted for *virtue,* throughout his *Spirit of Laws."* Despite this cele-bration of property distribution in America, Webster emphasized the ne-cessity of "auxiliary supports," the principal one being the *"information of the people."* When Webster pursued the subject further in his essay "On the Education of Youth in America," he proclaimed that the two "fundamental articles, the *sine qua non* of the existence of the American republics," were, first, "such a distribution of lands and such principles of descent and alienation as shall give every citizen a power of acquiring knowledge and fitting himself for places of trust." [10]

Nowhere were these ideas more strikingly presented than in Robert Coram's *Political Inquiries: to Which Is Added a Plan for the General Establishment of Schools throughout the United States.* Coram, the editor and proprietor of the *Delaware Gazette,* began with a distinction be-tween the "savage" and "civilized" states of men, a discussion that paralleled Rush's observations of "Medicine Among the Indians of North America." In that oration Rush had argued that the inhabitants of civilized nations generally suffered from "artificial diseases," which were brought on by their abandonment of simple customs for the "modish practices of civilization." Coram, following Rush, affirmed "that the aborigines of the American continent have fewer vices, are less subject to diseases, and are a happier people than the subjects of any government in the Eastern World." But, just as Rush believed that good health could be attained and was in no way incompatible with civilization, Coram believed that the "proneness to vice . . . in civilized nations" must be the "effect of bad government" because "it is plain, if men are virtuous without laws, they may be virtuous with good laws." [11]

What, then, could account for the wretched condition of civilized man, and the perplexing fact that government, instituted for the public good and happiness, promoted instead human misery and vice? "In the com-parative view of the civilized man and the savage," Coram asserted, "the most striking contrast is the division of property. To the one, it is the source of all his happiness; to the other, the foundation of all his misery." While savages, abiding by the prescriptions of "holy writ," shared a com-mon "dominion over the earth," human laws in civilized nations arbitrar-ily parceled out the general stock of land to certain orders and classes of men. Employing the reasoning of Locke, and specifically refuting the doc-trine of Blackstone, Coram argued that labor ought to constitute the "right of property in moveables and the right of possession in lands." "The fruit growing on a tree was common, but when collected it became the exclusive property of the collector; land uncultivated was common, but when cultivated, it became the exclusive possession of the cultivator." Labor, and not mere occupancy as Blackstone would have it, was the only just foundation of private property; "in other words, a man has a right to as much as he cultivates and no more." Without this restriction, a few persons can hoard, and have hoarded, most of the available land. "In fact, the whole of Blackstone's chapter on property was artfully contrived to countenance the monopoly of lands as held in Europe." [12]

Notwithstanding this belief that the exclusive possession of land "in its origin seems to have been arbitrary," Coram did not advocate the enactment of agrarian laws. He agreed, in part, with Thomas Dawes, who remarked that an equal distribution, if effected by law, had the unmistakable tendency of deadening the "motives of industry." Much more favorable to liberty and republicanism was the "happy mediocrity" that prevailed in America. Besides, said Coram, "I am not quite so visionary as to expect that the members of any civilized community will listen to an equal division of lands." Had that been the object of his essay, the effort would surely have been made in vain, Coram acknowledged. "But a substitute" for such a division, "and perhaps the only one, is highly practicable." There was a way to alleviate the miseries of civilized man "without disturbing the established rules of property." The substitute was "A SYSTEM OF EQUAL EDUCATION." [13]

"In the savage state . . . the system of education is perfect," Coram said. Because all property was held in common, and because a livelihood could be obtained from nature, personal independence was relatively secure. In civil society, however, men no longer had a common right to property; they "submitted to exclusive property in lands." Civilized men were thus deprived of their natural means of subsistence and, in order to maintain some semblance of autonomy, had to be equipped with a proper education. If men in civil society were miserable and sometimes depraved beings, Coram declared, then it was due to "some fundamental error . . . common to all civilized nations, and this error appears to me to be in education." Indeed, while education in the savage state was perfect, "in the civilized state education is the most imperfect part of the whole scheme of government." [14]

By offering education as an alternative to the freehold, Coram hoped in essence to reinforce the classical ideal of the citizen. Education meant the "instruction of youth in certain rules of conduct by which they will be enabled to support themselves when they come to age and to know the obligations they are under to that society of which they constitute a part." Foremost, it would ensure that youths can maintain a "becoming independency when they shall arrive to years of maturity." A properly educated citizen, like the proprietor of a freehold, possessed a commodity that enabled him to avoid a dependence upon others, and, therefore, enhanced his capacity for virtuous action. Coram was certain that in order to remedy "all the evils attendant on an abuse of civilization" and to secure the ends for which governments were instituted—namely, the public good and happiness—the "first step" was to make men independent. "For if they are dependent, they can neither manage their private concerns properly, retain their own dignity, or vote impartially for their country; they can be but tools at best." Education was a practical substitute for the freehold because it not only supported a "becoming independency," but was also a permanent possession and, consequently, a durable foundation for republican citizenship.[15]

II

Autonomous participation in the great machine of the state was a crucial part of Benjamin Rush's conceptualization of a "republican machine." But alone it fell short of that ideal. To be complete, the "becoming independency" of the citizens had to be complemented with a binding attachment to the republic itself. The very survival of the commonwealth depended upon it. A "government is like every thing else," Montesquieu said, "to preserve it we must love it." Monarchies endured over long periods of time and, unfortunately, even despotic governments were prone to be long-lived, because kings and princes were fond of the states over which they ruled. For a republic to be equally resilient the people, as sovereign, must be similarly disposed. Their personal independence notwithstanding, citizens had to be infused with a "love of the laws and of . . . [their] country." "Every thing," Montesquieu concluded, depended upon "establishing this love in a republic"; therefore, "to inspire it ought to be the principal business of education."[16]

It should be apparent that Rush's exegesis of the business of republican education was founded on this notion of civic love. One of the first lessons to be taught to the children of the republic, Rush advised, was a "SUPREME REGARD TO THEIR COUNTRY." Family, friends, and property were all dear, to be sure, but none must take precedence over "our country." Others were as committed to this proposition as Rush was. The Revolutionary generation was especially insistent in this regard because most were convinced that the diverse social and economic factions that were sure to thrive in the bountiful and extensive American republic constituted one of the gravest challenges to its survival. "Among those means, which are calculated to destroy a free government," Thomas Day declared, "none will be found more efficient than PARTY SPIRIT." Americans were already suffering under the schemes of men who placed their own well-being above the interests of the republic, Day observed, and unless the "most vigorous exertions are made to exterminate" this factional temper "our nation, bright as its prospects have appeared, will . . . soon be convulsed with a civil war." To David Daggett writing in 1787, the "whole political frame" of independent America seemed to be "convulsed and threatened . . . with an immediate dissolution" because too many citizens lacked the necessary love of country.[17]

The histories of other nations provided ample and incontrovertible evidence of the dangers of factional strife. "Party spirit, a spirit of jealousy and discord," proved to be fatal to the ancient republics of Greece, warned Samuel Wales. "If the same spirit prevail among us we have no reason to suppose but it will produce the most unhappy consequences," for, Wales explained by resorting to the logic of David Hume and the Scottish moralists, "Human nature is the same in every age, and similar causes will produce similar effects." William Wyche contended that the "pernicious spirit of party" existed in a "thousand different shapes." Yet, "let party assume what name it will, it is at all times attended with the same ill consequences" because it uniformly produced "hatred and animosity." As an "immediately analogous" example, Wyche asked, "what caused the fall of Athens? Faction: the spirit of discord prevailed, and liberty was destroyed." This "fatal shore, on which so many nations have been stranded, is destined to produce the same fate to America, unless the spirit of party be repressed." Repeating the essence of Hume's axiom, Wyche announced that the "inevitable destruction arising from disunion must, in all situations, have a uniform tendency." In the end, Donald Fraser agreed, partisan clashes produce so much "spleen and rancour" in a nation that they were "very fatal both to men's morals and to their understandings." In spite of this acknowledged truth, however, the "minds of many good men among us, appear so heated with party principles, and alienated from one another in such a manner as seems altogether incompatible with the sound dictates of reason and religion." The national government itself, John Taylor hinted, showed signs of being the "prostitute of a faction."[18]

Complaints such as these indicate that the Madisonian synthesis notwithstanding, the traditional arguments against parties and factions still worked with considerable force among the new republicans. Madison's famous doctrine, it will be remembered, attributed stability to the existence of numerous countervailing factions. In an extended republic comprising a great variety of diverse and competing interests the formation of an unjust combination constituting a majority of the whole was highly improbable. The separate factions would lack either a common motive or a convenient opportunity to form a self-interested majority capable of subverting minority rights. Civic action "could seldom take place on any other principles than those of justice and the general good." Underlying all of this, however, was the assumption that the competing interests would, in the end, recognize the general good and make the private concessions necessary to secure it. This meant that, as Madison acknowledged, disparate interests must be contained within manageable limits. Despite the logic of the argument favoring a vast and diversified republic, there remained a real concern, even in Madison, over the extent of a "practicable sphere." [19]

The problem of containing factional disputes within Madison's "practicable sphere" was part of a larger challenge confronting the American populace. As George Eacker put it, there could be an "infinite variety" of individual interests in a state of nature, "yet when mankind unite under one system of laws and government, a similar tone" must be "given to their actions" because this was the hallmark of a "national character." That the American scene at times seemed to be so strife-ridden might be accounted for in precisely these terms. Having only recently gained their independence from the imperial mother, the new republicans had not yet managed to forge a separate national identity. "People of the UNITED STATES OF AMERICA will you form a national character and naturalize the arts and sciences in your own country as a source of happiness to your future generations and of glory to a polished nation?" Lafitte du Courteil demanded to know. Joel Barlow was motivated by a concern over national character when he produced his patriotic allegory *The Vision of Columbus.* Similarly, Timothy Dwight was moved by this concern in writing *The Conquest of Canaan,* a performance whose merit, according to Webster, "cannot fail to recommend it to every friend of America and of virtue." Meanwhile, Jedidiah Morse, displeased with European accounts of the subject, completed his book on American geography and prefaced it with a candid indictment: "We have humbly received from Great Britain our laws, our manners, our books, and our modes of thinking, and our youth have been educated rather as subjects of a British king, than as citizens of a free and independent republic." [20]

The very nature of the problem readily suggested a solution. With a view to the special circumstances that obtained in America, in particular the diverse "elements which form the population of the United States," Lafitte remarked that "an institution of national education is there evidently more necessary to form a proper character than it was in the republics of antiquity." Noah Webster was more specific. "Our national character is not yet formed," he announced, therefore, "it is an object of vast magnitude that systems of education should be adopted and pursued which may not only diffuse a knowledge of the sciences but may implant in the minds of the American youth the principles of virtue and of liberty and inspire them with just and liberal ideas of government and with an inviolable attachment to their own country." [21]

This concern over diversity and the national character surfaced in Samuel Knox's plan for a national system of education. "In a country circumstanced and situated as the United States of America," Knox observed, "a considerable local diversity in improvement, whether with respect to morals or literature, must be the consequence of such a wide extent of territory inhabited by citizens blending together almost all the various manners and customs of every country in Europe. Nothing, then, surely, might be supposed to have a better effect towards harmonizing the whole in these important views than an *uniform system of national education.*" Rush, too, was apprehensive about the extent of American diversity. The enemies of the republic were claiming that the new nation was too extensive, and the habits of its citizens too contrary, to support a republican form of government, Rush said. Regardless of how offensive such opinions and predictions might be to the majority of Americans, "they will certainly come to pass unless the people are prepared for our new form of government by an education adapted to the new and peculiar situation of our country." First and foremost for political survival, "one general and uniform system of education" must render the "mass of the people more homogeneous and thereby fit them more easily for uniform and peaceable government." [22]

The political impulse behind this drive for homogeneity was brought sharply into focus in Noah Webster's painstaking attempts to fashion a uniform national language. If America was to be culturally as well as politically independent, Webster argued, it was necessary, first, to dispense with the English standards of propriety and to consolidate the disparate American linguistic hybrids. The "language of this country should be reduced to such fixed principles, as may give its pronunciation and construction all the certainty and uniformity which any living tongue is capable of receiving." That Webster was concerned with more than mere convenience or accuracy in communication is beyond question. Linguistic uniformity had a considerable bearing on national affection, he insisted. The "sameness of pronunciation," for example, was of "considerable consequence in a political view" because "provincial accents are disagreeable to strangers and sometimes have an unhappy effect upon social affections." Even the seemingly innocuous differences of local dialects tended to excite "reciprocal ridicule" and to encourage mutual disrespect, with dire political as well as literary results. "Our political harmony is therefore concerned in a uniformity of language," Webster concluded. [23]

Webster's observations were made more compelling by the common belief in the singularity of the American historical moment. The Revolutionary generation had the "fairest opportunity of establishing a national language, and of giving it uniformity and perspicuity, in North America, that ever presented itself to mankind." Reflecting the general mood, Webster urged: "Now is the time to begin the plan. The minds of the Americans are roused by the events of a revolution; the necessity of organizing the political body and forming constitutions of government that shall secure freedom and property, has called all the faculties of the mind into exertion; and the danger of losing the benefits of independence, has disposed every man to embrace any scheme that shall tend, in its future operation, to reconcile the people of America to each other, and weaken the prejudices which oppose a cordial union." [24]

The quest for harmony and homogeneity prompted many of the proposals for a national university. Among the principal benefits of a national university, the Commissioners of the Federal District told Congress, was the "removal, or at least the diminution, of those local prejudices which at present exist in the several States, by the uniformity of education and the opportunity of a free interchange of sentiments and information among the youth from all the various parts of the Union." Such an institution, Rush confirmed, would become a place "where the youth of all the states may be melted (as it were) together into one mass of citizens after they have acquired the first principles of knowledge in the colleges of their respective states." "Till this is done," he warned American legislators, "you will undertake to make bricks without straw. Your supposed union" of independent men "will be a rope of sand." [25]

Washington, likewise convinced of the importance of a national university, offered as an endowment the fifty shares in the Potomac Company that were given to him by the Virginia legislature in 1784. The development of sectional "prejudice" in the union must be arrested, Washington advised, by assembling the "youth of every part [of the country] under such circumstances, as will, by the freedom of intercourse and collision of sentiment, give to their minds the direction of truth, philanthropy and mutual conciliation." That the diffusion of knowledge was essential in a country where the "measures of Government receive their impression so immediately from the sense of the community as in ours" was undeniable. Equally important, however, Washington said, was the diminution of "local prejudices & habitual jealousies." This could best be accomplished through the establishment of an institution capable of homogenizing the "principles, opinions, and manners of our countrymen, by the common education of a portion of our youth from every quarter." Washington's basic premise was that the "more homogeneous our citizens can be made in these particulars, the greater will be our prospect of permanent union." [26]

The proposed remedy for the problem of factionalism reflects the Revolutionaries' abiding faith in the power of education. As Jefferson asserted, education generated "habits of application, of order, and the love of virtue," and thereby controlled "any innate obliquities in our moral organization." Man was not fixed "by the law of his nature, at a given point." Moral improvement was within the scope of education, Jefferson assured the American public. "As well might it be urged that the wild and uncultivated tree, hitherto yielding sour and bitter fruit only, can never be made to yield better; yet we know that the grafting art implants a new tree on the savage stock, producing what is most estimable both in kind and degree. Education, in like manner, engrafts a new man on the native stock, and improves what in his nature was vicious and perverse into qualities of virtue and social worth." [27]

If, therefore, men succumbed to the temptations of parties and factions, there had to be some fundamental error in their education. It was well known, Enos Hitchcock noted, that where education was neglected, freedom degenerated into "licentious independence" and men fell prey "to their own animosities and contentions." If "notions of liberty . . . are not guided and limited by good education," Jeremy Belknap agreed, they tend to "degenerate into a savage independence." Charles Nisbet offered a terse explanation of this relationship between ignorance and factionalism. "To the crude thoughts of simple and unlettered men," he said, "mankind appear as so many loose, independent & unconnected individuals, having each a separate interest, and naturally disposed to make war with one another. Such inaccurate views tend to nourish a selfish spirit, a neglect of the duties of society, & a total indifference for the public." [28]

It logically followed, therefore, as Webster argued, that a good education had a propensity "gradually [to] eradicate" factional disputes. "Discord and strife have always proceeded from, or risen upon, ignorance and passion," Samuel Harrison Smith declared. If ignorance could be eliminated and passion "virtuously directed" the "great result will be harmony." It was precisely this sort of harmony that a general system of education aimed to achieve, for, as Rush pointed out, it would dispense knowledge and, at the same time, seek to "prevent the irregular action of the passions, to regulate, compose, and harmonize them." [29]

For these Revolutionaries the establishment of a system of education capable of shaping the American character by providing the people with a common "tone" was "fundamental," as Webster declared, to the "existence of the American republics." An arrangement of the institutions of government, even an arrangement as prudential as the synthesis achieved under the American constitutions, could not by itself guarantee the survival of the nation. The "preservation of any republican form of government" depended, Enos Hitchcock said, more on its educational system "than on the form itself." The best foundation "on which to rest the welfare of a community," Timothy Dwight concurred, was the "natural conscience" of the people "carefully cultivated by education into habit." [30]

The criteria put forth for constructing just such a system were varied and in a few cases even conflicting. But on two points the Revolutionaries were in unanimous agreement. In the first place, the institutions of a general system of education must be located within the new republic. Opposition to the practice of sending American children abroad for their education had, of course, been voiced long before the Revolution. As early as 1699 a student orator at the College of William and Mary decried the practice. After the mid-eighteenth century, however, and especially after the relationship between the colonies and England began to deteriorate, the protests became more strident and more frequent. Lieutenant Governor William Bull captured the essence of a common sentiment when he told the South Carolina Assembly in 1770 that "seminaries of liberal Education" must be established in the province because the "expence and more particularly the anxiety of parents on account of danger to the Morals and lives of their Children . . . deter many from bestowing those inestimable advantages upon their Offspring, which are now not to be obtained but by sending them abroad." [31]

Radical Whig assumptions concerning the progressive advances of corruption in English society, and the decay of the European world in general, supported the most vigorous opposition to sending students abroad. Once independence was declared, however, this moral concern gained an additional and more distinctly political dimension. Republicans must cherish those hardy virtues of simplicity and frugality; therefore, according to Webster, a "foreign education is directly opposite to our political interests and ought to be discountenanced, if not prohibited." Abroad, Jefferson explained, the student invariably acquired a "fondness for European luxury and dissipation and a contempt for the simplicity of his own country." Indeed, the problem had already reared its ugly head: "Perhaps the greatest evil America now feels is an improvement of taste and manners" not suited to the state of the country, Webster testified. The "very source of this evil" was a foreign education. It instilled in the American students a "relish for manners and amusements" that became "fashionable," despite the incongruity of their presence in a republic.[32]

But the corruption of manners was not the sole, or even the principal, objection to a foreign education. It was a part of a more general concern inspired by the cathartic nature of the Revolution. The Revolutionaries were obliged, by the same advantages that fostered their grandiose visions of the American future, to establish schools that would be equal, if not superior, to the institutions of Europe. This same imperative, it will be recalled, affected and in large measure effected their commitment to republicanism. "If our universities and schools are not so good as the English or Scotch," Webster said, then "it is the business of our rulers to improve them." "Nature has been profuse to the Americans, in genius and in the advantages of climate and soil"; if, therefore, America "should long be indebted to Europe for opportunities of acquiring any branch of science in perfection, it must be by means of a criminal neglect of its inhabitants." As in the realm of politics and the quest for a durable republican system, failure in this enterprise would subject Americans to ridicule and condemnation. Because of the superiority of their situation, the Revolutionaries expected, and believed that it was expected of them, to extend the frontiers of knowledge. Anything less would have to be imputed to a wretched and criminal neglect.[33]

Besides, the bold projections of Americans were well known. The "era is at hand when America may hold the tables of justice in her hand and proclaim them to the unresisting observance of the civilized world," Samuel Harrison Smith boasted. The world, a proud Ezra Stiles said, was looking "to America for models of government and polity." With projections like these in mind, the Georgia legislature announced in 1785 that if Americans persisted in the practice of sending their students abroad, it would be "too humiliating an acknowledgment of the ignorance or inferiority of our own" institutions. Webster thought that nothing less than "our honor as an independent nation" was at stake in the effort to establish "literary institutions adequate to *all* our own purposes." Certainly, it would add very little luster to the "reputation of America to have it said abroad that after the heroic achievements of the late war these independent people" were forced to continue "sending boys to Europe for an education or sending to Europe" for books to "teach their children ABC."[34]

National honor necessitated an end to the servile adherence to European, especially English, ways of thinking. We have become "so habituated" to foreign "fashions and opinions," Jonathan Jackson complained, that "we have scarcely dared to wear our coats if not cut in their modes." Rush saw the "marks of the same incongruity of time and place in many other things" and was thus not surprised that English customs of education seemed to prevail in America. Similarly troubled, Robert Coram pleaded, "Let us keep nature in view and form our policy rather by the fitness of things than by a blind adherence to contemptible precedents from arbitrary and corrupt governments." [35]

What was required of Americans was clear: "It is now full time that we should assume a national character," Jackson proclaimed. "It is high time to awake from this servility—to study our own character—to examine the age of our country—and to adopt manners in everything that shall be accommodated to our state of society and to the forms of our government," Rush confirmed. George Eacker added that in "forming a complete national character we ought to avoid a servile imitation of foreign customs and manners, as inconsistent with true independence." Noah Webster elaborated. Before the Revolution, he said, the habit of imitating Europeans, emulating their modes of education, and sending American students abroad may have been proper, "at least so far as national attachments were concerned." But the propriety of these actions "ceased with our political relation to Great Britain." More specifically, "while these states were a part of the British Empire, our interest, our feelings, were those of Englishmen; our dependence led us to respect and imitate their manners and to look up to them for our opinions." This filial attachment was an acceptable posture for any state, as long as it remained in the hands of a "parent country." This, however, was no longer the condition of the American states. Webster assailed the mimetic impulse by imploring Americans to renounce all remnants of their former filial identity: "Americans, unshackle your minds and act like independent beings. You have been children long enough, subject to the control and subservient to the interest of a haughty parent. You now have an interest of your own to augment and defend; you have an empire to raise and support by your exertions and a national character to establish and extend by your wisdom and virtues." [36]

Elsewhere, Webster repeated this theme with equal conviction. In his *Sketches of American Policy,* Webster declared that America was an "independent empire" and thus "ought to assume a national character." "Nothing can be more ridiculous, than a servile imitation of the manners, the language, and the vices of foreigners." Indeed, "nothing can betray a more despicable disposition in Americans, than to be the apes of Europeans," Webster taunted. For his part, Webster laboriously undertook to reform the English language. To John Canfield, he wrote: "America must be as independent in *literature* as she is in *politics,* as famous for *arts* as for *arms.*" In a petition to the New York legislature, he affirmed this desire "to see America rendered as independent and illustrious in letters as she is already in arms and civil policy." Not only customs and habits, but "language . . . should be national," Webster explained in his *Dissertations on the English Language.* "America should have her *own* distinct from all the world," and especially distinct from England. A "blind imitation" of English manners and an "astonishing respect" for English art and literature were still too prevalent among independent Americans. This was unfortunate because their "habitual respect for another country, deserved and once laudable, turns their attention from their own interests, and prevents their respecting themselves." In short, said Webster, as an "independent nation, our honor requires us to have a system of our own" in language and education as well as in government.[37]

Impressed by conventional arguments concerning the sacrifices necessary for the support of republican forms of government, sacrifices made even more arduous by the bountiful and extensive American domain, the Revolutionaries could not help but be aware of the political significance of education. That they had committed themselves to a historically ephemeral form of government, and one that placed the old ligaments of the familial commonwealth, mutual affection and dependence, in low repute, only made the need for political education more acute. Thus a second point on which the Revolutionaries were wholeheartedly in agreement was their insistence that an American system of education must be self-consciously patriotic. With the decline of the social bonds of affection, "we have little else than the understanding and virtue of the people to combine them together in society, and gain their consent and subjection to necessary and just government," observed Enos Hitchcock. What was required was an educational system that would evoke these essential qualities by fortifying the people's love for their country—that is, by intensifying the bonds of patriotism.[38]

The effort to nurture a spirit of patriotism in Americans took on the aura of a "moral and a religious duty." And well it should, Rush declared, for patriotism was a "virtue . . . as necessary for the support of societies as natural affection is for the support of families." Jonathan Mason argued that "Patriotism is essential to the preservation and well being of every free government" because it encouraged the cultivation of every other social virtue and, in so doing, supported public liberty, security, and happiness. "Without some portion of this generous principle," Mason warned, the "jarring interests" of selfish individuals would lead directly to "anarchy and confusion" and bring about the "ruin and subversion of the state." Samuel Wales added that the jealousy and discord that had become so alarmingly commonplace since the end of the war were the effects of a "want of true patriotism." "Some semblances and imitations" of national affection were evident, but "genuine patriotism" had somehow vanished. "Pretended patriots," William Wyche sadly agreed, were responsible for precipitating much of the factional squabbling in America.[39]

It is important to note, as these statements suggest, that the Revolutionaries viewed patriotism as an artificial affection. Unlike the affection that prevailed in the family, which was "natural" because, as John Locke explained, "God hath woven into the Principles of Humane Nature . . . a tenderness for their Off-spring," patriotism had to be inculcated, sometimes forcibly. Furthermore, unlike the familial commonwealth, which was local and personal, the new republic was extensive and impersonal; therefore, the scope of this national affection was vastly larger, temporally as well as geographically, than its earlier social counterpart. As Rush put it, patriotism "comprehends not only the love of our neighbors but of millions of our fellow creatures, not only of the present but of future generations." [40]

The desire to inculcate this intangible and artificial, but nevertheless essential, bond of national affection in the citizenry, strengthened the Revolutionaries' conviction that an "education in our own is to be preferred to an education in a foreign country." The "principle of patriotism," Rush declared, "stands in need of the reinforcement of *prejudice,* and it is well known that our strongest prejudices in favor of our country are formed in the first one and twenty years of our lives." In particular, an "early attachment . . . to the laws and constitution" of the republic would be formed, and the bonds of patriotism thereby tempered, by an American education. Noah Webster, whose efforts at "forming" the American mind were unsurpassed, proposed an educational exercise that was unabashedly patriotic. One of the first lessons in Webster's program of instruction was a kind of political catechism for the American child: "As soon as he opens his lips, he should rehearse the history of his own country; he should lisp the praise of liberty and of those illustrious heroes and statesmen who have wrought a revolution in her favor." [41]

This was, of course, a form of political indoctrination. In the Revolutionary perspective, however, with the fate of the republic hanging in the balance, this emphasis on "Americanism" hardly needed to be excused. It was true, Rush acknowledged, the argument had been made that children be kept free of all prejudices so that "after they arrived at an age in which they are capable of judging for themselves" they might "choose their own principles." If it were possible to "preserve the mind in childhood and youth a perfect blank," then "this plan of education would have more to recommend it, but this we know to be impossible. The human mind runs as naturally into principles as it does after facts." The "young mind cannot be stationary," Simeon Doggett agreed. "As soon as the powers and capacities of the mind begin to unfold, the directing and fostering hand of education" must "turn the mind right"; otherwise, indulgence and bad examples will "turn it wrong." Webster was certain that it was "extremely dangerous to suffer young men to pass the most critical period of life, when the passions are strong, the judgment weak, and the heart susceptible and unsuspecting, in a situation where there is not the least restraint upon their inclinations." [42]

Thus it was because, in the words of David McClure, "youth is a susceptible age," that a republican catechism was necessary. The "HUMAN MIND bears a strong resemblance to the wild and unmanured garden of nature," declared a Yale commencement speaker in 1772, "which (tho' amidst an infinite profusion of weeds and briers) by diligence and culture becomes fertile, fair and flourishing." This proposition was by no means novel. In 1699 a student orator at the College of William and Mary had employed a similar comparison to support his contention that "Education helps Nature." "In a word as a field w[hi]ch of it Selfe is Barren & brings forth nothing but Bryars & weeds by Manuring & Tillage may be made fertill [,] Soe a vitious disposition by discipline & good Literature may be made vertuous." The analogy of the mind and the garden remained popular with the Revolutionaries, perhaps because it conveyed the need for constant care and cultivation even more compellingly than did the traditional simile that likened the mind to wax. "Youth are daily growing up to manhood," Jeremy Belknap cautioned, "and if good principles are not early implanted in their minds, bad ones will assume their place like noxious weeds in a neglected garden." The "active nature" of the child's mind necessitated the "most assiduous care with respect to its earliest stages, lest rank and poisonous weeds spontaneously shoot forth their baneful influence," warned an anonymous writer. "The human mind is like a rich field," Webster concluded, "which, without constant care, will ever be covered with a luxuriant growth of weeds." [43]

If, in other words, an American education did not inspire American youths with an affection for their country and its republican principles, then a foreign education would give rise, like weeds in a neglected garden, to an attachment to a foreign government or to principles foreign to America. Washington, certainly, was troubled by this prospect. "It has always been a source of serious reflection and sincere regret with me," he confessed, "that the youth of the United States should be sent to foreign countries for the purpose of education. Although there are doubtless many, under these circumstances, who escape the danger of contracting principles unfavorable to republican government, yet we ought to deprecate the hazard attending ardent and susceptible minds, from being too strongly and too early prepossessed in favor of other political systems, before they are capable of appreciating their own." If youths were sent abroad "before their minds were formed," or before they had "imbibed any adequate ideas of the happiness" engendered by the republican form of government, Washington recorded in his will, they adopted "too frequently, not only habits of dissipation & extravagance, but principles unfriendly to Republican Governm[en]t . . . which, thereafter are rarely overcome." [44]

Noah Webster was even more strident in his insistence that an "attachment to a *foreign* government, or rather a want of attachment to our *own,* is the natural effect of a residence abroad during the period of youth." Nearly all, "ninety-nine persons of a hundred," who spend these formative years in a foreign country develop a preference for its people, manners, and laws, Webster declared. Moreover, because the impressions received during this critical period usually lasted a lifetime, it was a matter of "infinite importance that those who direct the councils of a nation should be educated in that nation." This did not mean that citizens must restrict their acquaintances to their own country. Such provincialism was contrary to the spirit of the Revolution. What it did mean, however, was that "their first ideas, attachments, and habits should be acquired in the country which they are to govern and defend." [45]

Clearly, then, patriotism needed the support of a national educational system. As Rush remarked, "young men who have trodden the paths of science together, or have joined in the same sports" in school, usually formed "such ties to each other as add greatly" to the strength of the republic. Alternatively, Jefferson observed, a youngster educated in a foreign country "loses the season of life for forming in his own country those friendships which of all others are the most faithful and permanent." Fond of luxury and dissipation, fascinated by the privileges and trappings of nobles and kings, and firmly attached to distant friends, the student "returns to his own country, a foreigner." The Georgia legislature summarized and officially sanctioned these sentiments. In 1785 it ruled that residents who, prior to their sixteenth birthday, had spent three or more years studying in a foreign country would be "considered and treated as aliens" for as many years as they had been abroad.[46]

In a very real sense, this notion of patriotism, and of the prejudice needed to reinforce patriotic principles, were merely extensions of those unseemly and unrepublican passions, pride and selfishness. Individual vices, however, did not always translate into corresponding national vices. "There is indeed such a thing as a predilection for *one's own* country . . . which, although it savours of prejudice, is the basis of patriotism," assured a contributor to the *Columbian Magazine.* "This, so far from being reprehensible, is an exalted virtue." It was not prejudice proper, or a "preference . . . founded on real merit and superior excellence," but "*ill-founded* prejudice" that was the bane of mankind. Benjamin Rush endorsed this distinction. "Prejudices are of two kinds, true and false," he argued, and "in a world where *false* prejudices do so much mischief, it would discover great weakness not to oppose them, by such as are *true.*" A well-founded preference, one that promoted the public good and opposed error, was, Jonathan Mason observed, a "noble passion." So noble was this patriotic spirit, Rush added, that "even our Savior himself gives a sanction to this virtue." After all, the Savior as a true patriot had "confined his miracles and gospel at first to his own country." [47]

If the Revolutionaries seemed preoccupied with the task of inculcating patriotism it was also because they believed that in the monarchical world of the eighteenth century, the rather solitary American republic had a special need for a patriotic citizenry. "While we are conversant with the people of other nations, and are visited by men who hold by inheritance, or by indefeasible grant, high offices, to which large emoluments are annexed, we are not to feel ourselves as inferior to them," advised James Sullivan. "There is a kind of republican pride, that must be cherished in our minds, if we mean to support a free government." [48]

III

Benjamin Rush knew all about the demands of republican pride in the face of monarchical glitter. A self-professed republican in the late 1760s, the youthful Rush had nevertheless been overwhelmed by the trappings of royalty during a visit to the House of Lords. The experience made a lasting impression on him, for after Independence Rush worried that Americans, having "knocked up the substance of royalty," might still be awed into worshiping its "shadow." This regrettable reminder of filial dependency, an "impurity we contracted by laying so long upon the lap of Great Britain," had to be "purge[d] away." [49]

The salutary effect of knowledge in displacing even the shadow of royalty in the new republic magnified the political significance of education. Rush in 1786 pleaded with Richard Price, the influential English radical, to write a general treatise on education addressed to Congress and the state legislatures. In his *Observations on the Importance of the American Revolution,* Price had worried openly about the spread of false refinement and luxury in America, which he thought threatened to abort the republican experiment. Rush tailored his appeal to Price's principled uneasiness. Only a plan of "general education" structured to promote the public good, Rush said, would "render the American Revolution a blessing to mankind." [50]

Price endorsed Rush's assessment of the importance of republican education—"nothing, certainly, can be of more importance"—but politely declined the invitation to submit a separate essay on the subject. *Observations* was "intended as a last testimony of my goodwill to the American states" and contained the "best advice I am capable of giving them on Education." Although Price refused to pursue the matter, there was no dearth of proposals emanating from the Revolutionaries themselves. Indeed, since knowledge, virtue, and independence were essential to the success of the rising empire, support for public education became a kind of measure of individual and institutional commitment to republican principles. "Whenever we have an opportunity of observing any state, legislature, or commonwealth, or even any distinguished characters unsolicitous about the means of disseminating public instruction, there, we may be assured," Samuel Knox declared, "the principles of despotism and ambitious encroachment have taken root." [51]

The proponents of public education in the new nation were in agreement on the arrangement most likely to secure its full benefits. To begin with, a republican system of education had to be inclusive. Public order could be maintained, and the good of the whole advanced, only if the people-at-large were generally enlightened. Because wisdom and virtue were inseparably connected, with, as Samuel Harrison Smith had pointed out, the "degree and efficiency of the one" directly affecting the "measure and vigor of the other," it stood to reason that a republican polity "cannot possibly be too enlightened." A broad dissemination of the rudiments of knowledge increased the likelihood of ordinary inhabitants acting the part of responsible citizens: informed enough to recognize their respective offices and duties, independent enough to act upon those obligations, and intelligent enough to elect men of real merit to civil offices. [52]

Even the most modest participants in the 1795 contest sponsored by the American Philosophical Society to promote the best plan of "liberal Education . . . adapted to the genius of the United States," touted the importance of educational inclusiveness. Because the ill effects of ignorance could not be confined among the ignorant, and because talent was not a monopoly of the wealthy, "in a republic, there should be every means used, in order to diffuse information, that every Citizen, even those of the poorest parents, and smallest connections, should have it in their power, in case they have the ability, and are industrious" to rise to the very "summit of information," explained one contributor. It was essential, said another, not only to seek "genius wherever [it is] to be found" but also to improve the "sort of each in its proper sphere." Whenever access to the sources of knowledge were confined to a few privileged souls, a third concluded, the "liberties of the state" were rendered precarious.[53]

A system of education that embraced every part of the community would be incomplete, however, if it did not include a procedure for the filtration of talent. An expansive network of primary institutions must be oriented to instill the basic lessons of citizenship in the commonalty, but it should also be designed to serve as the first step in the process of identifying the natural aristocracy in a one-class republic. Jefferson, in a letter to John Adams, pointed out that a major goal of his "Bill for the More General Diffusion of Knowledge" was the discovery of "Worth and genius . . . from every condition of life." By allowing increasingly exclusive institutions to succeed the inclusive ones established at the primary level, the truly meritorious inhabitants of the state would continually advance and, ultimately, be "compleatly prepared by education for defeating the competition of wealth and birth for public trusts."[54]

Jefferson was not alone in his appreciation of the utility of selective promotions. God had dispensed natural abilities in unequal portions, Josiah Bridge noted, "to some he giveth wisdom and understanding exceeding much. . . . The powers of others seems formed upon a lesser scale." Thus "Providence, as with a sun-beam," had already singled out those who should be "vested with ruling powers" and those who were best restricted to a "lower line of duty." A judicious system of general education ought to complement this natural order. It must reflect the "natural diversity in the human composition." Samuel Harrison Smith, working from the same premise, made the progressive search for talent a basic part of his plan of republican education. And Samuel Knox argued that a hierarchical arrangement of institutions geared for the advancement of "such as discovered the brightest genius" was in the best interest of America. Each level of education might then be structured to accommodate a particular group of citizens whose natural abilities could carry them no further. Accordingly, with the schools of any one level "endowed, furnished, and conducted in such a manner as to complete one uniform course," every citizen would theoretically be prepared to assume his station in the compound republic.[55]

Given the political connotations of these educational proposals, it comes as no surprise to find that the effort to promote public education in America figured prominently when it came to the cataloging of patriotic endeavors. The cause of public education deserved the highest order of "patriotic exertions," Knox declared, because the interest, character, freedom, and happiness of the nation depended upon it. Hoping to encourage his fellow citizens further to commit themselves to what promised to be an enormous undertaking, Knox elaborated upon the example set by Washington, the "most illustrious living character which America or the world can now boast." Washington's contributions as a "Warrior" to the welfare and happiness of this "infantine" country were unmatched. But these "trophies of the field" were "secondary" to his "noble and disinterested exertions" on behalf of public education. "No trait or feature" in Washington's physical or moral constitution "afforded a more convincing proof of his pure regard for civil liberty." His work to establish "literature and science" on a sure national footing was the best evidence of Washington's "uncorrupted spirit of patriotism and republican virtue." Washington's actions and achievements in this realm would preserve his reputation through the "lapse of ages." Americans anxious over the apparent moral declension of their countrymen could do no better than to emulate the "illustrious example" of this "truly *great man.*" [56]

IV

When the Rush children were unruly their famous father sought to "frighten them" back in line "by telling them the king . . . will catch them." In the first decades of the nineteenth century, as American faith in the durability of the republic firmed up and the bogeyman of monarchy retreated into the background, some of the force behind the politics of education was lost. The "shadow" of royalty increasingly gave way to the specter of democracy, and the public school system finally established in the age of egalitarianism might be attributed as much to social as to political impulses. [57]

But the impact of the Revolutionary ferment over education was still far reaching. In addition to institutional reforms and what Tocqueville observed to be the wearisome "garrulous patriotism" of Americans, the heightened political significance attached to education in Revolutionary America contributed to the decline of traditional authority within the family. [58] It sharpened the already discernable distinction between civil and familial responsibilities, and enlarged the scope of the former at the expense of the latter. "Wisdom and knowledge, as well as virtue, diffused generally among the body of the people, being necessary for the preservation of their rights and liberties," declared the Massachusetts constitution of 1780, it is the "duty of legislatures and magistrates" to extend the "opportunities and advantages of education in the various parts of the country." This theme, that it was a solemn civil "duty" of the state to supervise and expand the realm of education, was a favorite of the Revolutionaries. "Are ye aware, legislators," demanded Robert Coram, "that in making knowledge necessary to the subsistence" of the people, "ye are in duty bound to secure to them the means of acquiring it?" Before the great body of citizens could participate responsibly in the affairs of the republic, Samuel Harrison Smith said, "one principle must prevail. Society must establish the right to educate, and acknowledge the duty of having educated, all children." "If it is the duty and interest of the State to avail itself of the capacities of all its citizens," Jeremy Belknap explained, "it is then their duty and interest to cultivate those capacities." "Much has been done already to enlighten our citizens," Rush noted, "but much more may be done." And, Du Pont de Nemours added, "if improvement is a possibility, it is a duty."[59]

It was the "duty of a nation," in particular, according to Samuel Harrison Smith, "to superintend and even to coerce the education of children." Circumstances not only justified, they dictated the "establishment of a system which shall place under a control, independent of and superior to parental authority, the education of children." The dissemination of knowledge was "so momentously important" that it "must not be left to the negligence of individuals." Consequently, it must "be made punishable by law in a parent to neglect offering his child to the preceptor for instruction." Robert Coram fully endorsed these sentiments. "Education should not be left to the caprice or negligence of parents, to chance," he cautioned. The anonymous essayist who proposed to make the business of "education . . . wholly a public concern even to the exclusion of the parent from interference therewith" was thus simply repeating a common refrain.[60]

In addition to the desire to minimize the possible ill effects of parental negligence, this sentiment for making the student "public property" was supported by the Revolutionaries' understanding of the life of the mind. It was widely acknowledged, as Rush remarked, that "first impressions upon the mind are the most durable." Indeed, Smith exclaimed, "first impressions are almost omnipotent." This meant that the "first great object of a liberal system of education should be the admission into the young mind of such ideas only as are either absolutely true or in the highest degree probable; and the cautious exclusion of all error." It also meant, said Rush, that the moral character of men and the moral fiber of the republic were formed in nurseries, and by women because the "*first* impressions upon the minds of children are generally derived from the women." As Smith put it, the "virtue or the vice of an individual, the happiness or the misery of a family, the glory or the infamy of a nation, have had their sources in the cradle, over which the prejudices of a nurse or a mother have presided." "Mothers and school-masters plant the seeds of nearly all the good and evil which exist in our world," Rush emphasized.

[191]

If, therefore, American mothers did not "concur in all our plans of education for young men . . . no laws will render them effectual."[61]

A partial solution to this predicament was obvious: because mothers played such a crucial role in forming the dispositions of children and were thus instrumental in "controlling the manners of a nation," women should be qualified for this purpose. Noah Webster, who believed that the "only way to make good citizens" was to "nourish them from infancy," argued that in constructing a truly comprehensive system of education the "female sex" must "claim no inconsiderable share of our attention." Moreover, the "usual branches of female education" were no longer adequate. Music, drawing, dancing, and household economics had to be complemented with studies that would enable women to "implant in the tender mind such sentiments of virtue, propriety, and dignity as are suited to the freedom of our governments." Republican mothers must, Rush insisted, be qualified to a certain degree to instruct "their sons in the principles of liberty and government." In order for them to do this some of the conventional subjects taught to women had to be supplanted by concentrations of "history, philosophy, poetry, and the numerous moral essays." This substitution, Rush thought, was suited to the state of American society. It was essential for a republican system of education to include a "Peculiar mode of education proper for WOMEN in a republic."[62]

But female education was not a sufficient guarantee against the introduction of error into the young mind. It was still the "duty" of the state to "coerce" the education of all children. Unless education was handled by public institutions, there was always the danger that private "prejudices" would become "as hereditary as titles." "Error is never more dangerous than in the mouth of a parent," Samuel Harrison Smith declared, because children customarily accepted without question the opinions of their parents. Ill-founded prejudices become hereditary simply "by the mechanical adoption of parental error or vice." A public system of education "remote from parental influence" was best, for it would encourage the exercise and development of the mental faculties of children and remove them "from an *entire* dependence on . . . [their] parents." This argument alone was a powerful motive for republicans who distrusted all forms of dependence. "Above every other consideration," Smith said, the "spirit of independent reflection and conduct" that it inspired "must give an undeniable ascendancy to the public over the private plan" of education in America. Ultimately, the Revolutionaries reversed the earlier colonial priorities of familial and civil responsibilities. The colonists had viewed public intrusion into the realm of parental obligations in education as a matter of last resort; the Revolutionaries came to accept it as a matter of first consequence.[63]

The very idea of an educational system independent of and superior to parental authority was new. Under the old familial paradigm such a prospect was unthinkable, if only because of the fusion of civil and domestic concerns. With the establishment of the republic, however, civil authority could no longer be viewed as parental authority writ large. As a result, the Revolutionaries had to posit conceptual distinctions that once were unnecessary. At the time they were beginning to emphasize the need for educational systems outside of the family circle, they were hard pressed to define the appropriate mode of governing those systems.

This problem was expertly reviewed in a letter written by Eliphalet Pearson in 1789. As a member of the Harvard faculty, Pearson was troubled by the rising tide of student disturbances in colleges throughout the new nation. The unrest, he thought, was rooted in a basic ambiguity in the minds of most Americans. Political theorists had distinguished between two kinds of societies, "*domestic & civil.*" The former included "husband & wife, parents & children, master & servants" and was "governed by the father." As such, Pearson noted, it was proper to label this "form of government *patriarchal, parental,* or *family.*" Civil societies, on the other hand, comprised "magistrates & subjects, in all the numerous forms of *civil polity.*" The forms themselves, "*monarchy, aristocracy,* or *democracy;* or certain mixtures of these," outlined the respective rights and duties of rulers and ruled, governors and governed. The problem in America, Pearson said, stemmed from the uncertainty of fitting educational institutions within this scheme. Were schools properly to be "denominated *domestic,* or *civil,* or *sui generis,* or mixed"? Some would argue that the school was a civil society analogous to the republic and ought, therefore, to be governed accordingly. In that case, students must be given the same rights bestowed upon citizens. Others were just as vehement in their insistence that the school was a domestic society. Pupils, then, were children subject to the rulings of a parental surrogate. The ensuing confrontations between these two groups of partisans resulted in charges and countercharges that only deepened the confusion already evident in American education and further encouraged the student rioters. An examination must be conducted, Pearson pleaded, into the nature of the schools in order to determine "what *species* of society" they were.[64]

Pearson's remarks are indicative of the splintering of American social perceptions that came about after the familial paradigm of society and the patriarchal model of affectionate authority had lost much of their explanatory power. It should be pointed out, however, that this splintered situation was transitional. Independent Americans, having made the commitment to republicanism, soon discovered the revolutionary implications of that commitment. It was impossible to confine the impact of the republican paradigm strictly to the sphere of civil relations. The school and the family had to accommodate the leveling forces set in motion by the Revolutionary experiment in politics. In the course of the nineteenth century, as classical republicanism was engulfed by egalitarian nationalism, the "republic" itself became symbolically important as the standard by which to measure all forms of social interaction. The republican paradigm eventually came to exert from above the kind of influence that the familial paradigm had once exerted from below.[65] In the end, the world of order and affection, of filial fear and paternal faithfulness, a world arranged in conformity with the social imperatives contained in the Fifth Commandment, would give way to a world in which autonomy and personal independence were among the most cherished social virtues and equality was enshrined as a principal axiom of political discourse.

Epilogue: Father of His Country

In 1788 a French traveler to the United States, Brissot de Warville, commented that Americans by and large spoke of Washington "as they would of a father." Thus even before his death Washington was being touted as the father of his country. After his death in 1799 virtually all came to praise him. This acclaim, the burgeoning legend of the founding father, would seem to invalidate the assertion that in the wake of Independence the familial paradigm was supplanted by republicanism. It is important, then, to deal with the Washington myth to see if it indeed represented a continuation of the pre-Revolutionary ideal of the familial commonwealth founded on affectionate authority.[1]

Brissot himself provided some clues for understanding the phenomenon of the founding father. According to Brissot, Washington possessed "all the qualities and all the virtues of the perfect republican." He also noted, however, that of all places it was in Washington's home state that the hero seemed least appreciated. "Virginia is perhaps the only state where he does have enemies." These seemingly conflicting circumstances were quite probably complementary. For the very process of creating the myth of the "perfect republican" may have alienated those who knew Washington best. As early as 1777 John Adams was already expressing some misgivings over the "superstitious veneration that is sometimes paid to General Washington." To Abigail he complained, "We can allow a certain Citizen to be wise, virtuous, and good, without thinking him a Deity." It is not too much to suggest that fellow Virginians shared similar regrets as the historical Washington was transformed into the symbolic founding father.[2]

The reasoning behind the transformation was straightforward enough. Americans were not only embarking on an independent course but had committed themselves to an experiment in republicanism. Despite their proud boasts of Enlightened progress, they remained acutely aware of the hazards, rooted essentially in an unchanging human nature, that had brought down the republics of the past. The role of the "perfect republican" was to promote stability by serving as a virtuous example truly worthy of imitation. The exemplary character of the mythical

[195]

founder, if widely imitated, would become the basis of the emerging American character. Once this occurred the republic was sure to be long-lived.

What were the principal virtues of this remarkable republican? There were, of course, the obvious ones popularized by Mason Locke Weems in his *Life of Washington*. The good parson enshrined forever in the minds of generations of Americans the angelic integrity of Washington by re-counting the dubious episode of the cherry tree. Weems also described, often with equally appealing anecdotes, the founding father's benevo-lence, charity, dedication to duty, religious commitment, agrarian instincts, courage, justice, selflessness, and patriotism—that "grand re-publican virtue." Less obvious, although certainly no less important in the list of republican virtues, was the mythical Washington's sense of order and obedience. For example, Weems pointed out that Washington's conduct during the French and Indian War was beyond reproach. "To a man of his uncommon military mind, and skill in the arts of Indian warfare, the pride and precipitance of general Braddock must have been excessively disgusting and disheartening." Yet even in the face of such pompous incompetence, Washington never once threatened to leave the service or to supersede Braddock's command. "On the con-trary, he nobly brooked his rude manners, gallantly obeyed his rash orders, and, as far as in him lay, endeavoured to correct their fatal tenden-cies." [3]

Washington's dedication was similarly tested during the Revolutionary War when his intentions were constantly thwarted by a well-meaning but, according to Weems, nevertheless incompetent Congress. Indeed, Weems said, Congress was responsible not only for "dragging out the war—dispiriting the nation," but also for personally "disgracing" Washington. Again, however, Washington was a model of order and obe-dience. The founding father, we are told, refused to give in to "gusts of passion." He steadfastly refused to entertain any notion of supplanting congressional authority; rather, he actively opposed even the slightest suggestion of such "dark intrigues." Washington continued "to treat con-gress as a virtuous son his respected parents." As in the case of his experi-ence with General Braddock, Washington, despite all manner of provoca-tion, calmly pointed out "wiser measures, but in defect of their adoption, makes the best use of those they give him." [4]

Other contributors to the Washington myth likewise emphasized the founder's commitment to maintaining order. Washington, summarized one eulogist, was a constant opponent of the "restless disorganizers of civil society." Stable and secure, methodical and regular, orderly and systematic, the mythical Washington was the finest example of Benjamin

Rush's "republican machine." For the ordinary citizen, this aspect of Washington's character was perhaps more compelling than any other. Few, certainly, could aspire to achieve such lofty heights of selflessness and courage displayed by the founder, but all had experienced the sometimes unpleasant duty of submitting to properly constituted authorities. Washington's example proved, in the first place, that steadiness and dependability in the face of disorder were as valuable as any of the other virtues of man. But it also did much more than that. By providing Washington with these attributes these writers were elevating the mundane to the level of the heroic. Gallantry and self-sacrifice in combat were qualities highly esteemed by the people, and quite properly so; but, some might be tempted to ask, Was mere obedience to lawfully appointed authorities as estimable? Popularizers such as Weems enthusiastically answered yes. Washington was never more courageous than when he demonstrated his *"courage to obey,"* never more noble than when he performed the "noble acts" of compliance to the wishes of Congress. The association with Washington had transformed the ordinary into the extraordinary.[5]

Washington quickly became a vital part of the public domain. As one panegyrist remarked, the "history of his life is the history of his country's glory." The line between the historical and the mythical, never very distinct even while Washington lived, was blurred forever after his death. The "perfect republican," the ideal American, personified the nation itself, but personification was a dehumanizing process. The human personality was subsumed under the heroic. Again, this may be why Virginians, who in general must have had greater first-hand knowledge of the man than all other Americans, were more circumspect about adopting the mythical Washington. At any rate, the life of Washington soon took its place among the moral advice literature of the nineteenth century. Cast as the "great preceptor to his country," the name Washington called to mind not the image of a man, but rather a catalogue of virtues. And because those virtues were supposedly the very essence of republicanism, Washington's "name and that of our country," as the eulogist Jeremiah Smith said, "are inseparable."[6]

What all of this suggests is that post-Independence references to Washington as the founding father do not stand as evidence of the continuing strength of the familial paradigm. Instead, they mark the symbolic end to the relevance of that model. In the popular mind, "Washington" was synonymous with "the Republic," more an institution than a man. Noah Webster had advised that as soon as the American child "opens his lips, he should rehearse the history of his own country." He should be taught at that early age to "lisp praise of liberty." Several influential nineteenth-century schoolbooks offered the same advice: "Begin with the infant in his cradle / Let the first word he lisps be WASHINGTON." Lisping praises of liberty and country had become interchangeable with lisping praises of Washington. Furthermore, symbolically, if not literally, the American child would be taught to call out first not to his natural father, but to the Father of His Country. The first lesson in republican education tended to undermine the very substance of the older model of affectionate authority. This was clearly in line with Rush's statement concerning the first duty to be taught to a sturdy republican: "Let him be taught to love his family, but let him be taught, at the same time, that he must forsake and even forget them, when the welfare of his country requires it." In short, the recognition accorded to Washington as the founding father was tantamount to an acknowledgment that all Americans were among "Columbia's proudest rising sons." The references to Washington as father thus represented not so much the persistence of the familial paradigm as its demise. All Americans were now children of the republic.[7]

Notes

Epigraphs

Affection, pp. 7–8

"A Narrative of the case of John Porter, Jun.," in Nathaniel B. Shurtleff, ed., *Records of the Governor and Company of the Massachusetts Bay in New England,* 5 vols. in 6 (Boston, 1853–54), 4, pt. 2, pp. 216–18.

Demeanor, pp. 31–32

Samuel Willard, *Ne Sutor Ultra Crepidam. Or Brief Animadversions upon the New England Anabaptists Late Fallacious Narratives* (Boston, 1681), pp. 18–21.

Disaffection, p. 85

John Adams to H. Niles, 13 February 1818, ed. L. H. Butterfield, in Daniel Boorstin, ed., *An American Primer* (Chicago, 1966), pp. 229–30; but see also pp. 227–38.

Republicanism, pp. 139–40

Benjamin Rush to Ebenezer Hazard, 22 October 1768, in L. H. Butterfield, ed., *Letters of Benjamin Rush,* 2 vols. (Princeton, 1951), 1: 68; George W. Corner, ed., *The Autobiography of Benjamin Rush: His "Travels Through Life" together with his Commonplace Book for 1789–1813* (Princeton, 1948), pp. 45–46.

1: The Bonds of Affection

1. John Winthrop, "A Model of Christian Charity," in Edmund S. Morgan, ed., *Puritan Political Ideas, 1558–1794* (Indianapolis, 1965), pp. 76–77. Arthur O. Lovejoy, *The Great Chain of Being: A Study in the History of an Idea* (Cambridge, Mass., 1936), is the classic treatment of this idea.
2. William Perkins, "A Treatise of the Vocations or Callings of Men," in Morgan, ed., *Puritan Political Ideas,* pp. 39, 49; Nathaniel Chauncey, *The Faithful Ruler Described and Excited* (New London, 1734), p. 48. On the traditional images of the body politic, see Michael Walzer, *The Revolution of the Saints: A Study in the Origins of Radical Politics* (Cambridge, Mass., 1965), pp. 148–98; and more generally in Walzer, "On the Role of Symbolism in Political Thought," *Political Science Quarterly* 82 (1967): 191–204.
3. William Balch, *A Publick Spirit . . . Recommended to Rulers and People* (Boston, 1749), pp. 16, 22; Abraham Williams, *A Sermon Preach'd at Boston, Before the Great and General Court* (Boston, 1762), pp. 11, 13–14.

4. Ibid., p. 14; Joseph Huntington, *A Discourse . . . on the Health and Happiness, or Misery and Ruin, of the Body Politic, in Similitude to that of the Natural Body* (Hartford, 1781), pp. 4–8, 13–15, 17–20.
5. Perkins, "Treatise of the Vocations or Callings," pp. 51, 53, 50. J. E. Crowley, *This Sheba, Self: The Conceptualization of Economic Life in Eighteenth-Century America* (Baltimore, 1974), pp. 50–75; and James Axtell, *The School upon a Hill: Education and Society in Colonial New England* (New Haven, 1974), pp. 100–165, discuss some of the social implications of the concept of "calling."
6. Perkins, "Treatise of the Vocations or Callings," pp. 50, 52; Williams, *Sermon Preach'd at Boston,* pp. 3–5; Peter Clark, *The Rulers Highest Dignity, and the People's Truest Glory* (Boston, 1739), p. 13.
7. Williams, *Sermon Preach'd at Boston,* pp. 1–2; Samuel Willard, *A Compleat Body of Divinity* (1726; New York, 1969), p. 598; Thomas Foxcroft quoted in Edmund S. Morgan, *The Puritan Family: Religion and Domestic Relations in Seventeenth-Century New England,* rev. ed. (New York, 1966), p. 94; Sewall quoted in Stephen Foster, *Their Solitary Way: The Puritan Social Ethic in the First Century of Settlement in New England* (New Haven, 1971), p. 20.
8. Jonathan Todd, *Civil Rulers the Ministers of God, for Good to Men* (New London, 1749), pp. 10, 40; Noah Hobart, *Civil Government the Foundation of Social Happiness* (New London, 1751), pp. 1, 3.
9. William Welsteed, *The Dignity and Duty of the Civil Magistrate* (Boston, 1751), p. 9; Charles Chauncy, *Civil Magistrates Must Be Just, Ruling in Fear of God* (Boston, 1747), pp. 8–9; Daniel Lewis, *Good Rulers the Fathers of Their People* (Boston, 1748), p. 8. Also, Williams, *Sermon Preach'd at Boston,* pp. 6–7; Jared Eliot, *Give Cesar His Due, or, Obligation that Subjects are Under to Their Civil Rulers* (New London, 1738), p. 25.
10. Samuel Phillips, *Political Rulers Authoriz'd and Influenc'd by God . . .to Decree and Execute Justice* (Boston, 1750), pp. 6, 7, 33; Perkins, "Treatise of the Vocations or Callings," p. 60; Henry Bullinger, *The Decades,* in Morgan, ed., *Puritan Political Ideas,* p. 16; Todd, *Civil Rulers the Ministers of God,* p. 30; "Journal of John Winthrop," in Morgan, ed., *Puritan Political Ideas,* p. 137.
11. Bullinger, *The Decades,* p. 16; Balch, *Publick Spirit Recommended,* p. 13; Samuel Whittelsey, *A Publick Spirit Described and Recommended* (New London, Conn., 1731), p. 13; Hobart, *Civil Government the Foundation,* p. 3; Elnathan Whitman, *The Character and Qualifications of Good Rulers* (New London, Conn., 1745), p. 14.
12. Welsteed, *Dignity and Duty,* p. 17; Chauncy, *Civil Magistrates Must Be Just,* pp. 12, 13; "Original Righteousness" appears in the "Shorter Catechism" of the Westminster Assembly included in *The New-England Primer,* ed. Paul Leicester Ford (New York, 1962).
13. Whittelsey, *Publick Spirit Described,* pp. 3, 9; Clark, *Rulers Highest Dignity,* p. 13; Williams, *Sermon Preach'd at Boston,* p. 23; Jeremiah Wise,

Rulers the Ministers of God for the Good of Their People (Boston, 1729), pp. 36, 52; William Burnham, *God's Providence in Placing Men in Their Respective Stations & Conditions Asserted & Shewed* (New London, 1722), p. 18.

14. Whittelsey, *Publick Spirit Described,* pp. 1, 3; Balch, *Publick Spirit Recommended,* pp. 13, 15; Phillips, *Political Rulers Authoriz'd by God,* pp. 20, 17; Nathaniel Appleton, *The Great Blessing of Good Rulers* (Boston, 1742), p. 23.
15. Winthrop, "Model of Christian Charity," pp. 83–87, 90. Also, Perkins. "Treatise of the Vocations or Callings," p. 50; Williams, *Sermon Preach'd at Boston,* pp. 4, 5; John Barnard, *A Call to Parents and Children, or, the Great Concern of Parents; and the Important Duty of Children* (Boston, 1737), pp. 57–58.
16. Williams, *Sermon Preach'd at Boston,* p. 4; Jonathan Edwards, *The Religious Affections,* ed. John E. Smith (New Haven, 1959), pp. 96, 98, 99. More important for our purposes, as we shall see in chapter 2, "filial fear" and "faithfulness" were complex affections.
17. Edwards, *Religious Affections,* pp. 98, 107–8.
18. Ibid., pp. 96, 97, 99, 101, 448.
19. Ibid., p. 98.
20. John Taylor, *The Value of a Child, or, Motives to the Good Education of Children* (Philadelphia, 1753), p. 7; Robert Ashton, ed., *The Works of John Robinson* (Boston, 1851), 1: 217. Also, Josiah Smith, *The Duty of Parents to Instruct Their Children* (Boston, 1730), pp. 12, 25; and Smith, *The Young Man Warn'd: or, Solomon's Counsel to his Son* (Boston, 1730), p. 20; Chauncey, *Faithful Ruler Described,* p. 5; John Wise, *A Vindication of the Government of New England,* in Morgan, ed., *Puritan Political Ideas,* pp. 256–57.
21. *New-England Primer,* "Shorter Catechism" and passim; John Barnard, *The Throne Established by Righteousness* (Boston, 1734), p. 9; Chauncey, *Faithful Ruler Described,* p. 2.
22. Welsteed, *Dignity and Duty,* p. 10; Todd, *Civil Rulers the Ministers of God,* p. 40; Barnard, *Throne Established by Righteousness,* p. 9; Eliot, *Give Cesar His Due,* p. 26.
23. Winthrop, "Model of Christian Charity," pp. 76–77; Hobart, *Civil Government the Foundation,* p. 1.

2: Honor Thy Father

1. Abraham Williams, *A Sermon Preach'd at Boston, Before the Great and General Court* (Boston, 1762), p. 6; Stephen White, *Civil Rulers Gods by Office, and the Duties of Such Considered* (New London, Conn., 1763), pp. 5, 21; Jonathan Ingersoll, *A Sermon Preached Before the General Assembly* (New London, Conn., 1761), pp. 17, 21.
2. Samuel Whittelsey, *A Publick Spirit Described and Recommended* (New

London, Conn., 1731), p. 12; William Balch, *A Publick Spirit . . . Recommended to Rulers and People* (Boston, 1749), p. 21; Peter Clark, *The Rulers Highest Dignity, and the People's Truest Glory* (Boston, 1739), p. 12. Gordon J. Schochet, *Patriarchalism in Political Thought: The Authoritarian Family and Political Speculation and Attitudes Especially in Seventeenth-Century England* (New York, 1975), is an excellent study of the interaction of familial perceptions and political imperatives; the Lawson quote appears on p. 181; see also, Michael Walzer, *The Revolution of the Saints: A Study in the Origins of Radical Politics* (Cambridge, Mass., 1965), pp. 183–98.

3. Schochet, *Patriarchalism in Political Thought*, p. 113; John Cotton, *Spiritual Milk for Boston Babes* (1656), in Robert H. Bremner, et al., eds., *Children and Youth in America: A Documentary History*, 2 vols. (Cambridge, Mass., 1970), 1: 32; Daniel Lewis, *Good Rulers the Fathers of Their People* (Boston, 1748), p. 24.

4. Richard Bushman, *From Puritan to Yankee: Character and the Social Order in Connecticut, 1690–1765* (Cambridge, Mass., 1967), p. 18.

5. William Gouge, *Of Domesticall Duties* (1622; Amsterdam and Norwood, N.J., 1976), pp. 428–29; Isaac Ambrose, *The Well-Ordered Family* (Boston, 1762), p. 23; Robert Ashton, ed., *The Works of John Robinson* (Boston, 1851), 1: 222.

6. Benjamin Wadsworth, *The Well-Ordered Family* (Boston, 1712), pp. 55, 90–91; Gouge, *Domesticall Duties*, p. 430; Samuel Willard, *A Compleat Body of Divinity* (1726; New York, 1969), p. 607.

7. Ambrose, *Well-Ordered Family*, p. 23.

8. Cotton Mather, *A Family Well-Ordered. Or An Essay to Render Parents and Children Happy In One Another* (Boston, 1699), p. 63. Also, Ebenezer Gay, *The Character and Work of a Good Ruler, and the Duty of an Obliged People* (Boston, 1745), p. 11; John Barnard, *The Throne Established by Righteousness* (Boston, 1734), p. 44.

9. Balch, *Publick Spirit Recommended*, p. 16; William Worthington, *The Duty of Rulers and Teachers in Unitedly Leading God's People* (New London, Conn., 1744), p. 26; Cotton, *Spiritual Milk for Boston Babes*, p. 32; "Shorter Catechism," in *The New-England Primer*, ed. Paul Leicester Ford (New York, 1962); Willard, *Compleat Body of Divinity*, pp. 600, 647–51, and more generally throughout Willard's discussion of Questions 63–66, pp. 597–655.

10. Gay, *Character and Work of a Good Ruler*, p. 1; Charles Chauncy, *Civil Magistrates Must Be Just, Ruling in Fear of God* (Boston, 1747), p. 46; Balch, *Publick Spirit Recommended*, p. 21; Jonathan Mayhew, *A Sermon Preach'd in the Audience of . . . William Shirley* (Boston, 1754), p. 13.

11. Lewis, *Good Rulers the Fathers*, pp. 13, 15, 19; Gay, *Character and Work of a Good Ruler*, pp. 17–18; Elnathan Whitman, *The Character and Qualifications of Good Rulers* (New London, Conn., 1745), pp. 11–12, 13.

12. Lewis, *Good Rulers the Fathers*, pp. 21–22; John Barnard, *A Call to Parents*

and Children, or, the Great Concern of Parents; and the Important Duty of Children (Boston, 1737), p. 34.

13. Nathaniel Chauncey, *The Faithful Ruler Described and Excited* (New London, Conn., 1734), pp. 8, 9, 26; Nathaniel Appleton, *The Great Blessing of Good Rulers* (Boston, 1742), p. 31.

14. Chauncey, *Faithful Ruler Described*, p. 10; Balch, *Publick Spirit Recommended*, p. 16; Ebenezer Devotion, *The Civil Ruler, A Dignify'd Servant of the Lord, But a Dying Man* (New London, Conn., 1753), pp. 39, 42–43.

15. Mayhew, *Sermon Preach'd*, pp. 25, 26; Chauncy, *Civil Magistrates Must Be Just*, p. 51; Robinson, *Works*, 1: 222.

16. Appleton, *Great Blessing of Good Rulers*, p. 32; Lewis, *Good Rulers the Fathers*, p. 18; Jonathan Marsh, *God's Fatherly Care of His Covenant Children* (New London, Conn., 1737), p. 10.

17. Samuel Phillips, *Political Rulers Authoriz'd and Influenc'd by God . . .to Decree and Execute Justice* (Boston, 1750), pp. 12, 20; Lewis, *Good Rulers the Fathers*, p. 23.

18. Lewis, *Good Rulers the Fathers*, pp. 14, 21.

19. Whitman, *Character of Good Rulers*, p. 29; Appleton, *Great Blessing of Good Rulers*, p. 58; White, *Civil Rulers Gods by Office*, p. 21.

3: Inward Esteem, Outward Expressions

1. M. Halsey Thomas, ed., *The Diary of Samuel Sewall, 1674–1729*, 2 vols. (New York, 1973), 1: 533–35, 544.

2. Samuel Willard, *A Compleat Body of Divinity* (1726; New York, 1969), p. 598.

3. Benjamin Wadsworth, *The Well-Ordered Family* (Boston, 1712), p. 92; Willard, *Compleat Body of Divinity*, p. 607; William Gouge, *Of Domesticall Duties* (1622; Amsterdam and Norwood, N.J., 1976), pp. 436–37; James Axtell, *The School upon a Hill: Education and Society in Colonial New England* (New Haven, 1974), p. 150.

4. Eleazar Moody, *The School of Good Manners. Composed for the Help of Parents in Teaching their Children How to Carry it in their Places during their Minority* (Boston, 1772), pp. 4–23; Robert H. Bremner et al., eds., *Children and Youth in America: A Documentary History*, 2 vols. (Cambridge, Mass., 1970), 1: 33–34.

5. Moody, *School of Good Manners*, pp. 5, 10, 11, 14, 15, 21.

6. Ibid., pp. 26–27.

7. [James Burgh], *Thoughts on Education* (Boston, 1749), p. 27; Charles Chauncy, *Civil Magistrates Must Be Just, Ruling in Fear of God* (Boston, 1747), p. 51; John Taylor, *The Value of a Child, or, Motives to the Good Education of Children* (Philadelphia, 1753), p. 16; Benjamin Wadsworth, *Exhortations to Early Piety* (Boston, 1702), p. 44.

8. Samuel Phillips, *Political Rulers Authoriz'd and Influenc'd by God . . . to Decree and Execute Justice* (Boston, 1750), pp. 56–57; Edmund S.

Morgan, *The Puritan Family: Religion and Domestic Relations in Seventeenth-Century New England*, rev. ed. (New York, 1966), pp. 20, 96; Josiah Smith, *The Duty of Parents to Instruct Their Children* (Boston, 1730), pp. 2, 39.

9. [Burgh], *Thoughts on Education*, pp. 7, 11; Smith, *Duty of Parents to Instruct*, p. 25; Wadsworth, *Well-Ordered Family*, pp. 53, 86.

10. Wadsworth, *Well-Ordered Family*, p. 55; Taylor, *Value of a Child*, pp. 5, 7, 10.

11. "The Dutiful Child's Promises," in *The New-England Primer*, ed. Paul Leicester Ford (New York, 1962); Taylor, *Value of a Child*, p. 25; John Barnard, *A Call to Parents and Children, or, the Great Concern of Parents; and the Important Duty of Children* (Boston, 1737), p. 28; Philip J. Greven, Jr., ed., *Child-Rearing Concepts, 1628–1861: Historical Sources* (Itasca, Ill., 1973), pp. 13–15.

12. Greven, ed., *Child-Rearing Concepts*, pp. 13–15. Also, Barnard, *Call to Parents and Children*, pp. 28–29; Richard Peters, *A Sermon on Education* (Philadelphia, 1751), pp. 5, 7, 14.

13. John Locke, *Some Thoughts Concerning Education*, ed. Peter Gay (New York, 1964), pp. 101, 26, 32. Cf. Locke, *Second Treatise of Government*, in Peter Laslett, ed., *Two Treatises of Government* (New York, 1963), pp. 348–49.

14. Locke, *Thoughts Concerning Education*, pp. 76, 28, 61, 62; Locke, *Second Treatise*, p. 348.

15. Locke, *Thoughts Concerning Education*, pp. 32, 33, 64, 68.

16. Ibid., pp. 97, 32, 26, 29, 86.

17. Ibid., pp. 87, 31, 32, 69, 80, 99ff.

18. [Burgh], *Thoughts on Education*, p. 10.

19. Wadsworth, *Early Piety*, p. 44; Locke, *Thoughts Concerning Education*, pp. 31, 101; Winthrop, "A Model of Christian Charity," in Edmund S. Morgan, ed., *Puritan Political Ideas, 1558–1794* (Indianapolis, 1965), p. 84.

20. Moody, *School of Good Manners*, pp. 26–27; Locke, *Thoughts Concerning Education*, p. 42.

21. Locke, *Second Treatise*, p. 354; Ebenezer Gay, *The Character and Work of a Good Ruler, and the Duty of an Obliged People* (Boston, 1745), p. 11; Isaac Ambrose, *The Well-Ordered Family* (Boston, 1762), p. 23; Cotton Mather, *A Family Well-Ordered. Or An Essay to Render Parents and Children Happy In One Another* (Boston, 1699), pp. 60–61.

22. Mather, *Family Well-Ordered*, p. 61; Moody, *School of Good Manners*, p. 26.

23. Robert Ashton, ed., *The Works of John Robinson* (Boston, 1851), 1: 229; Phillips, *Political Rulers Authoriz'd by God*, p. 18.

24. Morgan, *Puritan Family*, p. 103; Jonathan Marsh, *God's Fatherly Care of His Covenant Children* (New London, Conn., 1737), pp. 1, 5–6; Gouge, *Domesticall Duties*, pp. 550–55.

25. Gouge, *Domesticall Duties*, pp. 17–18; Samuel Whittelsey, *A Publick*

Spirit Described and Recommended (New London, Conn., 1731), pp. 13, 27; Nathaniel Chauncey, *The Faithful Ruler Described and Excited* (New London, Conn., 1734), p. 48; Wadsworth, *Well-Ordered Family,* p. 84; Mather, *Family Well-Ordered,* pp. 3, 4.

26. Gouge, *Domesticall Duties,* pp. 18, 499–500, 527, 558; Bremner, ed., *Children and Youth in America,* 1: 39–42; Robert F. Seybolt, *Apprenticeship and Apprenticeship Education in Colonial New England and New York* (New York, 1917), pp. 37, 39, 52–53, 54, 79, 80, 81, 114. On the governing of children and domestic advice literature, see Morgan, *Puritan Family,* pp. 65–108; John F. Walzer, "A Period of Ambivalence: Eighteenth-Century American Childhood," in Lloyd deMause, ed., *The History of Childhood* (New York, 1974), pp. 364–73; Axtell, *School upon a Hill,* pp. 97–165; Daniel Calhoun, *The Intelligence of a People* (Princeton, 1973), pp. 134–55; Peter Gregg Slater, *Children in the New England Mind in Death and in Life* (Hamden, Conn., 1977), pp. 93–158; and Philip Greven's highly suggestive *The Protestant Temperament: Patterns of Child-Rearing, Religious Experience, and the Self in Early America* (New York, 1977).

27. Locke, *Thoughts Concerning Education,* pp. 33, 34; Locke, *Second Treatise,* pp. 345–61. For a more general discussion of Locke's educational program and its impact in eighteenth-century America, see Calhoun, *Intelligence of a People,* pp. 139–55; and Slater, *Children in the New England Mind,* pp. 109–14.

28. Locke, *Thoughts Concerning Education,* pp. 33, 36, 60, 61, 68.

29. Ibid., pp. 30, 69, 68, 37, 60.

30. Excerpts from Samuel Hopkins, *The Life and Character of the Late Reverend, Learned, and Pious Mr. Jonathan Edwards* (Northampton, Mass., 1804), in Greven, ed., *Child-Rearing Concepts,* pp. 68–74; Jonathan Edwards, *The Religious Affections,* ed. John E. Smith (New Haven, 1959), p. 396.

31. Excerpts from Sereno E. Dwight, ed., *The Works of President Edwards: With a Memoir of His Life* (New York, 1829), in Greven, ed., *Child-Rearing Concepts,* pp. 74–80.

32. Ibid., pp. 77–78.

33. Ibid., p. 78; Mather, *Family Well-Ordered,* pp. 22–23; Josiah Smith, *The Young Man Warn'd: or, Solomon's Counsel to his Son* (Boston, 1730), p. 26; Taylor, *Value of a Child,* pp. 14–15.

34. Morgan, *Puritan Family,* pp. 105, 106; Greven, ed., *Child-Rearing Concepts,* p. 44; Mather, *Family Well-Ordered,* p. 22.

35. Robinson, *Works,* 1: 88; Edwards, *Religious Affections,* p. 96.

36. William Perkins, *Epiekeia, or a Treatise on Christian Equity and Moderation,* in Morgan, ed., *Puritan Political Ideas,* pp. 60, 61, 63–64, 70, 73; Smith, *Duty of Parents to Instruct,* p. 10.

37. Perkins, *Christian Equity,* pp. 62, 64.

38. Ibid., pp. 65, 66; Robinson, *Works,* 1: 215.

39. Whittelsey, *Publick Spirit Described,* p. 12; Willard, *Compleat Body of*

Divinity, p. 607; Moody, *School of Good Manners,* pp. 17–19; Locke, *Thoughts Concerning Education,* pp. 62, 71.

40. Locke, *Thoughts Concerning Education,* pp. 31, 43–44, 46.

41. The Theer case appears in C. F. Adams, "Some Phases of Sexual Morality and Church Discipline in Colonial New England," Massachusetts Historical Society, *Proceedings,* 2nd ser., 6 (1890–91): 483–84; Gouge, *Domesticall Duties,* p. 436.

42. Adams, "Sexual Morality and Church Discipline," pp. 483–84.

43. Ibid., pp. 485–86.

44. Joseph H. Smith, ed., *Colonial Justice in Western Massachusetts (1639–1702): The Pynchon Court Record, An Original Judges' Diary of the Administration of Justice in the Springfield Courts in the Massachusetts Bay Colony* (Cambridge, Mass., 1961), p. 285.

45. Ibid., p. 273.

46. Ibid., pp. 235–36.

47. The Sewall case appears in John James Currier, *History of Newburyport, Massachusetts, 1764–1909,* 2 vols. (Newburyport, 1906–9), 2: 580–83; Joshua Coffin, *A Sketch of the History of Newbury, Newburyport, and West Newbury, 1635–1845* (Boston, 1845), p. 61.

48. Michael Zuckerman, *Peaceable Kingdoms: New England Towns in the Eighteenth Century* (New York, 1970), pp. 85–122, contains the best discussion of the possible implications of the institutional inadequacies of colonial law enforcement.

49. On the evolution of the family and patriarchal authority in the eighteenth century, see Philip J. Greven, Jr., *Four Generations: Population, Land, and Family in Colonial Andover, Massachusetts* (Ithaca, 1970); Greven, *Protestant Temperament;* Kenneth A. Lockridge, *A New England Town: The First Hundred Years, Dedham, Massachusetts, 1636–1736* (New York, 1970); John Demos, *A Little Commonwealth: Family Life in Plymouth Colony* (New York, 1970); Daniel Blake Smith, *Inside the Great House: Planter Family Life in Eighteenth-Century Chesapeake Society* (Ithaca, 1980). Lawrence Stone, *The Family, Sex and Marriage In England, 1500–1800* (New York, 1977), pp. 85–480; and Gordon J. Schochet, *Patriarchalism in Political Thought: The Authoritarian Family and Political Speculation and Attitudes Especially in Seventeenth-Century England* (New York, 1975), offer suggestive accounts of the situation across the Atlantic.

4: *In Loco Parentis*

1. Herbert and Carol Schneider, eds., *Samuel Johnson: His Career and Writings,* 4 vols. (New York, 1929), 4: 278–80; Franklin Bowditch Dexter, *Biographical Sketches of the Graduates of Yale College, with Annals of the College History, 1701–1815,* 6 vols. (New York, 1885–1912), 2: 4;

Reuben Aldridge Guild, *Early History of Brown University Including the Life, Times, and Correspondence of President Manning, 1756–1791* (Providence, 1897), pp. 274, 357; Walter C. Bronson, *The History of Brown University, 1764–1914* (Providence, 1914), pp. 111–12; Franklin B. Dexter, ed., *The Literary Diary of Ezra Stiles,* 3 vols. (New York, 1901), 1: 161–62.

2. Anson Phelps Stokes, *Memorials of Eminent Yale Men: A Biographical Study of Student Life and University Influences during the Eighteenth and Nineteenth Centuries,* 2 vols. (New Haven, 1914), 2: 189–90.

3. Ibid., p. 247.

4. Ibid., pp. 190, 192.

5. Dexter, *Biographical Sketches with Annals,* 1: 351; 2: 4; John Maclean, *History of the College of New Jersey, From Its Origin in 1746 to the Commencement of 1854,* 2 vols. (Philadelphia, 1877), 1: 133; Guild, *Early History of Brown,* pp. 28, 264; Schneider and Schneider, eds., *Samuel Johnson,* 4: 225, 237; Trustees Minutes, University of Pennsylvania, 25 February 1788, 3: 241; and "Rules for the Good Government & Discipline of the Students & Schools in the University of Pennsylvania" (1791), both in the University of Pennsylvania Archives. On student life and the collegiate community, see Alexander Cowie, "Educational Problems at Yale College in the Eighteenth Century," Tercentenary Commission of the State of Connecticut *Publications* 55 (1936); Franklin B. Dexter, "Student Life at Yale in the Early Days of Connecticut Hall" (1908), and "Student Life at Yale College Under the First President Dwight" (1918), both reprinted in Dexter, *A Selection from the Miscellaneous Historical Papers of Fifty Years* (New Haven, 1918), pp. 266–73, 382–94; Louis Leonard Tucker, *Puritan Protagonist: President Thomas Clap of Yale College* (Chapel Hill, 1962), pp. 232–62; Edmund S. Morgan, *The Gentle Puritan: A Life of Ezra Stiles, 1727–1795* (New Haven, 1962), pp. 96–100, 360–75; David C. Humphrey, *From King's College to Columbia, 1746–1800* (New York, 1976), pp. 184–207.

6. Stokes, *Memorials of Eminent Yale Men,* 1: 215–16; Bronson, *History of Brown,* app. B, "Supplement to the Laws," p. 518.

7. Stokes, *Memorials of Eminent Yale Men,* 2: 190, 192; 1: 215–16; Guild, *Early History of Brown,* pp. 30, 31, 267; Wheeler quoted in Morgan, *Gentle Puritan,* p. 368. Dartmouth College laws required the removal of the hat at a distance of four rods (a rod equals five and a half yards) from a professor, and six rods from the president; see Frederick Chase, *A History of Dartmouth College and the Town of Hanover, New Hampshire,* ed. John K. Lord (Cambridge, Mass., 1891), p. 569; see also Richard P. McCormick, *Rutgers: A Bicentennial History* (New Brunswick, N.J., 1966), p. 20.

8. Stokes, *Memorials of Eminent Yale Men,* 1: 215; Bronson, *History of Brown,* "Supplement to the Laws," p. 519; Guild, *Early History of Brown,* p. 272; David McClure, *Diary of David McClure, Doctor of Divinity, 1748–1820,* ed. Franklin B. Dexter (New York, 1899), p. 9. Also, Chase, *History of Dartmouth,* p. 569.

9. Stokes, *Memorials of Eminent Yale Men,* 1: 215; Bronson, *History of Brown,* "Supplement to the Laws," p. 519.

10. Stokes, *Memorials of Eminent Yale Men,* 2: 16.

11. "Judgments and Acts of the President and Tutors," 18 June 1756, in ibid., 2: 165; Beecher quote, ibid., 1: 52.

12. Morgan, *Gentle Puritan,* pp. 369–70.

13. Guild, *Early History of Brown,* pp. 30, 270; Stokes, *Memorials of Eminent Yale Men,* 2: 190; 1: 214.

14. Dexter, *Biographical Sketches with Annals,* 2: 19; Stokes, *Memorials of Eminent Yale Men,* 1: 216.

15. Erving Goffman, *Relations in Public: Microstudies of the Public Order* (New York, 1971), pp. 29–32, 252–56; on "normal appearances" see pp. 238–333.

16. Stokes, *Memorials of Eminent Yale Men,* 1: 215; 2: 159; Bronson, *History of Brown,* p. 116; Dexter, *Biographical Sketches with Annals,* 2: 5.

17. Stokes, *Memorials of Eminent Yale Men,* 1: 216; Dexter, ed., *Diary of Stiles,* 2: 513–15. Cf. Norman H. Dawes, "Titles as Symbols of Prestige in Seventeenth Century New England," *William and Mary Quarterly,* 3rd ser., 6 (1949): 69–83.

18. Morgan, *Gentle Puritan,* p. 372; Dexter, ed., *Diary of Stiles,* 3: 135, 238, 365; Stokes, *Memorials of Eminent Yale Men,* 2: 16; Yale Corporation Records, 10 September 1760, ibid., 2: 165.

19. "Proceedings of the Trustees," 14, 15 September 1737, in Franklin B. Dexter, ed., *Documentary History of Yale University, 1701–1745* (1916; New York, 1969), p. 325; Yale Corporation Records, Stokes, *Memorials of Eminent Yale Men,* 2: 298. Also, William L. Kingsley, ed., *Yale College: A Sketch of Its History, with Notices of Its Several Departments, Instructors, and Benefactors Together with Some Account of Student Life and Amusements,* 2 vols. (New York, 1879), 1: 370.

20. "Proceedings of the Trustees," 8 September 1731, in Dexter, ed., *Documentary History of Yale,* p. 290; Yale Corporation Records, 10 September 1755, in Stokes, *Memorials of Eminent Yale Men,* 2: 165; Dexter, *Biographical Sketches with Annals,* 2: 15.

21. Dexter, *Biographical Sketches with Annals,* 2: 636–37; Tucker, *Puritan Protagonist,* pp. 248–50.

22. Walter Bradley to Henry P. Dering, September 1781, in Morgan, *Gentle Puritan,* p. 372.

23. Dexter, ed., *Diary of Stiles,* 1: 299; 3: 32, 130. Cf. Robert J. Dinkin, "Seating the Meeting House in Early Massachusetts," *New England Quarterly* 43 (1970): 450–64.

24. "Judgments and Acts of the President and Tutors," 21 January 1752, Stokes, *Memorials of Eminent Yale Men,* 1: 301–3. Compare the discussion that follows with Keith Thomas, *Rule and Misrule in the Schools of Early Modern England* (Stenton Lecture, University of Reading, 1976).

25. Stokes, *Memorials of Eminent Yale Men,* pp. 301–3.

26. Guild, *Early History of Brown,* pp. 30–31, 267, 357; Dexter, *Biographical Sketches with Annals,* 2: 4–5. Also, Maclean, *History of the College of New Jersey,* 1: 266; Kingsley, ed., *Yale College,* 1: 66.
27. Schneider and Schneider, eds., *Samuel Johnson,* 4: 226–29, 240.
28. Tucker, *Puritan Protagonist,* pp. 252, 253; Stokes, *Memorials of Eminent Yale Men,* 2: 173; 1: 37–38; Dexter, ed., *Diary of Stiles,* 3: 232; "Proceedings of the Trustees," 9 September 1741, in Dexter, ed., *Documentary History of Yale,* p. 351.
29. M. Halsey Thomas, ed., "The Black Book of King's College," *Columbia University Quarterly* 23 (1931): 4–5.
30. Yale Corporation Records, 10 September 1755, and 10 September 1760, in Stokes, *Memorials of Eminent Yale Men,* 2: 165; "Proceedings of the Trustees," 11 September 1734, in Dexter, ed., *Documentary History of Yale,* p. 309.
31. Dexter, *Biographical Sketches with Annals,* 2: 8; Stokes, *Memorials of Eminent Yale Men,* 1: 302.
32. Tucker, *Puritan Protagonist,* p. 238; Morgan, *Gentle Puritan,* p. 97; Dexter, *Biographical Sketches with Annals,* 5: 130–31; Dexter, ed., *Diary of Stiles,* 12 December 1793–18 March 1795, 3: 512, 514–15, 524, 555, 560.
33. Thompson's address is reprinted in Guild, *Early History of Brown,* pp. 99–107; quotation on p. 106; Stokes, *Memorials of Eminent Yale Men,* 2: 174.
34. Guild, *Early History of Brown,* p. 269; Dexter, *Biographical Sketches with Annals,* p. 8; Schneider and Schneider, eds., *Samuel Johnson,* 4: 240. At Queen's College, the student was charged for repairs to such broken doors; see McCormick, *Rutgers,* p. 20.
35. Dexter, *Biographical Sketches with Annals,* 2: 9.
36. Eliphalet Pearson to Edward Holyoke, 28 April 1789, in James McLachlan, "The *Choice of Hercules:* American Student Societies in the Early Nineteenth Century," Lawrence Stone, ed., *The University in Society,* 2 vols. (Princeton, 1974), 2: 464; Dexter, *Biographical Sketches with Annals,* 2: 16, 10; also, 2: 723–24; Bronson, *History of Brown,* "Supplement to the Laws," p. 518.
37. Maclean, *History of the College of New Jersey,* 1: 266.
38. Bronson, *History of Brown,* "Supplement to the Laws," p. 518; Dexter, ed., *Diary of Stiles,* 3: 12–13; Maxcy quoted in Guild, *Early History of Brown,* p. 359. Also, [Samuel Blair], *An Account of the College of New Jersey* (Woodbridge, N.J., 1764), p. 19.
39. Alexander Graydon, *Memoirs of His Own Time, with Reminiscences of the Men and Events of the Revolution,* ed. John S. Littell (Philadelphia, 1846), pp. 24–25; Joseph Jackson, "A Philadelphia Schoolmaster of the Eighteenth Century," *Pennsylvania Magazine of History and Biography* 35 (1911): 315–32. For other accounts, see Graydon, *Memoirs,* pp. 35–37; Walter Herbert Small, *Early New England Schools* (1914; New York,

1969), pp. 384–96; "Memoirs of a Senator from Pennsylvania: Jonathan Roberts, 1771–1854," ed. Philip S. Klein, *Pennsylvania Magazine of History and Biography* 62 (1938): 69, 70, 71; Warren Burton, *The District School As It Was, by One Who Went to It* (1833; Boston, 1850), pp. 63–68.

40. George W. Corner, ed., *The Autobiography of Benjamin Rush: His "Travels Through Life" together with his Commonplace Book for 1789–1813* (Princeton, 1948), pp. 29–31.

41. Benjamin Rush, "The Amusements and Punishments Which Are Proper for Schools," in Dagobert D. Runes, ed., *The Selected Writings of Benjamin Rush* (New York, 1947), pp. 109–12, 114–15; Rush, "Influence of Physical Causes upon the Moral Faculty," ibid., p. 205; Rush, "An Enquiry into the Effects of Public Punishments upon Criminals, and upon Society," in *Essays, Literary, Moral and Philosophical* (Philadelphia, 1798), p. 138.

42. According to Lawrence A. Cremin, *American Education: The Colonial Experience, 1607–1783* (New York, 1970), p. 510, Yale "served as the institutional model for the College of New Jersey, King's College, and the College of Rhode Island."

43. Dexter, *Biographical Sketches with Annals*, 2: 6–9.

44. [Blair], *Account of the College of New Jersey*, p. 21; Guild, *Early History of Brown*, pp. 270–71.

45. Stokes, *Memorials of Eminent Yale Men*, 1: 216; Dexter, *Biographical Sketches with Annals*, 2: 15; Guild, *Early History of Brown*, p. 268.

46. Guild, *Early History of Brown*, pp. 113–14.

47. Dexter, *Biographical Sketches with Annals*, 2: 9; [Blair], *Account of the College of New Jersey*, p. 21; Dexter, ed., *Diary of Stiles*, 3: 227.

48. [Blair], *Account of the College of New Jersey*, p. 21; Proceedings of the Trustees, 10 September 1729, and 9 September 1730, in Dexter, ed., *Documentary History of Yale*, pp. 281–82, 286.

49. Extracts of Ebenezer Baldwin's student diary are printed in Kingsley, ed., *Yale College*, 1: 445–46.

50. Morgan, *Gentle Puritan*, p. 100.

51. "Rules for the Good Government & Discipline of the Students," University of Pennsylvania Archives; Dexter, *Biographical Sketches with Annals*, 2: 16.

52. Dexter, ed., *Diary of Stiles*, 3: 36–37.

53. "Rules for the Good Government & Discipline of the Students," University Archives; Trustees Minutes, 25 February 1788, 3: 251, University Archives. The nature and impact of the demographic and intellectual changes have been described in David F. Allmendinger, Jr., *Paupers and Scholars: The Transformation of Student Life in Nineteenth-Century New England* (New York, 1975), and Allmendinger, "New England Students and the Revolution in Higher Education, 1800–1900," *History of Education Quarterly* 11 (1971): 381–89; McLachlan, "*Choice of Hercules*: American Student Societies in the Early Nineteenth Century," pp. 449–94; Humphrey, *From King's College to Columbia*, pp. 267–313; Steven J. Novak, *The Rights of Youth: American Colleges and Student Revolt,*

1798–1815 (Cambridge, Mass., 1977); Howard Peckham, "Collegia Ante Bellum: Attitudes of College Professors and Students toward the American Revolution," *Pennsylvania Magazine of History and Biography* 95 (1971): 50–72.

5: Revolution: The Alienation of Affection

1. Richard Eburne, *A Plain Pathway to Plantations* (1624), ed. Louis B. Wright (New York, 1962), pp. xxvi, 122; Francis Bacon, "Of Plantations" (1625), in Jack P. Greene, ed., *Settlements to Society, 1584–1763* (New York, 1966), pp. 9–11; [John White], *The Planters Plea. Or the Grounds of Plantations* (London, 1630), in Peter Force, ed., *Tracts and Other Papers Relating Principally to the Origin, Settlement, and Progress of the Colonies in North America*, 4 vols. (Washington, D.C., 1836–46), 2: no. 3.

2. [Robert Beverley], *An Essay upon the Government of the English Plantations on the Continent of America* (London, 1701), ed. Louis B. Wright (San Marino, Ca., 1945), p. 16; [Edward Littleton], *The Groans of the Plantations* (London, 1689), in Jack P. Greene, ed., *Great Britain and the American Colonies, 1606–1763* (Columbia, S.C., 1970), pp. 97–112. For discussions pertaining to the conceptual apparatus involved here, see Michael Walzer, "On the Role of Symbolism in Political Thought," *Political Science Quarterly* 82 (1967): 191–204; Thomas S. Kuhn, *The Structure of Scientific Revolutions* (Chicago, 1970), pp. 43–51; Fred Weinstein and Gerald Platt, *The Wish to Be Free: Society, Psyche, and Value Change* (Berkeley and Los Angeles, 1969), pp. 7–38; and Weinstein and Platt, *Psychoanalytic Sociology: An Essay on the Interpretation of Historical Data and the Phenomena of Collective Behavior* (Baltimore, 1973), pp. 91–112.

3. [Littleton], *Groans of the Plantations*, pp. 97–112.

4. Edwin G. Burrows and Michael Wallace, "The American Revolution: The Ideology and Psychology of National Liberation," *Perspectives in American History* 6 (1972): 167–306, provide the best analysis of the political significance of the parent-child metaphor in the Independence movement. See also J. M. Bumsted, " 'Things in the Womb of Time': Ideas of American Independence, 1633 to 1763," *William and Mary Quarterly*, 3rd ser., 31 (1974): 533–64; Jack P. Greene, "An Uneasy Connection: An Analysis of the Preconditions of the American Revolution," in Stephen G. Kurtz and James H. Hutson, eds., *Essays on the American Revolution* (Chapel Hill, 1973), pp. 32–80; Robert M. Weir, "Rebelliousness: Personality Development and the American Revolution in the Southern Colonies," in Jeffrey J. Crow and Larry E. Tise, eds., *The Southern Experience in the American Revolution* (Chapel Hill, 1978), pp. 25–54; Kenneth S. Lynn, *A Divided People* (Westport, Conn., 1977). On the "country" ideology, see J.G.A. Pocock, "Machiavelli, Harrington, and English Political Ideologies in the Eighteenth Century," and "Civic Humanism and Its Role in Anglo-American Thought," both reprinted in *Politics, Language and Time:*

Essays on Political Thought and History (New York, 1971), pp. 80–147. Weinstein and Platt, *Wish to Be Free,* pp. 30–31, employ the concept of desacralization to describe the process by which allegiances are repudiated. Greene, "Preconditions for American Republicanism," in *The Development of a Revolutionary Mentality* (Washington, D.C., 1972), pp. 119–23, applies this idea to the colonial crisis.

5. [Joseph Reed], *Four Dissertations on the Reciprocal Advantages of a Perpetual Union Between Great-Britain and Her American Colonies* (Philadelphia, 1766), diss. 3, p. 98. John Morgan, Stephen Watts, and Francis Hopkinson composed the first, second, and fourth essays.

6. Isaac Hunt, *The Political Family: Or a Discourse, Pointing Out the Reciprocal Advantages, Which Flow from an Uninterrupted Union between Great-Britain and Her American Colonies* (Philadelphia, 1775), p. 29; Richard Bland, *An Inquiry into the Rights of the British Colonies* (Williamsburg, 1766), p. 13; [Oxenbridge Thacher], *The Sentiments of a British American* (Boston, 1764), in Bernard Bailyn, ed., *Pamphlets of the American Revolution* (Cambridge, Mass., 1965), pp. 497–98; Reed, *Four Dissertations,* p. 103.

7. [Henry Barry], *The Advantages Which America Derives from Her Commerce, Connexion and Dependence on Britain* (Boston, 1775), p. 8; Hunt, *Political Family,* p. 15; [Reed], *Four Dissertations,* p. 100; [James Otis], *A Vindication of the British Colonies, Against the Aspirations of the Halifax Gentlemen* (Boston, 1765), in Bailyn, ed., *Pamphlets,* p. 565; Varnum commencement address reprinted in Reuben A. Guild, "First Commencement of Rhode Island College," *Collections of the Rhode Island Historical Society* 7 (1885): 287.

8. [Reed], *Four Dissertations,* p. 99; Hunt, *Political Family,* p. 13; [Barry], *Advantages Which America Derives,* p. 4.

9. Abigail Adams (cited hereafter as AA) to Isaac Smith, Jr., 20 April 1771, in L. H. Butterfield, ed., *Adams Family Correspondence,* 4 vols. (Cambridge, Mass., 1963–1973), 1: p. 76.

10. AA to Catharine Sawbridge Macaulay [1774], ibid., pp. 178–79.

11. AA to Edward Dilly, 22 May 17[75], ibid., pp. 200–201.

12. AA to Mercy Otis Warren, 5 December 1773, ibid., p. 88; AA to Macaulay [1774], ibid., p. 177; AA to Mercy Otis Warren [February 1775], ibid., p. 183; Mercy Otis Warren to AA, 28 January 1775, ibid., p. 181; AA to John Adams, 12 November 1775, ibid., p. 324. See also AA to John Adams, 19 August and 2 September 1774, ibid., pp. 142, 147; AA to Mercy Otis Warren, 2 May 1775, ibid., p. 190.

13. [John Dickinson], *The Late Regulations Respecting the British Colonies on the Continent of America Considered* (Philadelphia, 1765), in Bailyn, ed., *Pamphlets* pp. 688–90; [Martin Howard], *A Defense of the Letter from a Gentleman at Halifax* (Newport, 1765), p. 4. For an extended treatment of the filial implications of the imperial crisis, see Burrows and Wallace, "American Revolution," pp. 190–225.

14. Jonathan Mayhew, *The Snare Broken. A Thanksgiving-Discourse* (Boston, 1766), p. 28; John Joachim Zubly, *The Stamp Act Repealed* (Savannah, 1766), pp. 23, 25; Benjamin Throop, *A Thanksgiving Sermon, Upon . . . the Repeal of the Stamp Act* (New London, Conn., 1766), p. 15.

15. [Richard Wells], *A Few Political Reflections Submitted . . . by a Citizen of Philadelphia* (Philadelphia, 1774), p. 10.

16. George Mason to the Committee of London Merchants, 6 June 1766, in Edmund S. Morgan, ed., *Prologue to Revolution: Sources and Documents on the Stamp Act Crisis, 1764–1766* (Chapel Hill, 1959), pp. 158–59; [Silas Downer], *A Discourse Delivered in Providence* (Providence, 1768), p. 11.

17. In addition to the Pocock articles cited in note 4, above, see Bernard Bailyn, *The Ideological Origins of the American Revolution* (Cambridge, Mass., 1967); Gordon S. Wood, *The Creation of the American Republic, 1776–1787* (Chapel Hill, 1969); Isaac Kramnick, *Bolingbroke and His Circle: The Politics of Nostalgia in the Age of Walpole* (Cambridge, Mass., 1968); Caroline Robbins, *The Eighteenth-Century Commonwealthman: Studies in the Transmission, Development, and Circumstance of English Liberal Thought from the Restoration of Charles II until the War with the Thirteen Colonies* (Cambridge, Mass., 1959).

18. John Carmichael, *A Self-Defensive War Lawful, Proved in a Sermon* (Lancaster, 1775), pp. 24–25; [Anon.], *Some Observations of Consequences . . . Occasioned by the Stamp-Tax, Lately Imposed on the British Colonies* (Philadelphia, 1768), pp. 11, 44, 48; Samuel Langdon, *Government Corrupted By Vice, and Recovered By Righteousness* (Watertown, 1775), p. 19; Stephen Hopkins, *The Rights of Colonies Examined* (Providence, 1765), in Bailyn, ed., *Pamphlets,* p. 512.

19. [Anon.], *Some Observations of Consequence,* p. 46; Mayhew, *Snare Broken,* p. 25; John Morgan, *Four Dissertations,* diss. 1, pp. 25–26; Maurice Moore, *The Justice and Polity of Taxing the American Colonies, In Great-Britain, Considered* (Wilmington, 1765), p. 16.

20. [Anon.], *Some Observations of Consequence,* p. 66; Stephen Watts, *Four Dissertations,* diss. 2, pp. 52–53; Nicholas Ray, *The Importance of the Colonies of North America, and the Interest of Great Britain with Regard to Them* (New York, 1766), p. 6. Also, Jacob Duché, *The American Vine, A Sermon, Preached . . . before the Honourable Continental Congress* (Philadelphia, 1775), p. 16ff.

21. Hunt, *Political Family,* p. 30; Alexander Graydon, *Memoirs of His Own Time, with Reminiscences of the Men and Events of the Revolution,* ed. John S. Littell (Philadelphia, 1846), p. 116; Greene, "An Uneasy Connection," pp. 35–45; Pauline Maier, "The Beginnings of American Republicanism, 1765–1776," in *Development of a Revolutionary Mentality,* pp. 108–13; Wells, *A Few Political Reflections,* pp. 33–34.

22. Jack P. Greene, "Search for Identity: An Interpretation of the Meaning of Selected Patterns of Social Response in Eighteenth-Century America," *Journal of Social History* 3 (1970): 189–220; and William D. Liddle, "A

Patriot King, or None: American Public Attitudes Towards George III and the British Monarchy, 1754–1776" (Ph.D. diss., Claremont Graduate School, 1970), pp. 404–5, both use the term *catharsis* to describe the Revolutionaries' rejection of previously cherished social models. William Hull, *An Oration Delivered to the . . . Cincinnati . . . July 4, 1788* (Boston, 1788), pp. 8–9; Thomas Paine, "The Crisis III," in Philip S. Foner, ed., *The Complete Writings of Thomas Paine,* 2 vols. (New York, 1945), 1: 78–79; Joseph Buckminster, *A Discourse Delivered . . . After the Ratification of a Treaty of Peace* (Portsmouth, 1784), p. 7. David Ramsay, *The History of the American Revolution,* 2 vols. (London, 1793), 1: 345.

23. Jefferson, "Autobiography," in Paul Leicester Ford, ed., *The Writings of Thomas Jefferson,* 10 vols. (New York, 1892–1899), 1: 5; John Brooks, *An Oration, Delivered to the Society of the Cincinnati . . . July 4th, 1787* (Boston, 1787), p. 4; James Campbell, *An Oration, in Commemoration of . . . Independence* (Philadelphia, 1787), p. 12; David Daggett, *An Oration, Pronounced . . . in the City of New-Haven . . . It Being the Eleventh Anniversary of Independence* (New Haven, 1787), p. 8; Benjamin Rush, "On the Influence of Physical Causes in Promoting an Increase of the Strength and Activity of the Intellectual Faculties of Man," in *Sixteen Introductory Lectures, to Courses of Lectures upon the Institutes and Practice of Medicine* (Philadelphia, 1811), p. 110.

24. David Ramsay, *An Oration on the Advantages of American Independence,* in Robert L. Brunhouse, ed., *David Ramsay, 1749–1815: Selections from His Writings,* American Philosophical Society *Transactions* 55 (1965): 183–90; Ramsay, *The History of the American Revolution* 2: 315–18.

25. Rush to Mrs. Rush, 29 May 1776, in L. H. Butterfield, ed., *Letters of Benjamin Rush,* 2 vols. (Princeton, 1951), 1: 99; William King Atkinson, *An Oration: Delivered at Dover, New-Hampshire* (Dover, 1791), pp. 4, 16; Charles Backus, *A Sermon, Preached in Long-Meadow, at the Publick Fast* (Springfield, Mass., 1788), p. 7. Joseph J. Ellis, *After the Revolution: Profiles of Early American Culture* (New York, 1979), provides an excellent examination of the optimistic projections of the Revolutionaries.

26. Ramsay to Rush, 14 February 1776, and 6 August 1776, in Brunhouse, ed., *Ramsay Selections,* pp. 53–54; L. H. Butterfield, ed., "Dr. Rush to Governor Henry on the Declaration of Independence and the Virginia Constitution," American Philosophical Society *Proceedings* 95 (1951): 250–53; John Rodgers, *The Divine Goodness Displayed in the American Revolution* (New York, 1784), p. 32; John Lathrop, *A Discourse on the Peace; Preached on the Day of Public Thanksgiving* (Boston, 1784), pp. 5–6; George Duffield, *A Sermon Preached . . . on . . . December 11, 1783* (Philadelphia, 1784), p. 1.

27. W. Paul Adams, "Republicanism in Political Rhetoric Before 1776," *Political Science Quarterly* 85 (1970): 397–421, discusses the problems of eighteenth-century republicanism. See also Maier, "The Beginnings of American Republicanism," pp. 99–117; Greene, "Preconditions for Amer-

ican Republicanism" pp. 119–23; Cecelia M. Kenyon, "Republicanism and Radicalism in the American Revolution: An Old-Fashioned Interpretation," *William and Mary Quarterly,* 3rd ser., 19 (1962): 153–82. Jean-Jacques Rousseau, *The Social Contract or Principles of Political Right,* ed. and trans. Maurice Cranston (Baltimore, 1968), bk. 3, chap. 4, p. 113; for Rousseau's description of the democratic republic, bk. 2, chap. 6, and bk. 3, chap. 4, pp. 112–14. Robert Shackleton, *Montesquieu: A Critical Biography* (Oxford, 1961), pp. 272–77, argues quite convincingly that the discussion of the republic in the *Spirit of the Laws* was Montesquieu's excursion into idealism. For Montesquieu, republican systems were "unsatisfactory anachronisms" that "flourished in a former age when men were greater, bolder, and better." Thus, Shackleton contends, although the republic was an admirable form of government, "at no point . . . does Montesquieu offer the slightest suggestion that it has any relevance to eighteenth-century Europe."

28. David Tappan, *A Discourse, Delivered to the Religious Society in Brattle-Street, Boston* (Boston, 1798), pp. 18–19; Rush to John Adams, 21 July 1789, in Butterfield, ed., *Letters of Rush,* 1: 522–23. Also, Joseph Lathrop, *National Happiness, Illustrated in a Sermon, Delivered . . . February 19, 1795* (Springfield, Mass., 1795), p. 7; Thomas Barnard, *A Sermon, Delivered on the Day of National Thanksgiving, February 19, 1795* (Salem, 1795), pp. 21–23.

29. Backus, *A Sermon,* p. 9; Rush to Charles Nisbet, 5 December 1783; Rush to John Howard, 14 October 1789, in Butterfield, ed., *Letters of Rush,* 1: 315–16, 528; Rush to William Peterkin, 27 November 1784, in Butterfield, ed., "Further Letters of Benjamin Rush," *Pennsylvania Magazine of History and Biography* 78 (1954): 26, 27; Rush to Adams, 2 July 1788, in Butterfield, ed., *Letters of Rush,* 1: 468.

30. [David Tappan], *An Address to the Students of Philips' Academy in Andover* (Andover, 1791), p. 4; Rush to John Adams, 2 July 1788, in Butterfield, ed., *Letters of Rush,* 1: 469; Rush to Richard Price, 14 February 1787, in Butterfield, ed., "Further Letters," p. 28; Rush, *A Plan for the Establishment of Public Schools and the Diffusion of Knowledge in Pennsylvania; to Which Are Added, Thoughts upon the Mode of Education, Proper in a Republic* (Philadelphia, 1786), in Frederick Rudolph, ed., *Essays on Education in the Early Republic* (Cambridge, Mass., 1965), p. 23.

31. Charles Nisbet, *An Address to the Students of Dickinson College* (Carlisle, 1786), p. 6; David McClure, *An Oration on the Advantages of an Early Education, Delivered at . . . the Opening of the Philips Exeter Academy* (Exeter, N.H. 1783), p. 13; Simeon Doggett, *A Discourse on Education* (New Bedford, 1797), in Rudolph, ed., *Essays on Education in the Early Republic,* p. 158.

32. Enos Hitchcock, *A Discourse on the Causes of National Prosperity, Illustrated by Ancient and Modern History* (Providence, 1786), p. 23; Alexander Contee Hanson, *Political Schemes and Calculations* (Annapolis,

1784), p. 38; [Alexander Hamilton], *A Second Letter from Phocion to the Considerate Citizens of New-York* (New York, 1784), p. 41; Rush to John Howard, 14 October 1789, in Butterfield, ed., *Letters of Rush*, 1: 528.

33. Doggett, *Discourse on Education,* pp. 157–58; Jeremy Belknap, *An Election Sermon, Preached Before the General Court of New Hampshire* (Portsmouth, 1785), p. 22.

34. "An Essay on Education," *Columbian Magazine* (May 1789): 296; Barnard, *Sermon, Delivered on the Day of National Thanksgiving,* pp. 22–23; "Y.Z.," *Columbian Magazine* (September 1786).

35. See, for example, Harrison Gray Otis, *An Oration Delivered July 4, 1788* (Boston, 1788); Enos Hitchcock, *Discourse on the Causes of National Prosperity,* and Hitchcock, *An Oration, In Commemoration of the Independence of the United States* ([Providence], 1793); David Osgood, *Reflections on the Goodness of God . . . A Sermon Preached on the Day of Annual and National Thanksgiving* (Boston, 1784); Lathrop, *Discourse on the Peace;* John Marsh, *A Discourse Delivered at Wethersfield* (Hartford, 1784); [Timothy Dwight], *A Valedictory Address to the Young Gentlemen, Who Commenced Bachelor of Arts, at Yale-College* (New Haven, 1776); William Linn, *The Blessings of America, A Sermon, Preached . . . on the Fourth of July, 1791* (New York, 1791).

36. Rodgers, *Divine Goodness Displayed in the American Revolution,* p. 5.

37. Samuel Stillman, *An Oration, Delivered . . . at Boston, in Celebration of the Anniversary of American Independence* (Boston, 1789), pp. 29–30; Ramsay, *Oration on the Advantages of American Independence,* p. 190; McClure, *Advantages of Early Education,* p. 16; John Trumbull, *An Elegy of the Times,* p. 12; [Dwight], *Valedictory Address,* pp. 13–14; see also M. W. [Matthew Wilson], "On a Liberal Education," *Columbian Magazine* (February 1787); and "The Former, Present, and Future Prospects of America," *Columbian Magazine* (October 1787).

38. [Dwight], *Valedictory Address,* pp. 12–13; Backus, *Sermon Preached in Long-Meadow,* p. 12.

39. William Pierce, *An Oration Delivered at Christ Church, Savannah . . . In Commemoration of the Anniversary of American Independence* (Savannah, 1788), pp. 5–7; Joel Barlow, *An Oration Delivered . . . at the Meeting of the Cincinnati, July 4, 1787* (Hartford, 1787), p. 4; Noah Webster, *Sketches of American Policy,* ed. Harry R. Warfel (1785; New York, 1937), p. 23; also, Atkinson, *Oration Delivered at Dover,* pp. 20–21; Jonathan Jackson, *Thoughts upon the Political Situation of the United States of America* (Worcester, 1788), pp. 12–13; Ezra Stiles, *The United States Elevated to Glory and Honor* (New Haven, 1783), p. 15.

40. Osgood, *Reflections on the Goodness of God,* p. 31; Ramsay, *Oration on the Advantages of American Independence,* p. 189; Webster, *Sketches of American Policy,* p. 11; "Demophilus," *Pennsylvania Packet* (12 February 1776).

41. "The Former, Present, and Future Prospects of America," p. 84; Edward Bangs, *An Oration, Delivered at Worcester, on the Fourth of July, 1791*

(Worcester, 1791), p. 10; [Jackson], *Thoughts upon the Political Situation,* p. 19.

42. Webster, *Sketches of American Policy,* p. 24; Zabdiel Adams, *The Evil Designs of Men Made Subservient by God to the Public Good* (Boston, 1783), p. 25; [Anon.], *The Political Establishments of the United States . . . A Candid Review* (Philadelphia, 1784), p. 4; Buckminster, *Discourse . . . After the Ratification of a Treaty of Peace,* pp. 23–24; Josiah Bridge, *A Sermon Preached . . . Massachusetts, May 27, 1789. Being the Day of General Election* (Boston, 1789), p. 51; John Murray, *Jerubaal, or Tyranny's Grove Destroyed, and the Altar of Liberty Finished. A Discourse on America's Duty and Danger* (Newburyport, 1784), p. 55.

43. Buckminster, *Discourse . . . After the Ratification of a Treaty of Peace,* pp. 20, 23; [Anon.], *Rudiments of Law and Government, Deduced from the Law of Nature* (Charleston, 1783), p. v; Marsh, *Discourse Delivered at Wethersfield,* p. 19; Rodgers, *Divine Goodness Displayed in the American Revolution,* pp. 10–11, 37; Stillman, *Oration Delivered at Boston in Celebration of American Independence,* p. 28; William Jones, *An Oration, Pronounced at Concord, July 4th, 1794* (Concord, 1794), p. 16.

44. Samuel Wales, *The Dangers of Our National Prosperity; and the Way to Avoid Them* (Hartford, 1785), pp. 7, 16–29.

45. Rodgers, *Divine Goodness Displayed in the American Revolution,* pp. 37, 41; Silas Deane, *An Address to the Free and Independent Citizens of the United States* (Hartford, 1784), pp. 21–22; John Adams, *Defence of the Constitutions,* in Charles Francis Adams, ed., *The Works of John Adams,* 10 vols. (Boston, 1850–56), 4: 290; Robert R. Livingston, *An Oration Delivered Before the . . . Cincinnati of the State of New-York* (New York, 1787), p. 4; Jonathan Loring Austin, *An Oration Delivered . . . In Celebration of the Anniversary of American Independence* (Boston, [1786]), p. 17; David Tappan, *A Discourse Delivered at the Third Parish in Newbury . . . Occasioned by the Ratification of a Treaty of Peace* (Salem, 1783), p. 17.

46. Atkinson, *Oration Delivered at Dover,* p. 16; [Aedanus Burke], *Considerations on the Order of Cincinnati . . . with Remarks on its Consequences to the Freedom and Happiness of the Republick* (Charleston, 1783), p. 14; [John Taylor], *An Enquiry into the Principles and Tendency of Certain Public Measures* (Philadelphia, 1794), p. 49.

47. Rodgers, *Divine Goodness Displayed in the American Revolution,* pp. 37–38; Livingston, *Oration Delivered Before the Cincinnati,* pp. 12–13; Levi Hart, *The Description of a Good Character Attempted and Applied to the Subject of Jurisprudence and Civil Government* (Hartford, [1786]), p. 17; Elias Boudinot, *An Oration, Delivered at Elizabeth-Town, New Jersey . . . On The Fourth of July, 1793* (Elizabeth-Town, 1793), p. 13.

48. Backus, *Sermon Preached in Long-Meadow,* p. 8; Livingston, *Oration Delivered Before the Cincinnati,* p. 17.

49. Bridge, *Sermon Preached the Day of General Election,* p. 52; Hanson *Polit-*

ical Schemes and Calculations, p. v; Thomas Day, *An Oration on Party Spirit, Pronounced Before the Connecticut Society of Cincinnati* (Litchfield, 1798), p. 6.

50. Ramsay to John Eliot, August 1785; Ramsay to Rush, 6 August 1786, in Brunhouse, ed., *Ramsay Selections,* pp. 90, 105; Daggett, *Oration Pronounced in New-Haven,* p. 5.

51. Rush to John Coakley Lettsom, 8 April 1785, in Butterfield, ed., *Letters of Rush,* 1: 350; Ramsay, *History of the American Revolution,* 2: 324; Ramsay to Rush, 18 July 1779; Ramsay to Rush, 3 June 1779; Ramsay to Benjamin Lincoln, 13 August 1781, in Brunhouse, ed., *Ramsay Selections,* pp. 62, 60, 67.

52. Rush to Adams, 22 January 1778; Rush to Adams, 23 October 1780; Rush to Nathanael Greene, 15 April 1782, in Butterfield, ed., *Letters of Rush,* 1: 191, 255, 268.

53. L. H. Butterfield, ed., "Dr. Rush to Governor Henry," American Philosophical Society *Proceedings,* p. 251; Jones, *Oration Pronounced at Concord,* p. 6; John Gardiner, *An Oration . . . in Celebration of the Anniversary of American Independence* (Boston, 1785), p. 33; Pierce, *Oration Delivered at Christ Church,* pp. 8–9; "Thoughts on the Present Situation of the Federal Government of the United States of America," *Columbian Magazine* (December 1786): 173.

54. Rush to Adams, 22 January 1778, in Butterfield, ed., *Letters of Rush,* 1: 191; Daggett, *Oration Pronounced in New-Haven,* pp. 9, 13; Elbridge Gerry, *Observations on the New Constitution* (1788), in P. L. Ford, ed., *Pamphlets on the Constitution of the United States, Published during Its Discussion by the People, 1787–1788* (Brooklyn, 1888), p. 22. These statements, in context, contrast sharply with the "selective perception" of the loyalists; see Burrows and Wallace, "American Revolution," pp. 295–99.

55. Ramsay, *History of the American Revolution,* 2: 315, 324–25.

56. Brooks, *Oration Delivered to the Cincinnati,* p. 7; Joseph Lathrop, *A Sermon, Preached in . . . West-Springfield, December 14, 1786, Being the Day . . . for Publick Thanksgiving* (Springfield, Mass., 1787), p. 16.

57. Bangs, *Oration Delivered at Worcester,* p. 5; "Prospects of America," *Columbian Magazine* (October 1786): 86; Campbell, *Oration in Commemoration of Independence,* p. 18; David Rittenhouse, *An Oration, Delivered . . . Before the American Philosophical Society* (Philadelphia, 1775), p. 20. On the cyclical implications of societal growth, see also Tappan, *Discourse Delivered to the Religious Society in Brattle-Street;* Backus, *Sermon Preached in Long-Meadow;* Barnard, *Sermon Delivered on the Day of National Thanksgiving;* Samuel Stanhope Smith, *The Divine Goodness to the United States of America* (Philadelphia, 1795); and Samuel Williams, *A Discourse on the Love of Our Country* (Salem, 1775). Stow Persons, "The Cyclical Theory of History in Eighteenth-Century America," *American Quarterly* 6 (1954): 147–63, provides a good summary of this idea.

58. Daggett, *Oration Pronounced in New-Haven,* p. 15; Thomas Dawes, *An Oration Delivered July 4, 1787* (Boston, 1787), p. 16.

6: Depersonalization: The Law Is King

1. In addition to the items cited in note 49 of chapter three, above, the significant themes and trends of the literature on the family have been reviewed in James Henretta, "The Morphology of New England Society in the Colonial Period," *Journal of Interdisciplinary History* 2 (1971): 379–95; Robert V. Wells, "Family History and Demographic Transition," *Journal of Social History* 9 (1975): 1–20; Daniel Blake Smith, "The Study of the Family in Early America: Trends, Problems, Prospects," *William and Mary Quarterly,* 3rd ser., 39 (1982): 3–28. Jack P. Greene, "The Social Origins of the American Revolution: An Evaluation and An Interpretation," *Political Science Quarterly* 88 (1973): 1–22, examines the issues and arguments pertaining to social change and the development of political radicalism in eighteenth-century America. The most suggestive account of the possible links between the evolution of the family and the commitment to Revolutionary politics is in Philip J. Greven, Jr., *Four Generations: Population, Land, and Family in Colonial Andover, Massachusetts* (Ithaca, 1970), pp. 222–58, 279–82.

2. On the gap between ideals and reality, and its possible significance in Revolutionary America, see Jack P. Greene, "Search for Identity: An Interpretation of the Meaning of Selected Patterns of Social Response in Eighteenth-Century America," *Journal of Social History* 3 (1970): 189–220; and Greene, "An Uneasy Connection: An Analysis of the Preconditions of the American Revolution," in Stephen G. Kurtz and James H. Hutson, eds., *Essays on the American Revolution* (Chapel Hill, 1973), pp. 32–80; Bernard Bailyn, "Political Experience and Enlightenment Ideas in Eighteenth-Century America," *American Historical Review* 67 (1962): 339–51; Robert M. Weir, "Who Shall Rule at Home: The American Revolution as a Crisis of Legitimacy for the Colonial Elite," *Journal of Interdisciplinary History* 6 (1976): 679–700.

3. John Locke, *Two Treatises of Government,* ed. Peter Laslett (New York, 1963), pp. 345–61, 374–94; quotations on pp. 361, 380–81. For an elaboration of Locke's arguments on the family and the origins of the state, see Gordon J. Schochet, *Patriarchalism in Political Thought: The Authoritarian Family and Political Speculation and Attitudes Especially in Seventeenth-Century England* (New York, 1975), pp. 244–67.

4. Thomas Paine, *Common Sense,* in Philip S. Foner, ed., *The Complete Writings of Thomas Paine,* 2 vols. (New York, 1945), 1: 29. See also Winthrop D. Jordan, "Familial Politics: Thomas Paine and the Killing of the King, 1776," *Journal of American History* 60 (1973): 294–308.

5. R. R. Palmer, *The Age of the Democratic Revolution: A Political History of Europe and America, 1760–1800,* vol. 1, *The Challenge* (Princeton,

1959), pp. 213–35; Charles Howard McIlwain, *Constitutionalism: Ancient and Modern,* rev. ed. (Ithaca, 1947), pp. 1–22.

6. William Livingston, *The Independent Reflector,* ed. Milton M. Klein (Cambridge, Mass., 1963), no. 33, p. 288; Charles Francis Adams, ed., *The Works of John Adams,* 10 vols. (Boston, 1850–56), 4: 358, 440. On the development of the classical English constitution and the mixed government and separation of powers doctrines, see Corinne C. Weston, *English Constitutional Theory and the House of Lords, 1556–1832* (New York, 1965); Weston, "Beginnings of the Classical Theory of the English Constitution," American Philosophical Society *Proceedings* 100 (1956): 134–44; and Weston, "The Theory of Mixed Monarchy Under Charles I and After," *English Historical Review* 75 (1960): 426–43; M.J.C. Vile, *Constitutionalism and the Separation of Powers* (Oxford, 1967); W. B. Gwyn, *The Meaning of the Separation of Powers: An Analysis of the Doctrine from Its Origin to the Adoption of the United States Constitution* (New Orleans, 1965); Kurt von Fritz, *The Theory of the Mixed Constitution in Antiquity: A Critical Analysis of Polybius' Political Ideas* (New York, 1954). On the significance of the classical tradition in early America, see Richard Gummere, *The American Colonial Mind and the Classical Tradition: Essays in Comparative Culture* (Cambridge, Mass., 1963), and Gummere, "The Classical Ancestry of the United States Constitution," *American Quarterly* 14 (1962): 3–18; Gilbert Chinard, "Polybius and the American Constitution," *Journal of the History of Ideas* 1 (1940): 38–58; Zera S. Fink, *The Classical Republicans: An Essay in the Recovery of a Pattern of Thought in Seventeenth Century England* (Evanston, Ill., 1950).

7. Joseph Warren, *Oration Delivered at Boston, March 5, 1772;* and *Oration Delivered at Boston, March 5, 1775,* both in Hezekiah Niles, ed., *Principles and Acts of the Revolution in America* (New York, 1876), pp. 20–30; Ramsay to John Eliot, 17 July, 17 October 1782, 2 January 1783, in Robert L. Brunhouse, ed., *David Ramsay, 1749–1815: Selections from His Writings,* American Philosophical Society *Transactions* 55 (1965): 70, 72, 73. Gordon S. Wood, *The Creation of the American Republic, 1776–1787* (Chapel Hill, 1969), pp. 11–13; and Jack P. Greene, "Political Mimesis: A Consideration of the Historical and Cultural Roots of Legislative Behavior in the British Colonies in the Eighteenth Century," *American Historical Review* 75 (1969): 337–60, discuss the idealization of the English constitution in colonial America.

8. Livingston, *Independent Reflector,* p. 288; William Hooper to the Congress at Halifax, 26 October 1776, *The Colonial Records of North Carolina,* ed. William L. Saunders, 10 vols. (Raleigh, N.C., 1886–90), 10: 866; Allyn Mather, *The Character of a Well Accomplished Ruler Describ'd* (New Haven, 1776), p. 4; "Instructions of the Maryland Convention to their delegates in the Continental Congress, June 1776," in Peter Force, ed., *American Archives,* 6 vols. (Washington, D.C., 1837–46), 6: 1096–98.

9. The classical balance of the English constitution received its most systematic

analysis in the writings of Bolingbroke and Montesquieu; see Bolingbroke, *Remarks on the History of England,* Letter 7, in *The Works of Lord Bolingbroke,* 4 vols. (Philadelphia, 1941), 1: 332–33; *Dissertation on Parties,* Letters 9 and 13, ibid., 2: 85, 117–23; Isaac Kramnick, *Bolingbroke and His Circle: The Politics of Nostalgia in the Age of Walpole* (Cambridge, Mass., 1968), pp. 137–52; J. H. Burns, "Bolingbroke and the Concept of Constitutional Government," *Political Studies* 10 (1962): 264–76; Robert Shackleton, "Montesquieu, Bolingbroke, and the Separation of Powers," *French Studies* 3 (1949): 25–38; Shackleton, *Montesquieu: A Critical Biography* (Oxford, 1961), pp. 298–301; Gwyn, *Meaning of the Separation of Powers,* pp. 100–113; Vile, *Constitutionalism,* pp. 76–97; Henry J. Merry, *Montesquieu's System of Natural Government* (West Lafayette, Ind., 1970), pp. 338–80.

10. David Ramsay, *The History of the American Revolution,* 2 vols. (London, 1793), 1: 348–49.

11. Gwyn, *Meaning of the Separation of Powers,* pp. 40, 42, 131–33; Montesquieu, *The Spirit of the Laws,* ed. Franz Neumann, trans. Thomas Nugent (New York, 1949), bk. 11, chap. 6, p. 152; Francis D. Wormuth, *The Origins of Modern Constitutionalism* (New York, 1949), pp. 59–72. On the separation of powers doctrine and its theoretical independence from the social connotations of the theory of mixed government, see Gwyn, *Meaning of the Separation of Powers,* pp. 3–65; and Vile, *Constitutionalism,* pp. 21–52.

12. "Interest of America," in Force, ed., *American Archives* 6: 840–43; "To the People of North America on the Different Kinds of Government," ibid., 5: 180–83; General Sullivan to Meshech Weare, 11 December 1775, ibid., 4: 241–43. See also the proposed instructions of Mecklenburg and Orange counties to the Provincial Congress at Halifax, November 1776, *North Carolina Colonial Records,* 10: 239–42, 870a–870h; the returns of the towns of Greenwhich, Hardwick, and New Salem on the proposed 1778 Massachusetts constitution, in Oscar and Mary Handlin, eds., *The Popular Sources of Political Authority: Documents on the Massachusetts Constitution of 1780* (Cambridge, Mass., 1966), pp. 212–13, 215–16, 244; and "A Form of Government Proposed for the Consideration of the People of Anne Arundel County [Maryland]," 27 June 1776, in Force, ed., *American Archives,* 6: 1093–94.

13. Edward S. Corwin, "The Progress of Constitutional Theory between the Declaration of Independence and the Meeting of the Philadelphia Convention," *American Historical Review* 30 (1925): 512; "To the People of North America," in Force, ed., *American Archives* 5: 180–83; "Interest of America," ibid., 6: 840–43.

14. *The People the Best Governors* (1776), reprinted in Frederick Chase, *A History of Dartmouth College and the Town of Hanover, New Hampshire,* ed. John K. Lord (Cambridge, Mass., 1891), app. D, pp. 655, 660, 661; "Interest of America," in Force, ed., *American Archives* 6: 840–43.

15. Paine, *Common Sense,* in Foner, ed., *Writings of Paine,* 1: 6–7, 9.
16. Paine, *Rights of Man,* in Foner, ed., *Writings of Paine,* 1: 339–40; *Common Sense,* p. 6.
17. [John Taylor], *An Enquiry into the Principles and Tendency of Certain Public Measures* (Philadelphia, 1794), pp. 49–50.
18. John Taylor, *An Inquiry into the Principles and Policy of the Government of the United States* (1814; New Haven, 1950), pp. 31–34, 61–62, 94–97, 170–71, 356, 362–63, 374, 378; Taylor, *Enquiry into Public Measures,* pp. 1–3, 53.
19. Taylor, *Inquiry into the Principles of Government,* pp. 175, 378; Montesquieu, *Spirit of the Laws,* bk. 11, chap. 6, p. 152.
20. Taylor, *Inquiry into the Principles of Government,* pp. 36–37, 61–62, 79, 94, 358; Adams, ed., *Works of Adams,* 6: 466–67. Frederick Grimke in *The Nature and Tendency of Free Institutions* (1848), ed. John William Ward (Cambridge, Mass., 1968), pp. 70–71, 627–40, restated some of Taylor's arguments. Grimke believed that a classification of political systems based upon the mechanics of the several departments was necessarily faulty because it failed to deal with the vastly more important division "between the government and the power out of government." The legislative, executive, and judicial branches were formally organized and therefore highly visible, but, Grimke argued, it was certainly incorrect to assume that they contained all of the political powers of the community. The proper mode of classifying political systems was by taking into account the strength of those outside the formal structure itself. If the influence of the people out of government was "feeble," the system was either a "monarchy" or an "oligarchy"; if "moderate," the system was a "mixed form or limited monarchy"; if "very strong," the system must be a "representative republic." In a chapter addressing the question "Is the American Government a Balanced One?" Grimke concluded that "if by a balanced constitution we intend one in which the principal checks to power reside within the government, the American government is not a balanced one." Furthermore, it could never be so balanced, for America was "happily wanting" in the established orders that were the foundations of that type of a balanced constitution. If, however, we considered the checks that the people exercised over the various departments of government we would realize that the American system was balanced in a "higher sense" than the conventional notion founded upon internal dynamics would allow. External checks exercised by the people out of office made the American system "truly a balanced one."
21. Taylor, *Enquiry into Public Measures,* p. 53; Report of the Council of Censors, *Pennsylvania Gazette,* 6 October 1784. Cf. Isaac Kramnick's discussion of Bolingbroke in *Bolingbroke and His Circle,* pp. 163–69. The standard treatment of the struggles between the provincial assemblies and colonial governors is Jack P. Greene, *The Quest for Power: The Lower Houses of Assembly in the Southern Royal Colonies, 1689–1776* (Chapel Hill, 1963). The first state constitutions are discussed in Elisha P. Douglass,

Rebels and Democrats: The Struggle for Equal Political Rights and Majority Rule during the American Revolution (Chapel Hill, 1955); Jackson Turner Main, *The Sovereign States, 1775–1783* (New York, 1973); Allan Nevins, *The American States during and after the Revolution* (New York, 1924); William C. Webster, "Comparative Study of the First State Constitutions of the American Revolution," *Annals of the American Academy of Political and Social Science* 9 (1897): 380–420; William C. Morey, "The First State Constitutions," ibid., 4 (1893): 201–32; and most recently, Willi Paul Adams, *The First American Constitutions: Republican Ideology and the Making of the State Constitutions in the Revolutionary Era* (Chapel Hill, 1980).

22. Douglass Adair, "The Intellectual Origins of Jeffersonian Democracy: Republicanism, the Class Struggle, and the Virtuous Farmer" (Ph.D. diss., Yale University, 1943), p. 184. The notion of accountability of public officers is treated in my introduction to *Representative Government and the Revolution: The Maryland Constitutional Crisis of 1787* (Baltimore, 1975), pp. 1–32.

23. L. H. Butterfield, ed., *The Diary and Autobiography of John Adams,* 4 vols. (Cambridge, Mass., 1961), 3: 331, 356; Adams, ed., *Works of Adams,* 4: 287, 300; see also Adams to Abigail Adams, 19 March 1776, in L. H. Butterfield, ed., *Adams Family Correspondence,* 4 vols. (Cambridge, Mass., 1963–1973), 1: 363.

24. Adams, ed., *Works of Adams,* 4: 309, 382, 406, 409; 6: 10, 57, 61.

25. Adams, ed., *Works of Adams,* 4: 587–88. Adams's declining faith in the uniqueness of America and his emphasis on the universality of human experiences are examined in John R. Howe, Jr., *The Changing Political Thought of John Adams* (Princeton, 1966), pp. 102–55.

26. Adams to Roger Sherman, 17 July 1789, in Adams, ed., *Works of Adams,* 6: 428; Adams to Samuel Adams, 18 October 1790, ibid., 6: 417; Adams to John Taylor, 15 April 1814, ibid., 6: 448–49; also, Adams to Richard Henry Lee, 15 November 1775, ibid., 4: 186. The essence of the balance, according to Bolingbroke, was that "the legislative, or supreme power is vested by our constitution in three estates, whereof the king is one." Bolingbroke, *Dissertation on Parties,* Letter 13, in *Works of Bolingbroke,* 2: 117. Adams agreed that the glory of the English constitution derived from the fact that it promoted a balance among the functions of government as well as that "other balance which is in the legislature,—between the one, the few, and the many; in which two balances the excellence of that form of government must consist." Adams, ed., *Works of Adams,* 6: 429; 4: 380, 559.

27. Ibid., 4: 440, 557; 6: 117–18, 166–67, 171–72.

28. Ibid., 4: 380, 382, 392–97.

29. Adams to Taylor, 15 April 1814, ibid., 6: 451; Adams, *Defence of the Constitutions,* ibid., 5: 453; 6: 32, 65, 185–86; 5: 473; "Democraticus" [pseud.], "Loose Thoughts on Government" (1776), in Force, ed., *American Archives,* 6: 731.

30. [Theophilus Parsons], *Result of the Convention of Delegates Holden at Ipswich in the County of Essex* (Newburyport, 1778), reprinted in Handlin, ed., *Popular Sources of Political Authority,* pp. 324–26, 332–35, 337–38, 341, 343, 351, 360; Montesquieu, *Spirit of the Laws,* p. 156. Adams believed that "every man and every body of men is and has a rival. When the struggle is only between two . . . it continues till one is swallowed up or annihilated, and the other becomes absolute master." Because of this, because there could be "in the nature of things, no balance without three powers," the legislative branch must be divided into "three equiponderant, independent branches." Adams, ed., *Works of Adams,* 6: 323; 4: 354, 470.

31. Adams, ed., *Works of Adams,* 4: 216, 230, 231–32, 447.

32. *A Constitution or Frame of Government . . . State of Massachusetts-Bay,* in Handlin, ed., *Popular Sources of Political Authority,* pp. 447–48, 449.

33. "An address of the Convention, for Framing a New Constitution of Government, for the State of Massachusetts-Bay, to their Constituents," ibid., pp. 434–40.

34. *New Hampshire Provincial and State Papers,* ed. Nathaniel Bouton (Concord, 1875), 9: 837–42, 845–52, 858–59; see also ibid., pp. 877–95; 896–919; and Jere Daniell, *Experiment in Republicanism: New Hampshire Politics and the American Revolution, 1741–1794* (Cambridge, Mass., 1970), pp. 169, 177–78.

35. Madison, "Vices of the Political System of the United States," in Gaillard Hunt, ed., *The Writings of James Madison,* 9 vols. (New York, 1900–1910), 2: 366–69; Alexander Hamilton, James Madison, and John Jay, *The Federalist,* ed. Benjamin F. Wright (Cambridge, Mass., 1961), pp. 129–36, 355–59; *National Gazette,* 23 January 1792, in Hunt, ed., *Writings of Madison,* 6: 86; Madison to Jefferson, 24 October 1787, ibid., 5: 27–32. The best short treatment of the Madisonian synthesis is Douglass Adair, "That Politics May Be Reduced to a Science: David Hume, James Madison, and the Tenth Federalist," *Huntington Library Quarterly* 20 (1957): 343–60. For the context of the eighteenth-century "regard to reputation," see [Parsons], *Essex Result,* pp. 346–47; Gerald Stourzh, *Alexander Hamilton and the Idea of Republican Government* (Stanford, 1970), pp. 180–86; Arthur O. Lovejoy, "The 'Love of Praise' as the Indispensable Substitute for 'Reason and Virtue' in Seventeenth- and Eighteenth-Century Theories of Human Nature," in *Reflections on Human Nature* (Baltimore, 1961), pp. 153–93; Douglass Adair, "Fame and the Founding Fathers," in *Fame and the Founding Fathers: Essays by Douglass Adair,* ed. Trevor Colbourn (New York, 1974), pp. 4–26.

36. Caesar Rodney, *The Oracle of Liberty, and Mode of Establishing a Free Government* (Philadelphia, 1791), pp. 8–9; Hunt, ed., *Writings of Madison,* 2: 366, 368; Wright, ed., *Federalist,* pp. 351, 353, 356; Madison to Edmund Randolph, 10 January 1788, in Hunt, ed., *Writings of Madison,* 5: 81.

37. *National Gazette,* 5, 19 December 1791, in Hunt, ed., *Writings of Madison,* 6: 67–69, 70.
38. Wright, ed., *Federalist,* pp. 336–39, 343–44.
39. *National Gazette,* 5 December 1791, in Hunt, ed., *Writings of Madison,* 6: 67.
40. *National Gazette,* 5 December 1791, and 6 February 1792, ibid., 6: 67, 91–93; Wright, ed., *Federalist,* pp. 330, 356, 357–58.
41. David Osgood, *Reflections on the Goodness of God . . . A Sermon Preached on the Day of Annual and National Thanksgiving* (Boston, 1784), p. 31; [Timothy Dwight], *A Valedictory Address to the Young Gentlemen, Who Commenced at Yale-College* (New Haven, 1776), p. 15.
42. Jefferson to Cabell, 2 February 1816, in [Thomas Jefferson and Joseph C. Cabell], *Early History of the University of Virginia, as Contained in the Letters of Thomas Jefferson and Joseph C. Cabell* (Richmond, 1856), pp. 54–55; also Jefferson, "Autobiography," in Paul Leicester Ford, ed., *The Writings of Thomas Jefferson,* 10 vols. (New York, 1892–1899), 1: 113; Jefferson to Doctor Walter Jones, 2 January 1814, ibid., 9: 447; Jefferson to Samuel Kercheval, 12 July 1816, ibid., 10: 41.
43. Jefferson to M. D'Ivernois, 6 February 1795, ibid., 7: 4–5; Jefferson to the Governor of the Mississippi Territory (Robert Williams), 1 November 1807, ibid., 9: 167.
44. Jefferson to Kercheval, 12 July and 5 September 1816, ibid., 10: 41, 45; Jefferson to Cabell, 2 February 1816, [Jefferson and Cabell], *Early History of the University of Virginia,* p. 55.
45. Ibid., pp. 54–55; Adams to Zabdiel Adams, 21 June 1776, in Adams, ed., *Works of Adams,* 9: 401; Adams to Rush, 28 August 1811, ibid., 9: 636; Adams to Jefferson, 18 December 1819, ibid., 10: 386; Adams, *Defence of the Constitutions,* ibid., 6: 219; 4: 521, 556–58; 5: 29, 289–90; Adams, *Discourses on Davila,* ibid., 6: 263; Adams to Henry Marchant, 18 August 1789, ibid., 9: 560. See also Wood, *Creation of the American Republic,* pp. 91–124.
46. George Logan, *An Address on the Natural and Social Order of the World* (Philadelphia, [1798]), pp. 5–6, 11.
47. Ibid., pp. 4, 5–6.
48. Levi Hart, *The Description of a Good Character Attempted and Applied to the Subject of Jurisprudence and Civil Government* (Hartford, [1786]), p. 7.
49. Logan, *Natural and Social Order,* pp. 5–6.

7: Republican Machines

1. The body of literature on republicanism is large and still growing; see the review essays of Robert E. Shalhope, "Toward a Republican Synthesis: The Emergence of an Understanding of Republicanism in American

Historiography," *William and Mary Quarterly,* 3rd ser., 29 (1972): 49–80; and "Republicanism and Early American Historiography," ibid., 39 (1982): 334–56. The themes of independence and virtue in republican doctrine will be discussed in chapter eight; but see also J.G.A. Pocock, "Machiavelli, Harrington, and English Political Ideologies in the Eighteenth Century," and "Civic Humanism and Its Role in Anglo-American Thought," in *Politics, Language and Time: Essays on Political Thought and History* (New York, 1971), pp. 104–47, 80–103; and Pocock, *The Machiavellian Moment: Florentine Political Thought and the Atlantic Republican Tradition* (Princeton, 1975), pp. 462–552.

2. Benjamin Rush, *A Plan for the Establishment of Public Schools and the Diffusion of Knowledge in Pennsylvania; to Which Are Added, Thoughts upon the Mode of Education, Proper in a Republic* (Philadelphia, 1786), in Frederick Rudolph, ed., *Essays on Education in the Early Republic* (Cambridge, Mass., 1965), p. 9. David Freeman Hawke, *Benjamin Rush: Revolutionary Gadfly* (Indianapolis, 1971), is a good standard biography of Rush, but Donald J. D'Elia, *Benjamin Rush: Philosopher of the American Revolution,* American Philosophical Society *Transactions* 64 (1974), is the best intellectual biography.

3. Rush, *Mode of Education Proper in a Republic,* p. 15. On the struggle over the Pennsylvania constitution, see Robert L. Brunhouse, *The Counter-Revolution in Pennsylvania, 1776–1790* (Harrisburg, 1942); and J. Paul Selsam, *The Pennsylvania Constitution of 1776: A Study in Revolutionary Democracy* (Philadelphia, 1936).

4. Rush, *Mode of Education Proper in a Republic,* p. 15. See chapter 5, above, for an elaboration of this theme.

5. John Winthrop, "A Model of Christian Charity," in Edmund S. Morgan, ed., *Puritan Political Ideas, 1558–1794* (Indianapolis, 1965), p. 92.

6. Rush, *Mode of Education Proper in a Republic,* pp. 14–15.

7. Ibid., pp. 14, 17. For comments on Rush's statement concerning "republican machines," see David Tyack, "Forming the National Character: Paradox in the Educational Thought of the Revolutionary Generation," *Harvard Educational Review* 36 (1966): 29–41; Michael Kammen, *People of Paradox: An Inquiry Concerning the Origins of American Civilization* (New York, 1972), pp. 72–75; Rush Welter, *Popular Education and Democratic Thought in America* (New York, 1962), pp. 23–29.

8. Rush, "Lectures on Animal Life," in Dagobert D. Runes, ed., *The Selected Writings of Benjamin Rush* (New York, 1947), p. 175; Rush, "On the Education Proper to Qualify a Young Man for the Study of Medicine," in *Sixteen Introductory Lectures upon the Institutes and Practice of Medicine* (Philadephia, 1811), pp. 173, 175; Rush, "On the Study of Medical Jurisprudence," ibid., p. 363; Rush, "On the Duty and Advantages of Studying the Diseases of Domestic Animals and the Remedies Proper to Remove Them," ibid., p. 295; George W. Corner, ed., *The Autobiography of Benjamin Rush: His "Travels Through Life" together with his Commonplace Book for 1789–1813* (Princeton, 1948), p. 351.

9. Rush to Arthur Lee, 4 May 1774, in L. H. Butterfield, ed., *Letters of Benjamin Rush,* 2 vols. (Princeton, 1951), 1: 85; "Medicine Among the Indians of North America," in Runes, ed., *Writings of Rush,* p. 283; this important piece is also in Rush, *Medical Inquiries and Observations,* 4 vols., 5th ed. (Philadelphia, 1818), 1: 55–91.

10. Rush, "Medicine Among the Indians," in Runes, ed., *Writings of Rush,* pp. 255, 265, 259, 260, 267, 270, 273.

11. Ibid., pp. 271, 273, 274, 276, 282.

12. Ibid., pp. 278, 284, 285, 286–87; "Diseases from Employments and Amusements," Rush MSS, Historical Society of Pennsylvania, Philadelphia, (cited hereafter as HSP), Lectures on Pathology (cited hereafter as *Pathology,* followed by the appropriate document identification number), Yi2/7396/F23, pp. 320–21.

13. Rush, "Lectures on Animal Life," pp. 164–65, 166; Rush, "Diseases from Much Motion," *Pathology* Yi2/7396/F22, pp. 309–10, 266; Rush, *Medical Inquiries and Observations upon Diseases of the Mind* (1812; New York, 1962), p. 69.

14. Rush, "Diseases from Much Motion," pp. 310–11; Rush, *Diseases of the Mind,* pp. 68–70.

15. Rush, "Lectures on Animal Life," p. 168; "Animal Life," Rush MSS, HSP, Lectures on Physiology (cited hereafter as *Physiology,* followed by the appropriate document identification number), Yi2/7397/F3, pp. 110–11; Rush, "Diseases from Much Motion," pp. 312–13; David B. Lynds, "Lecture Notes on Pathology," student notebook, Rush MSS, Institute of the History of Medicine, Welch Library, Johns Hopkins University, p. 119; Rush, *Diseases of the Mind,* pp. 68–69.

16. Rush, "Medicine Among the Indians," pp. 286–87; Rush, "Lectures on Animal Life," p. 168; Rush, "Diseases from Much Motion," pp. 313–14; Lynds, "Notes on Pathology," p. 119.

17. Rush, "Observations and Reasoning in Medicine," in Runes, ed., *Writings of Rush,* pp. 252–53; "Introductory Lecture on the Certainty of Medicine," Rush MSS, HSP, Lectures of Rush (cited hereafter as *Lectures,* followed by the appropriate document identification number), Yi2/7400/F5, pp. 26–27; Rush, "On the Influence of Physical Causes in Promoting an Increase of the Strength and Activity of the Intellectual Faculties of Man," in *Sixteen Introductory Lectures,* p. 110; Valentine Seaman to Rush, 31 May 1793, Rush MSS, HSP, Correspondence, vol. 15. For the context in which to interpret Rush's medical doctrine, see Lester S. King, *The Medical World of the Eighteenth Century* (Chicago, 1958); and Corner, ed., *Autobiography of Rush,* app. 1, pp. 361–66.

18. Rush, "On Imposture in Medicine," Rush MSS, HSP, *Lectures* Yi2/7400/F5, p. 27; Corner, ed., *Autobiography of Rush,* pp. 44, 46, 87, 89. See also, Donald J. D'Elia, "Dr. Benjamin Rush and the American Medical Revolution," American Philosophical Society *Proceedings* 110 (1966): 227–34.

19. Rush, "The Progress of Medicine," in Runes, ed., *Writings of Rush,* p. 236; Rush, "On Imposture in Medicine," pp. 28–29; Rush, "Observations on

the Government of Pennsylvania," in Runes, ed., *Writings of Rush,* p. 60; "One of the Majority," *Pennsylvania Gazette,* 25 August 1784.

20. Rush, "The Progress of Medicine," in Runes, ed., *Writings of Rush,* pp. 238, 236; Rush, "On Imposture in Medicine," pp. 38–39, 42–43; Rush, "On the Practice of Medicine; on Nosology," Rush MSS, HSP, *Lectures,* Yi2/7400/F18, p. 21; Rush, "Duties of a Physician," in Runes, ed., *Writings of Rush,* p. 321; Rush, "On the Pains and Pleasures of a Medical Life," in *Sixteen Introductory Lectures,* p. 211; Rush, "On the Duties of Patients to their Physicians," ibid., pp. 318–19.

21. Rush, "The Progress of Medicine," p. 242; Rush, "Observations and Reasoning in Medicine," p. 253.

22. Rush, "An Account of the Influence of the Military and Political Events of the American Revolution upon the Human Body," in Runes, ed., *Writings of Rush,* p. 330; Rush, *Diseases of the Mind,* p. 114.

23. Rush, "Influence of the Military and Political Events of the Revolution upon the Human Body," pp. 330, 325–26, 328, 329; Rush, *Diseases of the Mind,* p. 113.

24. Rush, "Influence of the Military and Political Events of the Revolution upon the Human Body," pp. 330–31, 333.

25. Rush, "Lectures on Animal Life," p. 136; Rush, "Of Animal Life," Rush MSS, HSP, *Physiology* Yi2/7397/F1, p. 15; David B. Lynds, "Lecture Notes on the Human Mind," student notebook, Rush MSS, Institute of the History of Medicine, Welch Library, Johns Hopkins University, p. 6; Rush, "On the Application of Metaphysicks to Medicine," Rush MSS, HSP, *Lectures* Yi2/7400/F2, pp. 1–2, 5, 7; Russel Clark, "Notes on Dr. Rush's Lectures," student notebook, Rush MSS, Rare Book Collection, University of Pennsylvania Library, vol. 6, lecture 68; Rush, "Influence of Physical Causes on the Intellectual Faculties," p. 115. On the Jeffersonian philosophy and Rush's place in the Jeffersonian circle, see Daniel Boorstin, *The Lost World of Thomas Jefferson* (Boston, 1960); George Rosen, "Political Order and Human Health in Jeffersonian Thought," *Bulletin of the History of Medicine* 26 (1952): 32–44.

26. William Simonton, "Notes on Rush Lectures," student notebook, Rush MSS, Rare Book Collection, University of Pennsylvania Library, vol. 3, lecture 41, pp. 130, 131; Clark, "Notes on Dr. Rush's Lectures," student notebook, vol. 5, lecture 63; Rush, "On the Application of Metaphysicks to Medicine," pp. 12–13; Lynds, "Notes on the Human Mind," student notebook, p. 7.

27. Simonton, "Notes on Rush Lectures," student notebook, vol. 3, lecture 41, p. 130; Rush, *Diseases of the Mind,* pp. 184–85, 98–134, 192, 204, 342, 283, 301, 319, 326, 351, 364; Rush, "On the Utility of a Knowledge of the Faculties and Operations of the Human Mind, to a Physician," in *Sixteen Introductory Lectures,* p. 266; Rush, "Influence of Physical Causes on the Intellectual Faculties," pp. 88–89; Rush, "On the Proximate Cause of Disease," Rush MSS, HSP, *Pathology* Yi2/7396/F2, p. 8.

28. Rush, *Diseases of the Mind,* p. 11; Clark, "Notes on Dr. Rush's Lectures,"

student notebook, vol. 6, lecture 65; Rush's description of Roger Sherman and the others are in Corner, ed., *Autobiography of Rush,* pp. 318, 320, 145, 149.

29. Rush to John Witherspoon, 1 August 1767, in Butterfield, ed., *Letters of Rush,* 1: 45–46; Rush to Charles Nisbet, [April, 1784], p. 323; Rush to Nisbet, 5 December 1783, pp. 315–16; Rush to Nisbet, 15 May 1784, p. 334; Rush to John Montgomery, 8 June 1785, pp. 355–56; Rush to the Trustees of Dickinson College, 23 May 1785, p. 351.

30. Rush to John Montgomery, 14 June 1785, ibid., pp. 356–57; Rush to —, 27 June 1785, Rush MSS, HSP, Correspondence, vol. 41.

31. Charles Nisbet to Rush, 10 August 1785, Rush MSS, HSP, Correspondence, vol. 41; Rush to John Montgomery, 20 August 1785, in Butterfield, ed., *Letters of Rush,* 1: 361–63; Rush to Montgomery, 11 September 1785, pp. 369–70; Rush to John Erskine, 25 October 1785, pp. 373–74.

32. Charles Nisbet to Rush, — August 1785, Rush MSS, HSP, Correspondence, vol. 41; Nisbet to Rush, 24 August 1785, ibid.; Nisbet to Rush, 13 September 1785, ibid.; Tom Nisbet to Rush, — August 1785, ibid.; Rush mentioned Tom Nisbet's letter in his note to John Montgomery, 11 September 1785, in Butterfield, ed., *Letters of Rush,* 1: 370.

33. Eva V. Armstrong, "Portrait of Benjamin Rush from a Student's [Robert H. Maxwell] Note-Book," *University of Pennsylvania Library Chronicle* 5 (1937): 43; Rush, "Influence of the Military and Political Events of the Revolution upon the Human Body," pp. 328–29; Rush, *Diseases of the Mind,* p. 113; Rush to John Erskine, 25 October 1785, in Butterfield, ed., *Letters of Rush,* 1: 373; Rush, "On the Causes of Death, in Diseases that Are Not Incurable," in *Sixteen Introductory Lectures,* pp. 86–87.

34. Rush, "On Pathology," Rush MSS, HSP, *Pathology* Yi2/7396/F1, pp. 10, 11; Lynds, "Notes on Pathology," student notebook, pp. 2–3; Charles Nisbet to Rush, 24 August 1785, and 4 September 1785, Rush MSS, HSP, Correspondence, vol. 41. Cf. Rush's comment to Mrs. Rush: "It is, you know, through difficulties and trials that states as well as individuals are trained up to glory and happiness." Rush to Mrs. Rush, 18 September 1776, in Butterfield, ed., *Letters of Rush,* 1: 113.

35. Rush to John Erskine, 25 October 1785, ibid., 1: 373, 374; Rush to John Montgomery, 13 September 1785, Rush MSS, HSP, Correspondence, vol. 41.

36. John King to Rush, 6 December 1785, ibid.; Rush to John Montgomery, 28 November 1785, in Butterfield, ed., *Letters of Rush,* 1: 376; Rush to Montgomery, 18 June 1786, p. 393; Rush to Montgomery, 2 September 1785, Rush MSS, HSP, Correspondence, vol. 41; Rush to Montgomery, 19 August 1786, ibid., vol. 42; King to Rush, 30 September 1785, ibid., vol. 41; King to Rush, 2 February 1786, ibid., vol. 42.

37. Rush to Montgomery, 28 November 1785, in Butterfield, ed., *Letters of Rush,* 1: 376; Rush to the Trustees of Dickinson College, 21 October 1786, p. 398; Rush, *Diseases of the Mind,* p. 376.

38. Charles Nisbet to Rush, 30 January 1786, Rush MSS, HSP, Correspondence,

vol. 41; Nisbet to Rush, 15 March 1786, ibid., vol. 42; Rush to Montgomery, 11 September 1785, in Butterfield, ed., *Letters of Rush,* 1: 369;
Rush, *Diseases of the Mind,* pp. 268–69.

39. Rush, "An Inquiry into the Influence of Physical Causes upon the Moral
Faculty," in Runes, ed., *Writings of Rush,* pp. 181, 182; Lynds, "Notes on
the Human Mind," student notebook, p. 17. See also, Eric T. Carlson and
Meribeth M. Simpson, "Benjamin Rush's Medical Use of the Moral
Faculty," *Bulletin of the History of Medicine* 39 (1965): 22–33, for a useful
introduction to this subject.

40. Rush to Montgomery, 28 December 1785, in Butterfield, ed., *Letters of
Rush,* 1: 378; Butterfield's comment appears in footnote 5. Rush's oration
is also in *Medical Inquiries and Observations,* 1: 93–124.

41. Rush, "Influence of Physical Causes upon the Moral Faculty," in Runes,
ed., *Writings of Rush,* p. 182.

42. Ibid., pp. 136, 192–201, 203.

43. Ibid., p. 208.

44. Rush, "Causes of Death in Diseases that Are Not Incurable," p. 87; Rush,
"Influence of Physical Causes upon the Moral Faculty," pp. 191, 208–9,
189; Rush, *Mode of Education Proper in a Republic,* p. 15. Carlson and
Simpson, "Benjamin Rush's Medical Use of the Moral Faculty," pp. 22–33;
and Rosen, "Political Order and Human Health," pp. 32–44.

45. Rush, "Copied Lectures," Rush MSS, HSP, *Pathology* Yi2/7396/F3,
pp. 60.3, 60.5; Rush, "On the Application of Metaphysicks to Medicine,"
pp. 5–6; Rush, "On the Diseases of the Moral Faculty," Rush MSS, HSP,
Lectures Yi2/7400/F25; Rush, *Diseases of the Mind,* pp. 361, 362; Clark,
"Notes on Dr. Rush's Lectures," student notebook, vol. 6, lecture 67.

46. Clark, "Notes on Dr. Rush's Lectures," student notebook, vol. 6, lecture 68;
Rush, *Diseases of the Mind,* pp. 360, 209; Rush, "On the Diseases of the
Moral Faculty," *Lectures* Yi2/7400/F25; Rush, "On the Practice of
Medicine; on Nosology," p. 32; David B. Lynds, "Lecture Notes on the
Practice of Medicine," student notebook, Rush MSS, Institute of the
History of Medicine, Welch Library, Johns Hopkins University, p. 23ff.

47. Rush, "Facts and Documents on Moral Derangement as Exemplified Chiefly
in Murder," Rush MSS, HSP, *Lectures* Yi2/7400/F20, pp. 30, 33; Rush,
"Influence of Physical Causes upon the Moral Faculty," p. 191; Rush,
"Copied Lectures," p. 60.7; Rush, "Causes of Death in Diseases that Are
Not Incurable," p. 86; Rush, "On the Diseases of the Moral Faculty," *Lec-
tures* Yi2/7400/F25.

48. Rush, *Diseases of the Mind,* p. 259; Clark, "Notes on Dr. Rush's Lectures,"
student notebook, vol. 2, lecture 22; Simonton, "Notes on Rush
Lectures," student notebook, vol. 3, lecture 41, p. 134; Rush, "Copied
Lectures," pp. 60.5, 60.55, 60.6; Lynds, "Notes on the Human Mind," student notebook, p. 17; Corner, ed., *Autobiography of Rush,* p. 193.

49. Rush, "On the Application of Metaphysicks to Medicine," pp. 22, 25, 6;
Rush, "The Bible As a School Book," in Runes, ed., *Writings of Rush,*
p. 118; On Hartley, see Donald J. D'Elia, "Benjamin Rush, David Hartley,

and the Revolutionary Uses of Psychology," American Philosophical Society *Proceedings* 114 (1970): 109–18; and D'Elia, *Benjamin Rush,* pp. 74–75, 85–86, 96; Basil Willey, *The Eighteenth-Century Background: Studies on the Idea of Nature in the Thought of the Period* (New York, 1961), pp. 136–54.

50. Rush, *Diseases of the Mind,* pp. 333, 265; Rush, "Recapitulation of Lectures upon Animal Life," Rush MSS, HSP, *Physiology* Yi2/7397/F19, pp. 13–16; Rush, "Facts and Documents on Moral Derangement," pp. 21–23. Rush used the labels "voluntary" and "involuntary" to distinguish between conscious and unconscious (automatic and habitual if not instinctive) responses to stimuli, but he sometimes confused their usage, as evidenced in the manuscripts by his frequent corrections and transpositions. For example, when he described respiration he used "voluntary" to mean automatic; that is, the lungs through habit were made to move on their own without a conscious effort being made on the part of the individual. When he addressed the general phenomenon, however, Rush used "involuntary" to mean automatic, for actions that did not involve individual volition had to be habitual.

51. Rush, "Influence of Physical Causes upon the Moral Faculty," pp. 204, 202–3, 198–200, 195–96.

52. Rush to John Adams, 1 October 1777, in Butterfield, ed., *Letters of Rush,* 1: 154–57. Rush's complaints concerning the American military hospitals, and his quarrel with William Shippen, the director general, can be traced in his letters of 1777–1780. See especially, Rush to Adams, 21 October, 31 October 1777, and 8 February 1778, ibid., pp. 161, 164–65, 199–200; Rush to William Duer, 3 and 13 December 1777, pp. 171–74, 175–77; Rush to Washington, 26 December 1777, and 25 February 1778, pp. 180–82, 200–203; Rush to John Morgan, June 1779, pp. 225–29; Rush to Shippen, 18 November 1780, pp. 256–60. Also, Rush to Adams, 12 February 1812, ibid., 2: 1121–22.

53. Clark, "Notes on Dr. Rush's Lectures," student notebook, vol. 2, lecture 14; James Overton, "Notes on Lectures Delivered by Dr. Benjamin Rush on the Institutes and Practice of Medicine," student notebook, Rush MSS, Rare Book Collection, University of Pennsylvania Library, lecture 18; Rush, *Diseases of the Mind,* pp. 41, 206; Rush, "Of Local Diseases," Rush MSS, HSP, *Pathology* Yi2/7396/F25, p. 504; Rush, "On the Pleasures of the Mind," in *Sixteen Introductory Lectures,* pp. 445, 452, 453.

54. Rush, "On the Pleasures of the Senses," in *Sixteen Introductory Lectures,* pp. 399–400, 433, 434–35; Lynds, "Notes on Pathology," student notebook, p. 31; Lynds, "Notes on the Human Mind," student notebook, pp. 48, 66–67, 71–72; Rush, *Diseases of the Mind,* pp. 327–28, 117; Clark, "Notes on Dr. Rush's Lectures," student notebook, vol. 2, lectures 12 and 14; the phrase *"art of forgetting"* is in Rush, "The Amusements and Punishments Which Are Proper for Schools," Runes, ed., *Writings of Rush,* p. 115.

55. Rush, "Copied Lectures," p. 61; Rush, "Pleasures of the Mind," pp. 447–48.

56. Rush, "Demence," Rush MSS, HSP, *Lectures* Yi2/7400/F24, p. 1; Rush, *Diseases of the Mind,* pp. 259, 37; Overton, "Notes on Lectures," student notebook, lectures 18 and 19.
57. Rush, "Diseases from Much Motion," p. 312; Rush, *Diseases of the Mind,* pp. 297–98.
58. Rush, *Mode of Education Proper in a Republic,* pp. 15, 17.

8: The Bonds of Patriotism

1. Montesquieu, *The Spirit of the Laws,* ed. Franz Neumann, trans. Thomas Nugent (New York, 1949), bk. 4, pp. 29–34.
2. Noah Webster, *On the Education of Youth in America* (Boston, 1790), in Frederick Rudolph, ed., *Essays on Education in the Early Republic* (Cambridge, Mass., 1965), pp. 66, 72; Thomas Dawes, *An Oration Delivered July 4, 1787, at . . . the Town of Boston* (Boston, 1787), p. 11; David Osgood, *Reflections on the Goodness of God . . . A Sermon Preached on the Day of Annual and National Thanksgiving* (Boston, 1784), p. 32; Benjamin Rush, "To the Citizens of Philadelphia: A Plan for Free Schools," *Independent Gazetteer,* 28 March 1787, in L. H. Butterfield, ed., *Letters of Benjamin Rush,* 2 vols. (Princeton, 1951), 1: 413.
3. Simeon Doggett, *A Discourse on Education, Delivered at the Dedication and Opening of Bristol Academy* (New Bedford, 1797), in Rudolph, ed., *Essays on Education,* pp. 155–56; William Linn, *The Blessings of America. A Sermon, Preached . . . on the Fourth of July, 1791* (New York, 1791), p. 30; Samuel Knox, *An Essay on the Best System of Liberal Education, Adapted to the Genius of the Government of the United States* (Philadelphia, 1799), in Rudolph, ed., *Essays on Education,* p. 288; Benjamin Rush, *A Plan for the Establishment of Public Schools and the Diffusion of Knowledge in Pennsylvania; to Which Are Added, Thoughts upon the Mode of Education, Proper in a Republic* (Philadelphia, 1786), in ibid., p. 3.
4. Samuel Stillman, *An Oration, Delivered . . . at . . . Boston, in Celebration of the Anniversary of American Independence* (Boston, 1789), p. 25; Samuel Harrison Smith, *Remarks on Education: Illustrating the Close Connection Between Virtue and Wisdom* (Philadelphia, 1798), in Rudolph, ed., *Essays on Education,* pp. 170, 209, 174–75. Also, Samuel Magaw, "Concerning Education" (1797), MS, American Philosophical Society, Philadelphia.
5. Smith, *Remarks on Education,* pp. 174, 176; David McClure, *An Oration on the Advantages of an Early Education, Delivered at . . . the Opening of the Phillips Exeter Academy* (Exeter, N.H., 1783), p. 7; Charles Nisbet, *The Usefulness and Importance of Human Learning* (Carlisle, 1786), pp. 8–9; Webster, *Education of Youth in America,* pp. 63–64.
6. Nisbet, *Usefulness of Human Learning,* pp. 17, 28–29; Noah Webster, *Sketches of American Policy,* ed. Harry R. Warfel (1785; New York, 1937),

p. 28; Jefferson to Edward Carrington, 16 January 1787, in Julian P. Boyd, ed., *The Papers of Thomas Jefferson,* 19 vols. (Princeton, 1950–74), 11: 48–50; Jefferson, "A Bill for the More General Diffusion of Knowledge," ibid., 2: 526–27; Samuel Whitwell, *An Oration Delivered to the Society of the Cincinnati . . . July 4, 1789* (Boston, 1789), p. 8.

7. Jeremy Belknap, *An Election Sermon, Preached Before the General Court of New Hampshire* (Portsmouth, 1785), p. 19; Smith, *Remarks on Education,* pp. 220–21.

8. [Anon.], "Concerning Education in Pennsylvania: The Best Plan for Conducting a Liberal Education, Suited to the Government of the United States; or to a Republican Constitution in General," MS (ca. 1797), American Philosophical Society; Aristotle, *Politics,* ed. and trans. Ernest Barker (New York, 1974), bk. 3, pp. 92–110, quotation on p. 93. J.G.A. Pocock, "Civic Humanism and Its Role in Anglo-American Thought," in *Politics, Language and Time: Essays on Political Thought and History* (New York, 1971), p. 85; on the civic humanists, see Hans Baron, *The Crisis of the Early Italian Renaissance: Civic Humanism and Republican Liberty in an Age of Classicism and Tyranny* (Princeton, 1966).

9. McClure, *Oration on Early Education,* p. 13; Benjamin Hichborn, *An Oration, Delivered July 5th, 1784* (Boston, 1784), p. 8; Smith, *Remarks on Education,* pp. 177, 221. On the opposition of virtue ("active intelligence") and fortune ("passive unpredictability"), see J.G.A. Pocock, *The Machiavellian Moment: Florentine Political Thought and the Atlantic Republican Tradition* (Princeton, 1975), pp. 36–48. See chapter 7, above, for Rush's criticism of Charles Nisbet in these terms. Nisbet lacked the fortitude to withstand ill-fortune and, therefore, lacked the virtue necessary to remold his apparently disagreeable situation.

10. Pocock, "Civic Humanism and Its Role in Anglo-American Thought," p. 90; Noah Webster, *An Examination into the Leading Principles of the Federal Constitution* (Philadelphia, 1787), in Paul Leicester Ford, ed., *Pamphlets on the Constitution of the United States, Published during Its Discussion by the People, 1787–1788* (Brooklyn, 1888), pp. 59–60; Webster, *Sketches of American Policy,* p. 24; Webster, *Education of Youth in America,* pp. 65–66. Webster was not, however, forswearing the conventional requirement of virtue in a republic; on the contrary, he was appealing to the classical and civic humanistic tradition in which virtue was associated with independence and corruption with dependence. And since a freehold was the surest measure of personal independence, Webster was simply substituting the precondition ("lands in fee simple") for the product ("virtue") in Montesquieu's system. For a different reading of Webster, see Gordon S. Wood, *The Creation of the American Republic, 1776–1787* (Chapel Hill, 1969), pp. 610–12.

11. Benjamin Rush, "Medicine Among the Indians of North America," in Dagobert D. Runes, ed., *The Selected Writings of Benjamin Rush* (New York, 1947), p. 276; Robert Coram, *Political Inquiries: to Which is Added, a Plan for the General Establishment of Schools throughout the*

United States (Wilmington, 1791), in Rudolph, ed., *Essays on Education,* p. 81.

12. Ibid., pp. 91, 96–98.

13. Ibid., pp. 109, 91, 112, 111; Dawes, *Oration Delivered at Boston,* p. 10; Enos Hitchcock, *An Oration, In Commemoration of the Independence of the United States* ([Providence], 1793), p. 6; Webster, *Sketches of American Policy,* pp. 18, 20; Webster, *Examination of the Federal Constitution,* pp. 57–60.

14. Coram, *Political Inquiries,* pp. 82–83, 118.

15. Ibid., pp. 82, 113, 144, 143. According to the anonymous author of *Rudiments of Law and Government, Deduced from the Law of Nature* (Charleston, 1783), pp. 20, 26, "An equality of estate, will give an equality of power; and equality of power is a natural commonwealth." Having said this, however, he went on to explain that "to maintain a mediocrity and equipoise," which was important in a republic because "men in moderate circumstances are most virtuous," not only "must some be prevented from soaring too high, but others must be encouraged to elevate their ideas, and not be permitted to consider themselves as a grovelling, distinct species, uninterested in the general welfare. For the latter defect, education is the natural remedy." In his *Remarks on Education,* p. 192, Samuel Harrison Smith affirmed: "We are correct, therefore, in declaring a diffusion of knowledge, the best, perhaps the only, pledge of virtue, of equality, and of independence."

16. Montesquieu, *Spirit of the Laws,* bk. 4, p. 34.

17. Rush, *Mode of Education Proper in a Republic,* pp. 14–15; Thomas Day, *An Oration on Party Spirit, Pronounced Before the Connecticut Society of Cincinnati* (Litchfield, 1798), pp. 7, 9; David Daggett, *An Oration, Pronounced . . . in the City of New-Haven . . . It Being the Eleventh Anniversary of Independence* (New Haven, 1787), p. 15.

18. Samuel Wales, *The Dangers of Our National Prosperity; and the Way to Avoid Them* (Hartford, 1785), pp. 20–21; William Wyche, *Party Spirit: An Oration to the Horanian Literary Society* (New York, 1794), pp. 10–11, 15, 16; [Donald Fraser], *Party-Spirit Exposed, or Remarks on the Times* (New York, 1799), pp. 5–6, 8; [John Taylor], *A Definition of Parties* (Philadelphia, 1794), p. 4; also [Thomas Tudor Tucker], *Conciliatory Hints, Attempting, by a Fair State of Matters, to Remove Party-Prejudices* (Charleston, 1784); William Loughton Smith, *An Address from William Smith of South-Carolina to His Constituents* (Philadelphia, 1794). On David Hume and eighteenth-century historical thought, see Douglass G. Adair, "'Experience Must be Our Only Guide': History, Democratic Theory, and the United States Constitution," in Ray Allen Billington, ed., *The Reinterpretation of Early American History: Essays in Honor of John Edwin Pomfret* (New York, 1968), pp. 129–50; H. Trevor Colbourn, *The Lamp of Experience: Whig History and the Intellectual Origins of the American Revolution* (Chapel Hill, 1965). For general accounts concerning parties and political thought in the 1780s and 1790s, see Richard Hof-

stadter, *The Idea of a Party System: The Rise of Legitimate Opposition in the United States* (Berkeley, 1969), pp. 1–121; John R. Howe, Jr., "Republican Thought and the Political Violence of the 1790's," *American Quarterly* 19 (1967): 147–65. An alternative, but still complementary view, is presented by Patricia U. Bonomi, "The Middle Colonies: Embryo of the New Political Order," in Alden T. Vaughan and George Athan Billias, ed., *Perspectives on Early American History: Essays in Honor of Richard B. Morris* (New York, 1973), pp. 63–92.

19. James Madison, Federalist Numbers 10 and 51, in Benjamin F. Wright, ed., *The Federalist* (Cambridge, Mass., 1961), pp. 132–35, 358–59.

20. George I. Eacker, *Observations on the National Character of the Americans* (New York, 1798), p. 4; Lafitte du Courteil, *Proposal to Demonstrate the Necessity of a National Institution in the United States of America, for the Education of Children of Both Sexes* (Philadelphia, 1797), in Rudolph, ed., *Essays on Education,* p. 250; Webster to George Washington, 31 March 1786, in Harry R. Warfel, ed., *Letters of Noah Webster* (New York, 1953), p. 46; Morse quoted in Edgar W. Knight, "Early Opposition to the Education of American Children Abroad," *The Educational Forum* 11 (1947): 198. On Barlow, Dwight, and others, see Merrill Jensen, *The New Nation: A History of the United States During the Confederation, 1781–1789* (New York, 1950), pp. 88–110; Howard Mumford Jones, *O Strange New World: American Culture, The Formative Years* (New York, 1952), pp. 273–350; Jonathan Messerli, "The Columbian Complex: The Impulse to National Consolidation," *History of Education Quarterly* 7 (1967): 417–31.

21. Lafitte, *Necessity of a National Institution in the United States,* pp. 242, 243–44; Webster, *Education of Youth in America,* p. 45. For an analysis of corresponding ideas in Revolutionary France, especially the educational views of Condorcet, see Robert M. Stamp, "Educational Thought and Educational Practice During the Years of the French Revolution," *History of Education Quarterly* 6 (1966): 35–49; and Roland G. Paulston, "French Influence in American Institutions of Higher Learning, 1784–1825," ibid. 8 (1968): 229–45.

22. Knox, *Education Adapted to the Genius of the Government of the United States,* p. 311; Butterfield, ed., *Letters of Rush,* 1: 491; Rush, *Mode of Education Proper in a Republic,* p. 10.

23. Noah Webster, *Dissertations on the English Language,* ed. Harry R. Warfel (1789; Gainesville, Fla., 1951), pp. 18–20; Webster, "An Essay on the Necessity . . . of Reforming the Mode of Spelling," ibid., p. 397. See also, Messerli, "The Columbian Complex," pp. 420–21; and David Tyack, "Forming the National Character: Paradox in the Educational Thought of the Revolutionary Generation," *Harvard Educational Review* 36 (1966): 32–33.

24. Webster, *Dissertations on the English Language,* p. 36.

25. Edgar Knight, ed., *A Documentary History of Education in the South Before 1860,* 5 vols. (Chapel Hill, 1949–53), 2: 23; Rush to Richard Price, 25 May

1786, in Butterfield, ed., *Letters of Rush*, 1: 488; also, "A Plan for a Federal University," ibid., pp. 491–95; Rush, "On the Defects of the Confederation," in Runes, ed., *Writings of Rush*, p. 29.

26. Washington to Governor Robert Brooke of Virginia, 16 March 1795, in Knight, ed., *Documentary History of Education*, 2: 18; First Message to Congress, 8 January 1790, ibid., p. 14; extract from Washington's will, ibid., p. 26; Washington to Congress, 7 December 1796, ibid., pp. 21, 22.

27. "Report of the Commissioners Appointed to Fix the Site of the University of Virginia," in Roy J. Honeywell, *The Educational Work of Thomas Jefferson* (Cambridge, Mass., 1931), pp. 250–52.

28. Enos Hitchcock, *A Discourse on Education* (Providence, 1785), p. 10; Belknap, *Election Sermon . . . New Hampshire*, p. 18; Nisbet, *Usefulness of Human Learning*, p. 10; McClure, *Oration on the Advantages of an Early Education*, p. 7.

29. Webster, *Sketches of American Policy*, p. 44; Smith, *Remarks on Education*, p. 219; William Simonton, "Notes on Rush Lectures," student notebook, Rush MSS, Rare Book Collection, University of Pennsylvania Library, vol. 4, lecture 45.

30. Webster, *Education of Youth in America*, p. 66; Enos Hitchcock, *An Oration: Delivered July 4, 1788* (Providence, 1788), p. 20; Timothy Dwight, *Virtuous Rulers a National Blessing; A Sermon Preached at the General Election* (Hartford, 1791), p. 15.

31. "Speeches of Students of the College of William and Mary Delivered May 1, 1699," *William and Mary Quarterly*, 2nd ser., 10 (1930): 323–37; William Bull quoted in Knight, ed., *Documentary History of Education*, 2: 2; see also, Knight, "Early Opposition to the Education of American Children Abroad," pp. 193–204.

32. Webster, *Education of Youth in America*, pp. 72–73; Jefferson to John Banister, Jr., 15 October 1785, in Boyd, ed., *Papers of Jefferson*, 8: 635–37.

33. Webster, *Education of Youth in America*, p. 75. On the Revolutionaries' belief in the superiority of the American situation, and the impact of that belief on their commitment to Republicanism, see chapter 5, above.

34. Smith, *Remarks on Education*, p. 219; Ezra Stiles, *The United States Elevated to Glory and Honor* (New Haven, 1783), p. 55; Knight, ed., *Documentary History of Education*, 2: 3–4; Webster, *Education of Youth in America*, p. 72.

35. [Jonathan Jackson], *Thoughts upon the Political Situation of the United States of America* (Worcester, 1788), pp. 18, 16; Benjamin Rush, *Thoughts upon Female Education, Accommodated to the Present State of Society, Manners, and Government in the United States of America* (Boston, 1787), in Rudolph, ed., *Essays on Education*, p. 36; Coram, *Political Inquiries*, p. 145.

36. [Jackson], *Thoughts upon the Political Situation*, p. 18; Rush, *Thoughts upon Female Education*, p. 36; Eacker, *Observations on National Character*, p. 16; Webster, *Education of Youth in America*, pp. 72, 76–77. On the "mimetic" impulse, see Jack P. Greene, "Political Mimesis: A Consider-

ation of the Historical and Cultural Roots of Legislative Behavior in the British Colonies in the Eighteenth Century," *American Historical Review* 75 (1969): 337–67; and Greene, "Search for Identity: An Interpretation of the Meaning of Selected Patterns of Social Response in Eighteenth-Century America," *Journal of Social History* 3 (1970): 189–220.

37. Webster, *Sketches of American Policy,* p. 47; Webster to John Canfield, 6 January 1783, in Warfel, ed., *Letters of Webster,* p. 4; "Memorial to the Legislature of New York," ibid., p. 6; Webster, *Dissertations on the English Language,* pp. 179, 20, 398.

38. Hitchcock, *Discourse on Education,* p. 10.

39. [Rush], "To His Countrymen: On Patriotism," from the *Pennsylvania Journal,* 20 October 1773, in Butterfield, ed., *Letters of Rush,* 1: 83; Jonathan Mason, "Oration Delivered at Boston, March 6, 1780," in Hezekiah Niles, ed., *Principles and Acts of the Revolution in America* (New York, 1876), p. 42; Wales, *Dangers of Our National Prosperity,* pp. 19–20; Wyche, *Party Spirit,* p. 12.

40. John Locke, *Two Treatises of Government,* ed. Peter Laslett (New York, 1963), *Second Treatise,* p. 355; [Rush], "On Patriotism," p. 83.

41. Rush, *Mode of Education Proper in a Republic,* pp. 9, 10; Webster, *Education of Youth in America,* pp. 45, 68.

42. Rush, *Mode of Education Proper in a Republic,* p. 11; Doggett, *Discourse on Education,* pp. 157–58; Webster, *Education of Youth in America,* p. 54.

43. McClure, *Oration on the Advantages of an Early Education,* p. 13; [Anon.], *An Essay on Education; Delivered at the Public Commencement, at Yale College* (New Haven, 1772), p. 3; "Speeches of Students of the College of William and Mary," pp. 324–25; Belknap, *Election Sermon . . . New Hampshire,* p. 22; Philanthropedia [pseud.], "An Essay on Education," *Columbian Magazine* (May 1789): 296–97; Webster, *Education of Youth in America,* p. 54.

44. Washington to the Commissioners of the Federal District, 28 January 1795, in Knight, ed., *Documentary History of Education,* 2: 17; extract from Washington's will, ibid., p. 25; Washington to Governor Brooke of Virginia, 6 March 1795, quoted in Knight, "Early Opposition to the Education of American Children Abroad," p. 203.

45. Webster, *Education of Youth in America,* pp. 73, 72, 76.

46. Rush, *Mode of Education Proper in a Republic,* p. 10; Jefferson to John Banister, Jr., 15 October 1785, in Boyd, ed., *Papers of Jefferson* 8: 635–37; Knight, ed., *Documentary History of Education,* 2: 4.

47. "Y. Z.," *Columbian Magazine* (September 1786): 12; Rush, "The Bible As a School Book," in Runes, ed., *Writings of Rush,* p. 118; Mason, "Oration Delivered at Boston," p. 42; Rush, "On Patriotism," in Butterfield, ed., *Letters of Rush,* 1: 83.

48. James Sullivan, *Observations upon the Government of the United States of America* (Boston, 1791), p. 52.

49. Rush to Ebenezer Hazard, 22 October 1768, in Butterfield, ed., *Letters of*

Rush, 1: 68; Rush to Walter Jones, 30 July 1776, and Rush to John Adams, 8 August 1777, ibid., pp. 108, 152. Rush described his conversion to republicanism in his autobiography; see George W. Corner, ed., *The Autobiography of Benjamin Rush: His "Travels Through Life" together with his Commonplace Book for 1789–1813* (Princeton, 1948), p. 46.

50. Rush to Richard Price, 25 May 1786, in Butterfield, ed., *Letters of Rush,* 1: 388–89; Price, *Observations on the Importance of the American Revolution* (London, 1784), pp. 69–70; but pp. 54–70 passim.

51. Price to Rush, 30 July 1786 and 14 October 1787, Rush MSS, Historical Society of Pennsylvania, Correspondence, vol. 43; Knox, *Education Adapted to the Genius of the Government of the United States,* p. 288.

52. Smith, *Remarks on Education,* p. 209; Rush, "A Plan for Free Schools," Butterfield, ed., *Letters of Rush,* 1: 412–15.

53. [Anon.], "Concerning Education in Pennsylvania: The Best Plan for Conducting a Liberal Education, Suited to the Government of the United States; or to a Republican Constitution in General" (ca. 1797), MS, American Philosophical Society (hereafter APS); [Anon.], "Concerning Education in Public Schools" (ca. 1797), MS, APS; Academicus [pseud.], "A Few Outlines of a Plan for the Education of Youth Submitted to the Candid Inspection of the Philosophical Society of Philadelphia" (1797), MS, APS. See also Hiram [pseud.], "On Education and Public Schools" (1797), MS, APS. On the APS contest, see Merle M. Odgers, "Education and the American Philosophical Society," APS *Proceedings* 87 (1944): 12–24; Messerli, "The Columbian Complex," pp. 422–25.

54. Jefferson to John Adams, 28 October 1813, in Lester J. Cappon, ed., *The Adams-Jefferson Letters: The Complete Correspondence Between Thomas Jefferson and Abigail and John Adams,* 2 vols. (Chapel Hill, 1959), 2: 390; see also Jefferson, *Notes on the State of Virginia,* ed. William Peden (Chapel Hill, 1954), pp. 146–47; and Jefferson's "Bill for the More General Diffusion of Knowledge," in Gordon C. Lee, ed., *Crusade against Ignorance: Thomas Jefferson on Education* (New York, 1961), pp. 83–92.

55. Josiah Bridge, *A Sermon Preached . . . Massachusetts, May 27, 1789. Being the Day of General Election* (Boston, 1789), pp. 17–18; Smith, *Remarks on Education,* pp. 210–12; Knox, *Education Adapted to the Genius of the Government of the United States,* pp. 317–18, 335, 347; also Jeremy Belknap, *Election Sermon . . . New Hampshire,* p. 14.

56. Knox, *Education Adapted to the Genius of the Government of the United States,* pp. 287, 288–89.

57. Rush to Horatio Gates, 12 June 1781, in Butterfield, ed., *Letters of Rush,* 1: 264. On the development of public education in nineteenth-century America, see Michael B. Katz, *The Irony of Early School Reform: Educational Innovation in Mid-Nineteenth Century Massachusetts* (Cambridge, Mass., 1968); Rush Welter, *The Mind of America, 1820–1860* (New York, 1975), pp. 276–97; Robert H. Wiebe, "The Social Functions of Public Education," *American Quarterly* 21 (1969): 147–64.

58. Tocqueville's wonderfully descriptive phrase "garrulous patriotism"

appears in *Democracy in America,* ed. John Stuart Mill, 2 vols. (New York, 1961), 2: 268. Institutional reforms generated by the Revolution are discussed in Howard Miller, *The Revolutionary College: American Presbyterian Higher Education, 1707–1787* (New York, 1976); David Wendall Robson, "Higher Education in the Emerging American Republic, 1750–1800," (Ph.D. diss., Yale University, 1974); Robert Polk Thomson, "The Reform of the College of William and Mary, 1763–1780," American Philosophical Society *Proceedings* 115 (1971): 187–213; Francis L. Broderick, "Pulpit, Physics, and Politics: The Curriculum of the College of New Jersey, 1746–1794," *William and Mary Quarterly,* 3rd ser., 6 (1949): 42–68.

59. "Constitution or Form of Government for the Commonwealth of Massachusetts" (1780), chap. 5, sec. 2, in Robert J. Taylor, ed., *Massachusetts, Colony to Commonwealth: Documents on the Formation of Its Constitution, 1775–1780* (Chapel Hill, 1961), pp. 142–43; Coram, *Political Inquiries,* p. 113; Smith, *Remarks on Education,* p. 190; Belknap, *Election Sermon . . . New Hampshire,* p. 15; Rush to John Adams, 15 June 1789, in Butterfield, ed., *Letters of Rush,* 1: 517; Du Pont de Nemours, *National Education in the United States of America,* trans. B. G. Du Pont (Newark, Del., 1923), p. 5. See also the comments of William Manning in Samuel Eliot Morison, ed., "William Manning's *The Key of Libberty* [1798]," *William and Mary Quarterly,* 3rd ser., 13 (1956): 211, 217. On the reduction of the social space occupied by the family, see John Demos, *A Little Commonwealth: Family Life in Plymouth Colony* (New York, 1970); and Demos, "The American Family in Past Time," *American Scholar* 43 (1974): 422–46.

60. Smith, *Remarks on Education,* pp. 210, 190; Coram, *Political Inquiries,* p. 113; [Anon.], "Concerning Education in Public Schools," MS, APS.

61. Rush, *Mode of Education Proper in a Republic,* pp. 14, 13, 22, 21; Smith, *Remarks on Education,* pp. 192–93; Rush, "The Amusements and Punishments Which Are Proper for Schools," in Runes, ed., *Writings of Rush,* p. 114.

62. Webster, *Education of Youth in America,* pp. 69, 68, 71; Rush, *Thoughts upon Female Education,* pp. 28, 33–34; Rush, *Mode of Education Proper in a Republic,* p. 21. "At this eventful period of life the little folk are in the arms of their mothers," Simeon Doggett explained in his *Discourse on Education,* pp. 158–59. "Hence the maxim, as is the parent so is the child; and hence the inconceivable consequences of female education." Also Jefferson to Nathaniel Burwell, 14 March 1818, in Paul Leicester Ford, ed., *The Writings of Thomas Jefferson,* 10 vols. (New York, 1892–1899), 10: 104–6. The emphasis on female education in the republic is discussed in Mary Beth Norton, *Liberty's Daughters: The Revolutionary Experience of American Women, 1750–1800* (Boston, 1980), pp. 256–94; and Linda K. Kerber, *Women of the Republic: Intellect and Ideology in Revolutionary America* (Chapel Hill, 1980), pp. 189–231.

63. Smith, *Remarks on Education,* pp. 208, 209, 206, 207–8.

64. Eliphalet Pearson to Edward Holyoke, 28 April 1789, in James McLachlan, "The *Choice of Hercules:* American Student Societies in the Early Nineteenth Century," Lawrence Stone, ed., *The University in Society,* 2 vols. (Princeton, 1974), 2: 462–64. On student disturbances during these years, see Steven J. Novak, *The Rights of Youth: American Colleges and Student Revolt, 1798–1815* (Cambridge, Mass., 1977).

65. On the nature and direction of social and educational changes in the nineteenth century, see the items in note 58, above, and also David F. Allmendinger, Jr., *Paupers and Scholars: The Transformation of Student Life in Nineteenth-Century New England* (New York, 1975); Bernard Wishy, *The Child and the Republic: The Dawn of Modern American Child Nurture* (Philadelphia, 1968); Richard L. Rapson, "The American Child As Seen by British Travelers, 1845–1935," *American Quarterly* 17 (1965): 520–34. Tocqueville's analysis of these changes remains in many ways the most engaging; see especially *Democracy in America,* 2: 229–36.

Epilogue: Father of His Country

1. J. P. Brissot de Warville, *New Travels in the United States, 1788,* ed. Durand Echeverria (Cambridge, Mass., 1964), pp. 104, 344–45. For discussions of the Washington myth, see William Alfred Bryan, *George Washington in American Literature, 1775–1865* (New York, 1952); Lawrence J. Friedman, *Inventors of the Promised Land* (New York, 1975), pp. 44–78; Catherine L. Albanese, *Sons of the Fathers: The Civil Religion of the American Revolution* (Philadelphia, 1976), pp. 143–81; Daniel J. Boorstin, *The Americans: The National Experience* (New York, 1965), pp. 337–56; Robert P. Hay, "George Washington: American Moses," *American Quarterly* 21: 780–91; Kenneth Silverman, *A Cultural History of the American Revolution* (New York, 1976), pp. 598–608; Bernard Mayo, *Myths and Men: Patrick Henry, George Washington, Thomas Jefferson* (Athens, Ga., 1959), pp. 25–48; Edmund S. Morgan, *The Meaning of Independence: John Adams, Thomas Jefferson, George Washington* (New York, 1976), pp. 29–55.

2. Brissot, *New Travels in the United States,* pp. 344–45; Adams to the Continental Congress, 19 February 1777, quoted in Albanese, *Sons of the Fathers,* p. 148; Adams to Abigail Adams, 26 October 1777, in L. H. Butterfield, ed., *Adams Family Correspondence,* 4 vols. (Cambridge, Mass., 1963–1973), 2: 361.

3. Mason L. Weems, *The Life of Washington,* ed. Marcus Cunliffe (Cambridge, Mass., 1962), pp. 12, 172–226; Braddock episode recounted on p. 177.

4. Ibid., p. 178.

5. Eliab Stone, *A Discourse* (Boston, 1800), quoted in Friedman, *Inventors of the Promised Land,* p. 50; Weems, *Life of Washington,* pp. 178, 191.

6. Friedman, *Inventors of the Promised Land,* p. 51; Weems, *Life of Washington,* p. 213; Bryan, *Washington in American Literature,* p. 237.

7. Noah Webster, *On the Education of Youth in America* (Boston, 1790), in Frederick Rudolph, ed., *Essays on Education in the Early Republic* (Cambridge, Mass., 1965), p. 65; Ruth Miller Elson, *Guardians of Tradition: American Schoolbooks of the Nineteenth Century* (Lincoln, Neb., 1964), p. 203; Benjamin Rush, *A Plan for the Establishment of Public Schools and the Diffusion of Knowledge in Pennsylvania; to Which Are Added, Thoughts upon the Mode of Education, Proper in a Republic* (Philadelphia, 1786), in Rudolph, ed., *Essays on Education*, p. 14; George B. Forgie, *Patricide in the House Divided: A Psychological Interpretation of Lincoln and His Age* (New York, 1979), p. 28.

Bibliographical Essay

In 1782 the American farmer Hector St. John de Crevecoeur observed that the cultural underpinnings of any society were revealed in the "sort of education they [its members] give their children." This meant, Crevecoeur explained, that we must study "how they treat . . . [their children] at home, and what they are taught in their places of public worship." Crevecoeur's observation is worth pursuing and I can think of no better way to begin such a study of education than with Bernard Bailyn's suggestive essay *Education in the Forming of American Society* (Chapel Hill, 1960) and Edmund S. Morgan's solid monograph *The Puritan Family: Religion and Domestic Relations in Seventeenth-Century New England*, rev. ed. (New York, 1966). Although some of Bailyn's assumptions and conclusions have been called into question by the more recent works of social historians, his venture into the realm of "hypothetical history" remains a forceful argument against limiting the history of education to formal pedagogy. By defining education broadly as the "entire process by which a culture transmits itself across the generations," Bailyn is able to offer a provocative analysis of the evolution of early American society and of the impact of this evolution on the principal agents of education: family, community, and church. Morgan's examination of the imperatives of domestic life in colonial New England is a model summary. The recent deluge of monographs dealing with the family in early America notwithstanding, Morgan's description of the emotional bases of the familial order is unsurpassed. In addition to Bailyn and Morgan, Lawrence Cremin's *American Education: The Colonial Experience, 1607–1783* (New York, 1970) is an important study of the subject. Cremin finds Bailyn's definition of education too latitudinarian and posits in its stead a view of "education as the deliberate, systematic, and sustained effort to transmit or evoke knowledge, attitudes, values, skills, and sensibilities." Cremin's conclusions, however, tend to confirm and complement rather than contradict most of Bailyn's interpretation.

Crevecoeur also noted in 1782 that educational imperatives, and therefore cultural values, manifested themselves in "the modes of thinking, the rules of conduct, and the prevailing manners of any people." The study of such modes, rules, and manners often seems to be more familiar turf for the cultural anthropologist and sociologist than for the historian. Fortunately, important links between the disciplines have already been forged. The work of Clifford Geertz is especially important in this regard. In my treatment of the nonverbal modes of communication, I have benefited from Geertz's collection of essays *The Interpretation of Cultures* (New York, 1973). Geertz also offers an engaging analysis of symbols and rituals in *Negara: The Theatre State in Nineteenth-Century Bali* (Princeton, 1980). Erving Goffman's *Relations in Public: Microstudies of the*

[243]

Public Order (New York, 1971), *Interaction Ritual: Essays on Face-to-Face Behavior* (New York, 1967), *The Presentation of Self in Everyday Life* (New York, 1959), and *Frame Analysis: An Essay on the Organization of Experience* (Cambridge, Mass., 1974) contain some brilliant insights into the meanings of, and unspoken assumptions behind, everyday gestures. Basil Bernstein, *Class, Codes and Control: Theoretical Studies towards a Sociology of Language* (London, 1971); and Mary Douglas, *Natural Symbols: Explorations in Cosmology* (New York, 1973) are also useful.

Among historians, Rhys Isaac has perhaps been most successful in fusing anthropology with history. See, for example, his essays "Preachers and Patriots: Popular Culture and the Revolution in Virginia," in Alfred F. Young, ed., *The American Revolution: Explorations in the History of American Radicalism* (DeKalb, Ill., 1976), pp. 127–56; "Evangelical Revolt: The Nature of the Baptists' Challenge to the Traditional Order in Virginia, 1765 to 1775," *William and Mary Quarterly,* 3rd ser., 31 (1974): 345–68; and "Dramatizing the Ideology of Revolution: Popular Mobilization in Virginia, 1774 to 1776," *William and Mary Quarterly* 33 (1976): 357–85. Isaac has brought the themes of these pieces together in *The Transformation of Virginia, 1740–1790* (Chapel Hill, 1982), which also contains an essay on the methodology of historical ethnography (pp. 323–57). Isaac's emphasis on the "dramaturgical" aspects of evangelical religion, in particular, may prove most fruitful in illuminating the source of the appeal of New Light preachers during the Great Awakening. In this regard, Isaac has extended the insights of Alan Heimert, whose *Religion and the American Mind from the Great Awakening to the Revolution* (Cambridge, Mass., 1966) focuses on the effect that ideological commitments had on "modes of persuasion." Heimert's effort to describe the context of eighteenth-century communication, the "rhetorical stances and strategies of the spokesmen of the various colonial religious persuasions," serves as the inspiration for Harry S. Stout's examination of the social and political implications of the "new forms of public address" established during the Awakening. In "Religion, Communications, and the Ideological Origins of the American Revolution," *William and Mary Quarterly* 34 (1977): 519–41, Stout elaborates upon the emergence of a popular style of evangelical oratory and contrasts this new style with the more formal, print-oriented "modes of address preferred by upholders of established authority."

As Bailyn and Morgan have shown, family history is an essential part of the history of education. Colonial Americans were well aware of the educational responsibilities of this "First-born" of human societies. The standard treatment of the changing social perceptions of the family is Philippe Ariès, *Centuries of Childhood: A Social History of Family Life,* trans. Robert Baldick (New York, 1962). Edward Shorter's *The Making of the Modern Family* (New York, 1975) is valuable. I found his description of "emotionless" courtship in tradition-bound peasant societies and the indifference that characterized parental attitudes toward children to be a useful counterpoint to Morgan's *Puritan Family.* In *The Family, Sex and Marriage in England, 1500–1800* (New York, 1977), Lawrence Stone provides collateral evidence of the growth of affective individualism in the early modern family. However, it should be clear from my text that I think one needs to be aware of the metamorphosis of the very idea of "Affection" in order to appreciate the full extent of familial changes in the eighteenth century. John Demos, *A Little Commonwealth: Family Life in Plymouth Colony* (New York, 1970); Philip J. Greven, Jr., *Four Generations: Population, Land, and Family in Colonial Andover, Massachusetts* (Ithaca, 1970); and the first two chapters of Oscar and Mary F. Handlin, *Facing Life: Youth and the Family in American History* (Boston, 1971), describe the traditional and nontraditional aspects of the family in early America. Edmund S. Morgan, *Virginians at Home: Family Life in the Eighteenth Century* (Williamsburg, 1952); Michael Zuckerman, "William Byrd's Family," *Perspectives in American History* 12 (1979): 253–311; Daniel Blake Smith, *Inside the Great House: Planter Family Life in Eighteenth-Century Chesapeake Society* (Ithaca, 1980); Jan Lewis, *The Pursuit of Happiness: Family and Values in Jefferson's Virginia* (Cambridge, England, 1983); and Hunter Dickinson Farish, ed., *Journal and Letters of Philip Vickers Fithian: A Plantation Tutor of the Old Dominion, 1773–1774* (Charlottesville, 1968), offer some contrasts to the New England story. But what seems even more noteworthy are the similarities they describe in patterns of authority and affection, "fear mixt with love," in these eighteenth-century families.

Under the broad definition of education, child-rearing is certainly a subject that deserves a great deal of attention. For general discussions, see Frederick Elkin, *The Child and Society: The Process of Socialization* (New York, 1960), and Ronald D. Cohen, "Socialization in Colonial New England," *History of Education Quarterly* 13 (1973): 73–82. The best study of this subject is Philip Greven, *The Protestant Temperament: Patterns of Child-Rearing, Religious Experience, and the Self in Early America* (New York, 1977). Although my interpretation differs significantly from Greven's account of "Evangelical" family life, I found his analysis to be consistently intriguing. Elizabeth Bancroft Schlesinger, "Cotton Mather and His Children," *William and Mary Quarterly* 10 (1953): 181–89; Joseph Illick, "Child-Rearing in Seventeenth-Century England and America," in Lloyd de Mause, ed., *The History of Childhood* (New York, 1975), pp. 303–50; John F. Walzer, "A Period of Ambivalence: Eighteenth-Century American Childhood," ibid., pp. 351–82; and Monica Kiefer, "Early American Childhood in the Middle Atlantic Area," *Pennsylvania Magazine of History and Biography* 68 (1944): 3–37, are also instructive. Chronologically out of place, but nevertheless useful, are Richard L. Rapson's studies of the accounts of British observers: "The American Child As Seen by British Travelers, 1845–1935," *American Quarterly* 17 (1965): 520–34, and *Britons View America: Travel Commentary, 1860–1935* (Seattle, 1971).

The Puritans' commitment to order had obvious implications for the values they inculcated in and submission they demanded of their children. Arthur O. Lovejoy, *The Great Chain of Being: A Study of the History of an Idea* (Cambridge, Mass., 1936), is essential for background material. Stephen Foster, *Their Solitary Way: The Puritan Social Ethic in the First Century of Settlement in New England* (New Haven, 1971), describes the various manifestations of the ordered way of life. Ola Winslow, *Meetinghouse Hill* (New York, 1952), and Robert

Dinkin, "Seating the Meeting House in Early Massachusetts," *New England Quarterly* 43 (1970): 450–64, discuss the social importance of seating arrangements. Two older studies, often quaint but still useful, are Alice Morse Earle, *Customs and Fashions in Old New England* (New York, 1893), and Joseph B. Felt, *The Customs of New England* (New York, 1853).

Richard L. Bushman, *From Puritan to Yankee: Character and the Social Order in Connecticut, 1690–1765* (Cambridge, Mass., 1967), and Kenneth A. Lockridge, *A New England Town: The First Hundred Years, Dedham, Massachusetts, 1636–1736* (New York, 1970) detail the break up of the old order. Both Bushman and Lockridge corroborate the "declension" model of New England history that Perry Miller so eloquently described in *The New England Mind: From Colony to Province* (Cambridge, Mass., 1953). James A. Henretta, "The Morphology of New England Society in the Colonial Period," *Journal of Interdisciplinary History* 2 (1971): 379–95, rejects the "negative" connotations inherent in the declension theme and offers a more "positive vision of historical change."

Because communal ideals were founded on patterns of authority and submission, the mode of maintaining good order was a function as well as a manifestation of social education. Larzer Ziff offers some suggestive comments in this regard in "The Social Bond of Church Covenant," *American Quarterly* 10 (1958): 454–62. Emil Oberholzer deals with the problem of ecclesiastical discipline in "The Church in New England Society," in James Morton Smith, ed., *Seventeenth-Century America* (Chapel Hill, 1959), pp. 143–65, and in greater depth in *Delinquent Saints: Disciplinary Action in the Early Congregational Churches of Massachusetts* (New York, 1956). Edwin Powers, *Crime and Punishment in Early Massachusetts, 1620–1692: A Documentary History* (Boston, 1966), has carefully selected and organized a substantial array of source material. Darrett Rutman, "The Mirror of Puritan Authority," in George A. Billias, ed., *Law and Authority in Colonial America* (Barre, Mass., 1965), pp. 149–67, argues that the vision of a united "authority and cohesive, ordered society" is a construct of "intellectual historians who have turned to the writings of the articulate few—and little else." However, Rutman distinguishes too sharply between the "ideals of the articulate few" and the "actuality of the man in the street." A more satisfactory assessment of the relationship between ideals and actions is presented by Edward M. Cook, Jr., "Social Behavior and Changing Values in Dedham, Massachusetts, 1700 to 1775," *William and Mary Quarterly* 27 (1970): 546–80.

A survey of education in early America would be incomplete without a consideration of the popular *New England Primer*. An excellent edition of the *Primer* is edited by Paul Leicester Ford (New York, 1962). Samuel Eliot Morison's *The Puritan Pronaos* (New York, 1936), reprinted as *The Intellectual Life of Colonial New England* (New York, 1956), provides background information. Several older studies are still valuable; in particular, see Walter Small, *Early New England Schools* (1914; New York, 1969); Robert Seybolt, *The Private Schools of Colonial Boston* (Cambridge, Mass., 1935), and *Apprenticeship and Apprenticeship Education in Colonial New England* (New York, 1917); Marcus

Wilson Jernegan, *Laboring and Dependent Classes in Colonial America, 1607–1783* (New York, 1931); and Clifford K. Shipton, "Secondary Education in the Puritan Colonies," *New England Quarterly* 7 (1934): 646–61. Robert Middlekauff, *Ancients and Axioms: Secondary Education in Eighteenth-Century New England* (New Haven, 1963), describes the traditional patterns of schooling that prevailed in the colonial period, and the alteration of those patterns brought on by the Revolution. A brief but persuasive challenge to the conventional view that "wilderness" conditions accounted for the emphasis on education in New England can be found in Kenneth A. Lockridge, *Literacy in Colonial New England: An Enquiry into the Social Context of Literacy in the Early Modern West* (New York, 1974).

Higher education during the colonial and Revolutionary eras has not suffered from a lack of attention. There are enough college histories alone to fill a small library. A good survey text is Frederick Rudolph, *The American College and University: A History* (New York, 1962). Richard Hofstadter's general interpretation of the colonial college in *The Development of Academic Freedom* (New York, 1955) is an excellent synthesis. His discussion of college founding should be supplemented with Beverly McAnear, "College Founding in the American Colonies, 1745–1774," *Mississippi Valley Historical Review* 42 (1955): 24–44. Among the more useful of the individual college histories are: John Maclean, *History of the College of New Jersey from Its Origin in 1746 to the Commencement of 1854,* 2 vols. (Philadelphia, 1877); Thomas Jefferson Wertenbaker, *Princeton, 1746–1896* (Princeton, 1946); Francis L. Broderick, "Pulpit, Physics, and Politics: The Curriculum of the College of New Jersey, 1746–1794," *William and Mary Quarterly,* 3rd ser., 6 (1949): 42–68; Walter C. Bronson, *The History of Brown University, 1764–1914* (Providence, 1914); Reuben Aldridge Guild, *Early History of Brown University Including the Life, Times, and Correspondence of President Manning, 1756–1791* (Providence, 1897); Thomas Harrison Montgomery, *A History of the University of Pennsylvania from Its Foundation to A.D. 1770* (Philadelphia, 1900); Edward Potts Cheney, *History of the University of Pennsylvania, 1740–1940* (Philadelphia, 1940). However, none of these can equal Samuel Eliot Morison's distinguished account of *Harvard College in the Seventeenth Century,* 2 vols. (Cambridge, Mass., 1936). Morison's richly detailed history of the college and its social context is still unsurpassed. But Yale has been well-served by Richard Warch's excellent monograph *School of the Prophets: Yale College, 1701–1740* (New Haven, 1973). Warch's study should be followed by a reading of Louis Leonard Tucker, *Puritan Protagonist: President Thomas Clap of Yale College* (Chapel Hill, 1962), and Edmund S. Morgan, *The Gentle Puritan: A Life of Ezra Stiles, 1727–1795* (New Haven, 1962). Two other recent studies also deserve to be mentioned in particular, for they stand in the tradition established by Morison. David C. Humphrey, *From King's College to Columbia, 1746–1800* (New York, 1976), demonstrates the efficacy of relating the development of an institution to the wider social setting. Mindful of the "tensions besetting American society during the second half of the eighteenth century," Humphrey's first-rate study traces the evolution of King's College as both a reflection of and a response to those tensions. Howard

Miller, *The Revolutionary College: American Presbyterian Higher Education, 1707–1837* (New York, 1976) likewise deals with the history of education within the context of the social and political changes affecting eighteenth-century America. Indeed, Miller's interpretation of changing social perceptions, especially in regard to the accommodation of competition among disparate interest groups, parallels the argument posited by Gordon S. Wood in *The Creation of the American Republic, 1776–1787* (Chapel Hill, 1969).

Despite the abundance of institutional histories, studies of student life are still in short supply. The essays of Franklin B. Dexter, "Student Life at Yale in the Early Days of Connecticut Hall" (1908), and "Student Life at Yale College Under the First President Dwight" (1918), both reprinted in Dexter, *A Selection from Miscellaneous Historical Papers of Fifty Years* (New Haven, 1918), pp. 266–73 and 382–94, are worth reading, as is Alexander Cowie, "Educational Problems at Yale College in the Eighteenth Century," Tercentenary Commission of the State of Connecticut *Publications* 55 (1936). Tucker's biography of Thomas Clap, *Puritan Protagonist;* Morgan's study on Ezra Stiles, *Gentle Puritan;* and Humphrey's history of *King's College* all contain valuable discussions of the collegiate experience. James Axtell, *The School upon a Hill: Education and Society in Colonial New England* (New Haven, 1974), also has some important things to say about student life, but he overstates his case when he describes Yale in the last six years of Thomas Clap's presidency as a "guerrilla war zone." Furthermore, I think that Axtell's discussion of the presence of physical punishment—"Whipt Eminence"—in disciplinary proceedings must be qualified in the way that I have suggested. James McLachlan provides us with an insightful analysis of student values in "The *Choice of Hercules:* American Student Societies in the Early Nineteenth Century," in Lawrence Stone, ed., *The University in Society,* 2 vols. (Princeton, 1974), 2: 449–94. The best study of student unrest in the aftermath of the Revolution is Steven J. Novak, *The Rights of Youth: American Colleges and Student Revolt, 1798–1815* (Cambridge, Mass., 1977). An instructive comparison can be made with Keith Thomas, *Rule and Misrule in the Schools of Early Modern Europe* (Stenton Lecture, University of Reading, 1976). Demographic changes in the student population are dealt with in David F. Allmendinger, Jr., "New England Students and the Revolution in Higher Education, 1800–1900," *History of Education Quarterly* 11 (1971): 381–89; and Allmendinger, *Paupers and Scholars: The Transformation of Student Life in Nineteenth-Century New England* (New York, 1975).

Philip Greven in *Four Generations* suggests that "political independence in 1776 might have been rooted in the very character of many . . . American families." In Andover, Massachusetts, by the middle of the eighteenth century, Greven aruges, patriarchalism was on the wane and most fourth-generation sons had come to take the idea of personal independence for granted. For these sons, separation from the mother country may have been merely a matter of "common sense." Edwin G. Burrows and Michael Wallace, "The American Revolution: The Ideology and Psychology of National Liberation," *Perspectives in American History* 6 (1972): 167–306, examine the nature and implications of the familial understanding of the empire. Winthrop D. Jordan, "Familial Politics:

Thomas Paine and the Killing of the King, 1776," *Journal of American History* 60 (1973): 294–308; and Jack P. Greene, "An Uneasy Connection: An Analysis of the Preconditions of the American Revolution," in Stephen G. Kurtz and James H. Hutson, eds., *Essays on the American Revolution* (Chapel Hill, 1973), pp. 32–80, explore the meanings of and expectations created by the use of the familial paradigm. Robert M. Weir, "Rebelliousness: Personality Development and the American Revolution in the Southern Colonies," in Jeffrey J. Crow and Larry E. Tise, eds., *The Southern Experience in the American Revolution* (Chapel Hill, 1978), pp. 25–54; and Kenneth S. Lynn, *A Divided People* (Westport, Conn., 1977) offer more than a few hints about the possible relationship between family history and the origins of the American Revolution.

Recently, two related studies were completed independent of my own. Jay Fliegelman, *Prodigals and Pilgrims: The American Revolution against Patriarchal Authority, 1750–1800* (Cambridge, 1982); and Peter Charles Hoffer, *Revolution and Regeneration: Life Cycle and the Historical Vision of the Generation of 1776* (Athens, Ga., 1983) have approached the Revolutionary era along the lines suggested by Burrows and Wallace. Hoffer's interpretation of the "young men of the Revolution" is based primarily on Erik Erikson's concept of life-cycle challenges and their role in identity formation. More satisfying is Fliegelman's attempt to relate "eighteenth-century literary history to social, theological, and political events in America." However, Fliegelman's account of the coercive and imperious nature of "older patriarchal family authority" and the subsequent "emergence of a humane form of childrearing" in the eighteenth century is overdrawn. A servile "fear of the rod," as I have indicated, was not the ideal basis of filial obedience, even in the seventeenth century. The problem here seems to stem from an inclination to equate "affectionate" with "equalitarian" domestic arrangements.

The complex relationship between domestic and civil government is expertly described by Gordon J. Schochet in "Patriarchalism, Politics and Mass Attitudes in Stuart England," *Historical Journal* 12 (1969): 413–41; and more fully in *Patriarchalism in Political Thought: The Authoritarian Family and Political Speculation and Attitudes Especially in Seventeenth-Century England* (New York, 1975). Catherine L. Albanese, *Sons of the Fathers: The Civil Religion of the American Revolution* (Philadelphia, 1976), examines the role of familial imagery in the creation of a common faith among Independent Americans. Less successful but provocative nevertheless are the psychological studies of nineteenth-century America which assume that the familial paradigm persisted unchanged by the Revolution; see Michael Paul Rogin, *Fathers and Children: Andrew Jackson and the Subjugation of the American Indian* (New York, 1975); and George B. Forgie, *Patricide in the House Divided: A Psychological Interpretation of Lincoln and His Age* (New York, 1979).

That the Revolution was a "cathartic event" in the development of a "new conception of American identity" is the thesis of Jack P. Greene's "Search for Identity: An Interpretation of the Meaning of Selected Patterns of Social Response in Eighteenth-Century America," *Journal of Social History* 3 (1970): 189–220. Richard L. Bushman, " 'This New Man': Dependence and Independence, 1776," in Bushman, et al., eds., *Uprooted Americans: Essays to Honor Oscar Handlin* (Boston, 1979), pp. 77–96; and Robert M. Weir, "Who Shall Rule at Home: The American Revolution as a Crisis of Legitimacy for the Colonial Elite," *Journal of Interdisciplinary History* 6 (1976): 679–700, support the argument that the Revolution fundamentally altered the self-perceptions of Americans. Bernard Bailyn's important essay "Political Experience and Enlightenment Ideas in Eighteenth-Century America," *American Historical Review,* 67 (1962): 339–51, describes the legitimizing role played by "Enlightenment liberalism." The Revolution "destroyed the traditional sources of public authority" and thereby enabled Americans to "complete, formalize, systematize and symbolize what previously had been only partially realized, confused, and disputed matters of fact." The best discussion of the Enlightenment in America is Henry F. May's *The Enlightenment in America* (New York, 1976). Also helpful are Donald H. Meyer, *The Democratic Enlightenment* (New York, 1976), and Henry Steele Commager, *The Empire of Reason: How Europe Imagined and America Realized the Enlightenment* (New York, 1977).

The impact of the new American identity and the Enlightenment on education is the subject of several studies. Allen O. Hansen's *Liberalism and American Education in the Eighteenth Century* (New York, 1926) is dated but still useful. Jonathan Messerli, "The Columbian Complex: The Impulse to National Consolidation," *History of Education Quarterly* 7 (1967): 417–31; and David Tyack, "Forming the National Character: Paradox in the Educational Thought of the Revolutionary Generation," *Harvard Educational Review* 36 (1966): 29–41, are informative, although I would disagree with Tyack's interpretation of the "paradox." Douglas Milton Sloan, *The Scottish Enlightenment and the American College Ideal* (New York, 1971); and Miller, *The Revolutionary College,* provide insights into the problems and accomplishments of higher education. Aspects of republican education are also illuminated in studies dealing with the principal educational theorists of the period. For example, see Roy J. Honeywell, *The Educational Work of Thomas Jefferson* (Cambridge, Mass., 1931); and Charles F. Arrowood, *Thomas Jefferson and Education in a Republic* (New York, 1930). Benjamin Rush has received his share of attention in this regard; see Harry G. Good, *Benjamin Rush and His Services to American Education* (Berne, Ind., 1918); Hyman Kuritz, "Benjamin Rush: His Theory of Republican Education," *History of Education Quarterly* 7 (1967): 432–51; and the fine intellectual biography by Donald J. D'Elia, *Benjamin Rush: Philosopher of the American Revolution,* American Philosophical Society *Transactions* 64 (1974). Harry R. Warfel, *Noah Webster: Schoolmaster to America* (New York, 1936) should be read in conjunction with Warfel's edition of the *Letters of Noah Webster* (New York, 1953), and Richard M. Rollins's recent biography *The Long Journey of Noah Webster* (Philadelphia, 1980).

The new republicans, and educational thinkers in particular, were concerned about the roles that women normally played in the rearing of children. Carl N. Degler provides a survey of women's history in *At Odds: Women and the Family in America from the Revolution to the Present* (New York, 1980). Degler's chapter "Inducting Children into the Social Order" employs a broadly defined concept of education, but is helpful only as an introduction to the subject. Two fine recent studies, Mary Beth Norton, *Liberty's Daughters: The Revolutionary Experience of American Women, 1750–1800* (Boston, 1980); and Linda K. Kerber, *Women of the Republic: Intellect and Ideology in Revolutionary America* (Chapel Hill, 1980), examine the impact of republicanism on women's roles. The status of women in early America is also the subject of a number of recent articles. Among the more notable are: Nancy F. Cott, "Divorce and the Changing Status of Women in Eighteenth-Century Massachusetts," *William and Mary Quarterly* 33 (1976): 586–614; Cott, "Eighteenth-Century Family and Social Life Revealed in Massachusetts Divorce Records," *Journal of Social History* 10 (1976): 20–43; Alexander Keyssar, "Widowhood in Eighteenth-Century Massachusetts," *Perspectives in American History* 8 (1974): 83–119; Laurel Thatcher Ulrich, "Vertuous Women Found: New England Ministerial Literature, 1668–1735," *American Quarterly* 28 (1976): 20–40. Joan Hoff Wilson, "The Illusion of Change: Women and the American Revolution," in Young, ed., *The American Revolution,* pp. 383–445, argues that the Revolution "produced no significant benefits for American women." But clearly, in the new republic, the traditional perceptions of the woman's place were given new meanings as Kerber and Norton have shown. Barbara Welter, "The Cult of True Womanhood, 1820–1860," *American Quarterly* 18 (1966): 151–74, describes the antebellum ideal of womanhood, but this account must be read in the context provided by Nancy F. Cott, *The Bonds of Womanhood: "Women's Sphere" in New England, 1780–1835* (New Haven, 1977); and Kathryn Kish Sklar, *Catherine Beecher: A Study in American Domesticity* (New Haven, 1973).

On the beginnings of "garrulous patriotism" in the late-eighteenth and early-nineteenth centuries, I found Lawrence J. Friedman's *Inventors of the Promised Land* (New York, 1975) to be most suggestive. Also helpful are William Brock, "The Image of England and American Nationalism," *Journal of American Studies* 5 (1971): 225–45; Benjamin T. Spencer, *The Quest for Nationality: An American Literary Campaign* (Syracuse, 1957); Richard W. Van Alstyne, *Genesis of American Nationalism* (Waltham, Mass., 1970); and Joseph J. Ellis, *After the Revolution: Profiles of Early American Culture* (New York, 1979). America's struggle for self-definition during the first half of the nineteenth century is covered by Fred Somkin, *Unquiet Eagle: Memory and Desire in the Idea of American Freedom, 1815–1860* (Ithaca, 1967); Clinton Rossiter, *The American Quest, 1790–1860: An Emerging Nation in Search of Identity, Unity, and Modernity* (New York, 1971); Paul C. Nagel, *One Nation Indivisible: The Union in American Thought, 1776–1861* (New York, 1964); and Nagel, *This Sacred Trust: American Nationality, 1798–1898* (New York, 1971).

The Washington myth occupied a central place in the patriotic education of post-Revolutionary Americans. William A. Bryan, *George Washington in American Literature, 1775–1865* (New York, 1952) summarizes some of the major themes contained in this genre. Important observations are also made in the several chapters centering on Washington in the following works: Friedman, *Inventors of the Promised Land;* Bernard Mayo, *Myths and Men: Patrick Henry, George Washington, Thomas Jefferson* (Athens, Ga., 1959); Daniel J. Boorstin,

The Americans: The National Experience (New York, 1965); and Albanese, *Sons of the Fathers.*

The "sort of education" that Americans of the early national period gave their children can be viewed through Ruth Miller Elson's study of schoolbooks, *Guardians of Tradition: American Schoolbooks of the Nineteenth Century* (Lincoln, Neb., 1964); and Monica Kiefer's survey of children's literature, *American Children through Their Books, 1700–1835* (Philadelphia, 1948). Daniel Calhoun, *The Intelligence of a People* (Princeton, 1973), pp. 134–205; Peter Gregg Slater, *Children in the New England Mind in Death and in Life* (Hamden, Conn., 1977), pp. 93–158; and Bernard Wishy, *The Child and the Republic: The Dawn of Modern American Child Nurture* (Philadelphia, 1968), analyze the changing conceptions of childhood and childhood education in the eighteenth and early-nineteenth centuries. The nurturing of children is the subject also of Robert Sunley, "Early Nineteenth-Century American Literature on Child Rearing," in Margaret Mead and Martha Wolfenstein, eds., *Childhood in Contemporary Cultures* (Chicago, 1955), pp. 150–67; William G. McLoughlin, "Evangelical Childrearing in the Age of Jackson: Francis Wayland's Views on When and How to Subdue the Wilfulness of Children," *Journal of Social History* 9 (1975): 21–39; and Charles Strickland, "A Transcendentalist Father: The Child-Rearing Practices of Bronson Alcott," *Perspectives in American History* 3 (1969): 5–73.

The social and intellectual turmoil that attended the rise of democratic politics is beyond the scope of this study, but its importance to education as socialization is clear. David J. Rothman, *The Discovery of the Asylum: Social Order and Disorder in the New Republic* (Boston, 1971) traces the "revolution in social practice," which found Jacksonian Americans turning to institutional solutions for the problems of the insane, the criminal, and the orphan. The primary source of their inspiration, Rothman argues, was the desire to promote stability in a rapidly changing world. Michael B. Katz poses a similar kind of argument for school reform "by imposition" in *The Irony of Early School Reform: Educational Innovation in Mid-Nineteenth Century Massachusetts* (Cambridge, Mass., 1968). Rush Welter's chapter "The Uses of Education" in his work *The Mind of America, 1820–1860* (New York, 1975) and Robert H. Wiebe, "The Social Functions of Public Education," *American Quarterly* 21 (1969): 147–64, discuss education as an instrument of social control.

Finally, the broad scope of educational history is sometimes best measured in terms of personal experiences. The place to begin is with Robert Dawidoff's revealing account of *The Education of John Randolph* (New York, 1979); and Henry Adams's classic autobiography, *The Education of Henry Adams* (New York, 1931).

Index

Wolcott, Frederick, 60, 62
Wolcott, Oliver, 59–60, 62, 63, 64
Wright, Louis B., 87
Wyche, William, 175, 183–84

Yale College: commencement celebrations at, 67, 68, 73; and "fagging" custom, 64, 65, 73; government of, 59, 73, 74, 79; laws of, 61, 62, 63, 66, 73, 74, 77, 78, 80; rank of tutors in, 66–67; student behavior at, 61, 63, 67; and student drinking, 67–68; student interaction at, 65. *See also* Clap, Thomas; Stiles, Ezra

Zubly, John Joachim, 93

Melvin Yazawa teaches history at the University of New Mexico. He is the editor of *Representative Government and the Revolution: The Maryland Constitutional Crisis of 1787,* also published by Johns Hopkins.

THE JOHNS HOPKINS UNIVERSITY PRESS

From Colonies to Commonwealth

This book was composed in ITC Garamond type by Capitol Communication Systems, Inc., from a design by Tom Reeg. It was printed on S. D. Warren's 50-lb. Sebago Eggshell paper and bound in Holliston Roxite A by the Maple Press Company.